SAINT CATHERINE LABOURÉ

OF THE MIRACULOUS MEDAL

Apparition of the Blessed Virgin Mary to St. Catherine Labouré during the night of July 18-19, 1830. St. Catherine threw herself at Our Lady's knee and rested her hands on Mary's lap. Many years later St. Catherine stated that this was the sweetest moment of her life.

SAINT CATHERINE LABOURÉ

of the Miraculous Medal

JOSEPH I. DIRVIN, C. M.
ST. JOHN'S UNIVERSITY, NEW YORK

"Thou hast hidden these things from the wise and prudent, and hast revealed them to little ones. Yea, Father, for so it hath seemed good in thy sight."

—Luke *10:21*

TAN BOOKS AND PUBLISHERS, INC.
Rockford, Illinois 61105

Imprimi Potest: Silvester A. Taggart, C.M.
Visitator Provinciae Orientalis

Nihil Obstat: Martinus S. Rushford, Ph.D.
Censor Librorum

Imprimatur: ✠ Bryan Josephus McEntegart, D.D., LL.D.
Episcopus Bruklyniensis
Bruklyni
Die ii iunii, 1958

Reprinted in 1984 by TAN Books and Publishers, Inc. by arrangement with Farrar, Straus & Giroux.

Pictures used with the permission of the Vincentian Fathers and the Daughters of Charity. All rights of reproduction strictly reserved.

Library of Congress Catalog Card No.: 84-50466

ISBN: 0-89555-242-6

Printed and bound in the United States of America.

TAN BOOKS AND PUBLISHERS, INC.
P.O. Box 424
Rockford, Illinois 61105

1984

Anyone wishing to report favors received through the Miraculous Medal may write to the

Central Association of the Miraculous Medal
475 E. Chelten Avenue
Philadelphia, Pennsylvania 19144

To the Promoters and Members of The Central Association of the Miraculous Medal, who follow in the footsteps of Catherine Labouré by their devotion to the Miraculous Medal and their dedication to its diffusion throughout the world.

Contents

Foreword

THE PUBLISHERS say that this life of St. Catherine Labouré by Father Dirvin will be the *definitive* biography of St.
Catherine. Like many other people, I suppose, I have never
been quite certain of the meaning of this word as it is applied
to a biography. So I asked the publishers what they mean
when they say that Father Dirvin's book is definitive. Here is
their explanation.

This book is the full and authoritative story on the life and
works of St. Catherine, the Daughter of Charity to whom the
Miraculous Medal was manifested by the Blessed Virgin in
Paris in 1830. It contains much material never published before, since Father Dirvin had access to archives and places
never before opened to a biographer or a historian. These were
not only in Paris, but also in Rome and in the village of Fain-
les-moutiers, where Catherine was born and spent her childhood. Every statement of fact has been fully authenticated;
where evidence on any point is not fully conclusive, this is
clearly indicated. In this book you will read everything signifi-

cant that is recorded anywhere about St. Catherine and her
life's work.

How Father Dirvin was able to obtain so much previously
unpublished material can easily be understood by those who
know of the long and close association of the Vincentian
Fathers with the Miraculous Medal. For those who may not
know, a brief explanation should suffice.

St. Vincent de Paul founded two Communities: 1) the Congregation of the Mission (Vincentian Fathers) and 2) the
Daughters of Charity, sometimes called the Sisters of Charity.
At the time Mary manifested the design of the Medal of her
Immaculate Conception, Catherine Labouré was a novice in
the Paris motherhouse of the Daughters of Charity. When
the first Medals were cast two years later, it was only natural
that they should be distributed by the spiritual sons and
daughters of St. Vincent—first in France, and then throughout
the world.

The first organized effort to spread devotion to Mary
through her Medal was made in the United States, in 1915,
by the Vincentian Fathers of Germantown, Philadelphia.
Prompted by a desire to show our appreciation for a wonderful favor received through the Medal, the superiors of our
Community decided to establish an association to promote devotion to Mary Immaculate. This was the beginning of The
Central Association of the Miraculous Medal. For eleven years
prior to his transfer to St. John's University, Brooklyn, Father
Dirvin was on the office staff of the "Central Association" and
was associate editor of our magazine, *The Miraculous Medal*.

I hope that all this talk about definitive editions and schol-
arly research will not mislead anyone into thinking that Father
Dirvin's book is a dry compilation of facts. Far from it! Here
is a narrative that brings Catherine Labouré to vivid life—as
a child; as the little housekeeper in a motherless household; as
a girl seeking her vocation; as the young novice chosen by

Mary to give her Medal of grace to the world; as the humble Sister who insisted on remaining anonymous almost to the end. This is a book you will find very hard to lay aside until you have read the final sentence on the last page.

Rev. JOSEPH A. SKELLY, C.M., Director
The Central Association of the Miraculous Medal

Germantown, Philadelphia, Pa.
Feast of the Assumption, 1958

Acknowledgments

The author of any book is indebted to many people. It is impossible for him to thank them all publicly, but certain ones, whom he leaned upon heavily, cannot be passed over. My biggest debt of gratitude is to Father Joseph A. Skelly, C.M., who believed in the book from the first and was prodigal in giving me access to original sources. I am grateful to my confreres, who helped me by their encouragement, advice, and knowledge, especially to our Most Honored Father, William M. Slattery, Superior General of the Vincentian Fathers and the Sisters of Charity, and to Fathers William J. Casey, John J. Munday, and Joseph J. Symes. I am grateful also to my religious Sisters, especially Sister Mary Basil, Assistant General of the Sisters of Charity, and the Sisters Custodians of the Archives at Rue du Bac. Nor can I forget the kindness of M. l'Abbé Rochet, curé of the parish in which St. Catherine lived, and of Mme. Labouré-Gontard LeGrange, of Nuits St. Georges in Burgundy, a great grandniece of the saint. Special thanks are due Prof. William A. McBrien, of the Department of English of St. John's University, New York, for not counting the cost of time and labor in his careful and critical reading of the manuscript.

SAINT CATHERINE LABOURÉ

OF THE MIRACULOUS MEDAL

I

"Now You Will Be My Mother"

THE EVENING ANGELUS was ringing over Burgundy. The mild May breeze caught the sound from a hundred belfries and blew it across the mellowing fields and ripening vineyards. Workers in the fields stopped turning the ancient earth and straightened to bless themselves and pray. In the villages, housewives paused in their preparation of the evening meal. Even the children stood silent in the cobblestoned streets where they were at play. Everyone and everything was still, while the sweet bells told once more of the meeting of Gabriel and Mary.

This moment had not changed over the centuries. The lords and ladies of the Ducal court had known it, and the serfs toiling beneath the blue Burgundian skies, and the monks of St. Bernard and the nuns of St. Jane Frances de Chantal. Only the people and the dress and the customs had changed.

Now it was the second of May in the year of Our Lord 1806, and the evening Angelus was ringing.

In one house of the village of Fain-les-moutiers no one

paused for the evening prayer. It was the house of the prosperous farmer Pierre Labouré, and within its stout stone walls his wife, Madeleine Louise, was being delivered of a child. The bell of the little church across the lane had not ceased striking when the baby breathed its first breath and wailed. It was a girl, the second daughter of the household.

In the midst of all the to-do and bustle, the washings and exclamations of delight that all was well, the exhausted mother made herself heard. She had a startling request: that her newborn daughter's name be entered on the civil register at once. It was something that could wait: the official day was over; but, no, Madeleine Labouré would have it done now.

Nicolas Labouré, cousin to Pierre and mayor of the village, was summoned from his office. He brought with him his secretary, Baudrey, who carried the book and pen. The child's name was duly entered: "Catherine, daughter of Pierre Labouré and Madeleine Gontard his wife, was born this same day (May 2, 1806) at six o'clock in the evening." The mother raised herself resolutely to sign the record with her own hand. It was a marvel to her family. She had not done this for any other of her children, nor would she do it for those to come. Only for Catherine.

Thus it came about that the name of Catherine Labouré, saint of Burgundy and France, was inscribed in the written history of the world within a quarter of an hour of her birth. The very next day, the feast of the Finding of the Holy Cross, Catherine was baptized, and her name entered on the books of the Church. Her existence had now been noticed by both Church and State; both would have occasion to take note of her many times in the years ahead.

Abbé Georges Mamer poured the waters of baptism on the head of the little Catherine. He was the last Benedictine of the famed Fifth-Century Abbey of Moutiers, which lay outside the village. When his abbey had been suppressed and the monks dispersed during the French Revolution, Abbé Mamer had stayed on in the district to serve as pastor to the villages of Moutiers-Saint Jean, Fain and St. Just. He was honored by his people, for he had courageously refused the Constitutional Oath, that shameful pledge by which the taker denied his Master's Vicar in Rome for the bloody silver of the State.

According to legend, the lands of the Abbey of Moutiers had been the gift of Clovis, the first Christian King of the Franks. The first abbot, so the tale went, having found favor with the King, Clovis promised him all the land he could encircle in a day, riding on a donkey. Whether the charming legend is true or not, there is a poetic justice in the linking of Catherine, the maid of a new religious era, with the beginnings of French Catholicism fourteen hundred years before.

A coincidence like this—in fact, everything we call coincidence—is not one with God. It is part of His plan, a signpost He places along the way of a soul. It was not merely coincidence, for example, that Catherine was born at the ringing of the Angelus. It was God's charming touch, this heralding by the bells of Mary of the saint who was to usher in the Marian Age. Nor was it coincidence that, of all the Labouré children, Catherine's name alone received the prompt attention of the world: surely it was a holy mother's intuition that led Madeleine to call attention to her elected child. Even the feast of Catherine's baptism was prophetic, for Catherine was to "find" the Cross at every turning of her life, was to have a deep devotion for it, and was to see it in mysterious vision.

Catherine's baptismal name was rarely used by her family. They called her Zoé after an obscure saint whose feast fell on the day of Catherine's birth. St. Zoé must have enjoyed a certain local prominence, for the leading saint of the day on the calendar of the Church is Athanasius, the great champion of the Mother of God. Although entirely unofficial, the name Zoé was so much a part of Catherine that, when she served as godmother to a neighbor's child in 1826, she signed the baptismal register: *Catherine Labouré Zoé.*

Zoé Labouré came by her goodness honestly, for her father and mother were pious country folk. The father, Pierre, was born in 1767. He entered the seminary in his teens but, after a few years, gave up the idea of the priesthood and took to farming. His grandchildren, in testimony before the Beatification Tribunal of 1909, blamed the French Revolution for his change of heart. This was evidently a family tradition and must be respected as such; however, the facts indicate that the Revolution discouraged rather than obstructed the vocation of Pierre Labouré. He was already twenty-two when the Revolution broke out, an age when he would have been well along in his theological studies, and even in orders, were he still in the seminary. Furthermore, the Church was not hampered in her functioning, nor the seminaries closed, at once. The Constitutional Oath was not demanded until 1790, and the Days of the Terror, when persecution and martyrdom began in dead earnest, did not strike until 1793, some months after Pierre was married. Probably the shadow of the coming Revolution gave Pierre Labouré pause in his leanings toward the priesthood and, after an honest searching of his soul, he decided that God had other plans for him.

Zoé's mother, Madeleine Louise Gontard, was born in 1773, three years before the American Declaration of Independence. She came of cultured and respected people: the Gontards were looked up to as a sort of local aristocracy. When Pierre Labouré met her, she was living in the family home at Senailly, teaching school to support her widowed mother.

They were married on June 4, 1793. He was twenty-six; she was twenty. They were brave youngsters, to set up housekeeping in the reeling world of that day. The French Revolution had been disrupting normal living for four years. The King had been killed in January, and the Queen was to come to the scaffold in October. The heads of priests and nuns were soon to be falling into the blood-soaked baskets of the guillotine. The Labourés's daughter Catherine would come to revere the hallowed names of some of them: the Vincentian priests René Rogue, Louis François, and Henri Gruyer; the four martyred Sisters of Charity of Arras—all members of the double religious family Catherine was to join. Devilish cruelty, blasphemy, and lust were on the rampage, and even the far provinces and hidden villages like Senailly and Fain-les-moutiers felt the pangs of the frightful cancers that were eating away at France. But Pierre and Madeleine were young and in love, and young love knows no terrors or fears.

For the first seven years of their married life, the couple lived with Madeleine's mother in Senailly. Here the four oldest children were born: Hubert, in 1794; Marie Louise, in 1795; Jacques, in 1796; and Antoine, in 1797—and perhaps two of the six babies who died at birth or soon after. Madeleine Labouré had seventeen children in all: eleven lived, and one of these, Alexandre, died when a year old.

In 1800 old Mme Gontard died, and the Labourés moved to the farm in Fain-les-moutiers. Soon after their arrival in Fain the fourth son, Charles, was born. Then came Alexandre, in 1801; Joseph, in 1803; and Pierre, in 1805.

And in 1806, Catherine.

Catherine's parents were a study in contrasts. Pierre Labouré was a gruff, silent man, a devout and good Catholic, an able father, but one who ruled his children with a rod of iron. In all things a perfectionist, he saw to it that his farm and his household ran smoothly or he knew the reason why. It was this quality of management that made his land prosper and his children grow in courtesy and character. Madeleine Labouré was of a softer nature. She was truly the heart of her home, educated, genteel, and saintly.

They were a wonderful combination for the making of a

saint, this father and mother, and Zoé took the best qualities from each. She had her father's iron will and capable hand, her mother's gentleness and deep piety.

On October 21, 1808, when Zoé was nearly two and a half years old, Marie Antoinette, or Tonine, the sister who was to be the confidante of her childhood and adolescence, was born. And, in November 1809, the baby Auguste; he was born in poor health and was delicate all his life.

The little village of Fain-les-moutiers—there were scarcely 150 inhabitants—had honorable memories to recall, memories that bred in it a just and natural pride. It had once been part of the lands of the Abbey of Moutiers. St. Bernard and his holy brothers had been born and raised not far away and, later on, St. Jane Frances de Chantal. Some miles to the south lay Paray-le-monial, where the Sacred Heart of Jesus had unburdened Itself to St. Margaret Mary.

Fain was a charming village, perched on a shelf among the rolling hills, commanding a glorious view of the lovely Burgundian countryside stretching away beneath it. Just below, in the plain, lay the ruined abbey and, farther on, the larger village of Moutiers-Saint Jean. It was a good place to grow up in—healthful, quaint, and serene.

The Labouré farm was large, the house spacious. The sight of the prosperous farmstead was enough to tell the stranger to Fain that here lived the first family of the village. A dozen hired hands tilled the soil for Pierre Labouré. His barn was full, his granary bursting. Nearly 800 pigeons flew in and out of the large, stone dovecot which presided over the farmyard like a medieval battle-tower. Raising squabs for the market is a native French industry but, by ancient law, only one or two farmers in a given area may engage in it. Indoors as well, the polished oak and gleaming pewter reflected the comfortable station of the family. And, if further proof were needed, there was the tiny side chapel in the ancient village church, called the Chapel of the Labourés, and reserved for their use. Pierre Labouré was village mayor from 1811 to 1815.

The Labourés were prosperous because they worked hard and managed well. They knew simple comfort but never luxury. From sunup to sundown the father was in the fields, about his business of farming. At home, the mother was about hers, sewing and cooking, cleaning and dusting, managing her household. After Auguste was born, Mme Labouré had a servant to help her with the children and the housework. As the mother moved from room to room, the toddling Zoé tagged at her heels, taking in all the household tasks she would remember and do so well in the years to come. When the boys came home from the village school, they had chores to do to help their mother. As they grew older and stronger, they followed their father into the fields with plow and hoe.

Of course, there was time for play: the rollicking games in the barnyard or in the twisting streets, the leaping and wrestling in the high-piled hay of the barn. For Zoé and Tonine there were the dolls and the bits of bright cloth of little girlhood. When night had fallen and the whole family was gathered within the walls of the house, all was cozy with the sound of rattling dishes, chattering voices, and laughter.

While Zoé was still a tot, Marie Louise went off to live with an uncle and aunt in Langres. This aunt was Madeleine Labouré's sister, and Marie Louise had been named for her. Her husband was the commandant of the military post in the town. The couple was childless, and in their loneliness had asked the Labourés for Marie Louise. It does credit to the compassion and kindliness of Madeleine and Pierre that they gave her up. Her uncle and aunt raised the girl as their daughter, lavishing every care upon her, and giving her an excellent education with the Sisters of Charity at Langres.

In 1811, the oldest son, Hubert, enlisted in the army at the age of seventeen. Not long after, Jacques left home for Paris

to take a job as clerk in a business firm. The departure of these
two fired dreams in the eyes of the younger boys and they
yearned for the day when they, too, would set forth to make
their fortunes: their father was a hard man, and in the outside
world there was freedom and adventure. In the meantime,
however, the loving hand of their gentle mother kept them
tractable and together.

Zoé was growing up at her mother's knee, almost literally,
for the two were drawn to each other in a special way. Naturally enough, this grave little girl and her baby sister must have
been a comfort to Madeleine Labouré, surrounded and assailed for years by seven noisy boys. This womanly delight in
little girls, however, is not sufficient to explain the unusual relationship between Mme Labouré and Zoé. It would seem,
rather, that the native piety of the mother was quick to notice
the difference from the others in this chosen child, was quick to
detect in her an eager response to her own love of God. There
can be no doubt that the future saint learned the beginnings of
her sanctity from her mother. How well she learned, we know
from the lips of one who was a little girl with her.

The Labourés had relatives in the village of Cormarin, and
every year these cousins would invite the whole Labouré family to join them for the patronal feast of the village. The feast-
day celebration would begin with the singing of high Mass
in the village church. It was a long and trying ceremony for
the children, who had thoughts only for the good times to
come when it was over. Like children everywhere, they
squirmed, they fidgeted, they played with their fingers, they
looked this way and that. All except Zoé. She knelt up straight,
hands joined, eyes fixed on the altar where Calvary had come
again to a tiny hamlet in France. Her behavior was so different
from that of the other girls and boys, her attitude so proper
and attentive and grown-up, that it could not pass unnoticed.
And noticed it was, even by the children, for the old lady of

ninety who related it to the tribunal investigating the sanctity
of Zoé Labouré in 1895 was one of those children, and she
remembered all through the years.

There was another survivor of those feasts in Cormarin
who had more to tell. When Mass was over, the people would
pour into the village square, the grownups to chat and renew
acquaintanceship, the children to romp and play. Zoé was
there in the midst of the laughing, skipping, shrieking children.
Eighty years after, a playmate remembered her as "not pretty,
but pleasant and good, even when they teased her, as children
will." Teasing is hard for any child to take, for the teasing of
children can be cruel, but Zoé was not a sensitive little girl.
With her there was no hurting back or sobbing and running to
mama. She only laughed and passed it off.

In a short time, in fact, the competent Zoé had taken over
the group. Not that she organized the games and everyone
played them her way, or else. Her leadership showed itself
only when there was trouble—a quarrel or a downright fight.
Then she stepped in quickly and quietly and made peace, and
her peace terms were accepted and followed.

A wonderful treat for the children at the festival in Cormarin were the goodies—the candy and other sweets. It is
hard for us today, when candy is so plentiful and cheap, to
realize just how wonderful a treat it was for these simple
country children. There was no such thing as commercial
candy in the country provinces of France; it was all made at
home. And life was so hard and provisions so few and precious
that they could not be wasted on such a luxury as sweets, except on occasions like this.

There is no reason to suppose that Zoé Labouré was unlike the children of all ages in their common weakness for
candy. She, too, must have had a sweet tooth. Yet she would
give away her share of the feast-day goodies to the first poor
child who had been forgotten. This was a really remarkable

act of mortification for a little child, but there is sworn testimony that Zoé did it, and not once only.

Another banner expedition of Zoé's childhood was the annual trek to Senailly, where the Labouré family spent their summer vacation at the mother's old home. It was on one of these vacation trips that a tragic accident occurred. The horses bolted, or a wheel dropped into a deep hole in the rutty road, and one of the carriages overturned amid shrieks of fright and horror. When the dust had subsided, frail little Auguste lay oddly twisted, a cripple for life. Until his dying day, some twenty-two years later, he had to be waited on constantly and carried from place to place.

At home in Fain-les-moutiers the family circle kept getting smaller. Hubert and Marie Louise and Jacques were gone from the paternal roof. Antoine was the next to go. As soon as he was old enough, he apprenticed himself to a pharmacist in Paris. Charles was biding his time, waiting his chance to flee. Joseph and Pierre were in school most of the day. There was a village school for the boys of Fain; the girls had to travel to the school of the Sisters of Charity in Moutiers-Saint Jean.

Although Zoé and Tonine were old enough for school, their mother seemed loath to send them. It could not have been the distance that caused her reluctance: Moutiers-Saint Jean was little more than a half-hour's walk from Fain, and little country girls were used to such a walk. More likely, having suffered the separation from her older children, Madeleine Labouré was anxious to keep the youngest near her as long as possible; and perhaps she had a presentiment that she herself would not be with them much longer. It was a strange way for a former schoolteacher to act, and, even more strange, she does not seem to have given her little girls any schooling worthy of the name at home.

These years were pleasant ones for Zoé. Her pride in her home when she was its mistress and her deep, lifelong love for her family stem from them. She was the darling of her father and the comfort of her mother. Most fathers are helpless before the feminine wiles of their daughters, and Pierre Labouré was no exception. Zoé's only wile, however, was her goodness, which penetrated her father's hard shell and won his heart. Her mother's heart was easier to win, for Zoé carried a great part of it in her bosom: the loving kindness, the gentleness, the piety of Madeleine Labouré, all were copied faithfully in the heart of her little girl. Out of these years, too, sprang the single-souled friendship that always united Zoé and Tonine.

But, like every earthly happiness, it was not to last. On October 9, 1815, Madeleine Labouré died. She was only forty-two; she and her husband had been married twenty-two years.

There are no details of her death; we do not know whether it was sudden or long-drawn-out; we have no hint of the nature of her last illness. It has been suggested that she was worn out by her seventeen pregnancies, but this can only be a guess, and a dangerous and misleading one. After all, many a woman has borne a large family without dying of it. Madeleine Labouré could not have been a delicate woman. In an age when infant mortality was high, nine of her children grew to strong, healthy adulthood. Auguste, the youngest boy, was the only puny one, and he lived to be twenty-eight years old in spite of the crippling accident suffered in his childhood. Only Alexandre died in infancy, and his death need not be blamed on inherited frailty; any children's disease could have carried him off. Catherine lived to be seventy, and Marie Louise survived her, dying in her eighties. There is absolutely no indication that the Labourés were of weak stock, either on their father's side, or their mother's. Besides, Mme Labouré was not called upon to raise her family and keep her house single-handed. She had her mother with her when the older ones were babies, and a competent nurse and servant for the younger ones. To paint Madeleine Labouré as a poor, bedraggled creature, exhausted with babies and housework, is to paint a very false picture indeed.

The praises of this valiant woman could never be fully sung. She accepted fully the Christian duty of motherhood. She instilled in her children piety, honesty, and integrity of character: the children themselves have attested to it. The sanctity of Catherine is the crowning proof, for, as has been said, her mother taught Catherine the elements of holiness.

The greater the person, the greater the loss. Certainly the loss of Madeleine Labouré was a blow of major proportions to the Labouré family. It was like blowing out the light that had illumined the great square rooms, like tearing the heart out of the home. We do not know whether the three oldest boys were home when their mother died. Marie Louise came home from Senailly and stayed on after the funeral to manage the house. She was a young lady of twenty now, and her place was with her father.

He needed her. He needed every help, every consolation, for his way of life had changed suddenly and completely. The old familiar way was no more. It had started to crumble when the older children left home; now it broke up entirely. In the resulting chaos, Charles received his permission to go to Paris to learn the restaurant business. Joseph and Pierre were packed off to boarding school. Of all that large family there were left only the father, Marie Louise, Zoé, Tonine, and Auguste —and the servant. We do not even know the name of this good servant, but the fact that she earned from her little charges the name of Mama, speaks volumes.

Zoé was nine now, Tonine seven, and Auguste six. The poor little things wandered about, disconsolate, bewildered and unhappy. Of the three, Zoé seems to have taken her mother's death the hardest. She was just at that awakening time of childhood when the happenings of life, joyful and sad, are no longer things looked at idly like a play, but flesh-and-blood

experiences that touch and change the heart. Zoé had been especially attached to her mother; she had enjoyed the favored
dalliance of a mother who knows that she is near the end of
her bearing. Most of all, she had depended on her mother
for her spiritual food. Now there was an emptiness in her
breast. There was no mother to prattle to, to run to with
hurts to be kissed away; above all, to trust with her wise and
pious childish thoughts.

It was in this crisis that Zoé adopted Mary as her Mother.

It was on a day shortly after her mother's burial that the
extraordinary thing happened. A statue of Our Lady stood
on a shelf in the bedroom of her father and mother. It was
probably a cheap statue, battered and chipped. It might have
been of stone or wood or only of plaster, colored or plain—
it doesn't matter. What matters is that it was a statue of Our
Lady, perhaps the most important statue of Our Lady in modern times. That unknown, long-discarded statue was the instrument that ushered in the Marian Age.

Zoé was alone in the bedroom; she had looked carefully
about to make sure of that. She had a duty to perform, and
like all the solemn and decisive acts of life, it had to be done
alone. Of course even Zoé did not realize that what she was
about to do far transcended her personal life. It was vital to
countless millions yet unborn; and so she might have spared
herself her pains, for all the world was to see her. The Blessed
Virgin arranged for the servant to happen quietly on the scene
and to observe it all.

Zoé pulled a chair over beneath the shelf, for it was too high
for her to reach, even if she stood on tiptoe. Climbing up on
the chair, she stretched overhead and took down Our Lady's
image. She was too much engrossed in the ecstasy of her devotion to notice anything now. She did not even get down
from the chair; it would serve well enough for the altar of her
choosing and dedication. Throwing her arms about the statue,

she hugged it close to her little body, as a child might fondle her favorite doll or teddy bear.

But this was no doll. In a sense, it was no longer just a statue of Our Lady. It was Mary herself. Zoé's words showed that very clearly.

"Now, dear Blessed Mother," she said aloud with childlike fervor, "now you will be my Mother!"

Only that. She put the statue back in its familiar place and climbed down off the chair.

What Zoé meant to do, what she did, is clear enough. She missed her mother terribly, she felt deeply the need for someone to take her place. Yet how was it that, at the tender age of nine, she made the perfect choice?

It seems obvious that Zoé's instincts were, already, those of the saints. The great St. Teresa of Avila had made the same choice of Mary for Mother while praying before a statue of the Virgin, not long after her own mother's death. Certainly, Zoé's action was not just a cute, childish trick. As children say, this was "for real." Zoé had chosen Mary, the Mother of God, for her own mother—solemnly, surely, with a certain knowledge of what she was doing, of what she meant. Her whole life from this time on bears it out plainly.

From this day forward Zoé Labouré was truly the child of Mary and Mary was truly her mother. The reality of their relationship is evident in Zoé's simple, straightforward acceptance of it. Mary was as real to her as her father and brothers and sisters. This is the literal truth and it is the key to Zoé's life. It explains her intimate, her almost casual communion with the Mother of God. It explains how—whether now or a little later, we do not know—she could foster a desire that seems at first glance presumptuous, preposterous, nearly blasphemous: the desire to see the Blessed Virgin. She clung to that desire, made it the constant petition of her prayers, and, most amazing of all, was serenely confident that it would be realized. This little village girl *knew* that some day she would see the Mother of God.

It might be justly objected that, since children have marvelous imaginations and are adept at the game of make-believe, this whole business was but a child's fancy. Not so. Zoé Labouré was not an average child and her sister Tonine tells us, significantly, that Zoé disliked the games of childhood. Neither in her young years or later did she ever display the least tendency to daydream. She was singularly practical and unimaginative. If she spoke out loud to an inanimate statue, it was because she believed wholeheartedly in the living, breathing person the statue represented; it was because she felt, perhaps instinctively and without understanding, that this solemn choice must have a visible and sacramental form.

Probably the incident of the statue was almost entirely for the benefit of mankind, a way of serving public notice that the Marian Age had begun. Why else would Heaven have provided an eavesdropper in the person of the Labouré servant? Certainly the devotion of St. Catherine Labouré for the Immaculate Mother of God, with its enormous consequences for the human race, dated from this childhood dedication. It was the first act of homage of a new day, a day which was to dawn in a burst of glory with the Apparitions of the Miraculous Medal, was to grow steadily brighter with the Apparitions of Lourdes and Fatima, and was to reach its zenith in the solemn proclamation of the Assumption of Our Lady and in the intense, worldwide devotion of the Marian Year of 1954.

Having made her choice, Zoé was no longer lonesome. She had regained a mother. Her action did nothing to solve the family problems of the moment, however; indeed, it may have aggravated them, for, when the servant told Pierre Labouré of the touching scene she had witnessed, his heart must have been torn apart at this poignant evidence of the terrible loss his children had suffered in the death of their mother.

At this point Pierre's sister Marguerite came forward with a very generous offer. Marguerite Labouré was married to Antoine Jeanrot, who conducted a profitable vinegar distillery in the village of Saint Rémy. The Jeanrots had four daughters who would make perfect companions for the Labouré girls; and so Mme Jeanrot proposed to her brother that she take Zoé and Tonine into her home and family.

Pierre Labouré accepted his sister's offer. Perhaps he felt that it would be better all around. It would be a change for his little girls, and that in itself might help them to forget. Then they would be surrounded by a normal home life, complete with the tender ministrations of a mother. Certainly it would be a help to Marie Louise and the servant, who had all they could do to keep the house, feed the farm laborers, and nurse the invalid Auguste. At least it would be worth trying.

II

"Well, Then, Tell Him"

SAINT RÉMY was a village right out of a story book. It lay, pretty and peaceful, along a winding river, on the road from Fain to Montbard. The Jeanrot house was the first one you met after crossing the wooden bridge. The house had a lovely walled garden that ran down to the river and commanded a fine view of the ranging hills beyond. Here, in this country beauty, Zoé spent the years 1816 and 1817.

Zoé and Tonine were happy with their Aunt Marguerite. She was an aunt after a child's heart, tender and kind, with a fond reputation for charity among her neighbors—the sort of woman you turned to immediately when there was sickness or trouble. That her husband was a kindred spirit is evident from the generosity with which he welcomed his wife's two nieces into his home. The Jeanrot girls, who were older than their little cousins, doted upon them.

Life at Saint Rémy was, therefore, comfortable, cheerful, and pleasant. The Jeanrots seem to have been a carefree and lighthearted lot, and it was this sunny attitude toward living that drew from Fain certain disapproving hints that "at Saint Rémy the children did not receive all the useful attentions." Certainly the Jeanrot home was run very differently from the strict, precise, and efficient household of Fain, but that is probably the worst that can be said of it. It is possible that Antoine and Marguerite Jeanrot seemed slipshod when measured against the unyielding discipline of Pierre Labouré, but who is to say which view lay closer to the rule of the angels? The Jeanrot home was profoundly Christian; nor were Zoé and Tonine shamefully neglected there—a great deal to say.

Life was almost as before. The broken pieces were gathered and put together by the soothing hands of Aunt Marguerite, the emptiness in the hearts of the little girls wholly filled by her love. Of course they must have had a few bouts with homesickness in the beginning, but, no doubt, these soon passed. Fain was but a few miles away, and they saw their father, Marie Louise, Auguste, and the dear substitute Mama often enough. All this, with the healing power of time and the quickness of children to forget, turned the trick. The little Labourés were content.

One thing Zoé never forgot: that she had chosen Mary for her Mother. Nor the catechism of sanctity her earthly mother had taught her. She went right on building upon these foundations, laying prayer on prayer and devotion on devotion like so many bricks. It was of immense help to her that Saint Rémy possessed a resident priest. That meant many more church services than she had been used to, a whole new world of divine things. It was like turning a child loose in a huge, wonderful toyshop, for the things of the Lord were truly the toys of this holy child. The simplest object of piety, the crudest holy picture, or the most primitive statue, gave the same delight to her heart that a new ball or rag doll brought to other little girls.

Zoé's cousin Claudine, who was eighteen and so very

grown-up that Zoé called her "aunt," never got over Zoé's absorbed attention in church.

"What a pleasure it is to watch Zoé in church," she would say. "How alert she is when she prays!"

It is the testimony of Cormarin all over again. Nor did Claudine stop at admiring her little cousin, but went on to imitate her. Mentally she checked her own behavior in church: whether she knelt up straight, whether she folded her hands devoutly, whether she kept her eyes fixed on the Mass, as she should, as Zoé did. By her own testimony, Claudine's whole spiritual life grew better, all because of the artless piety of a little girl.

Among the "useful attentions" Zoé failed to receive at Saint Rémy was schooling. The Jeanrots cannot be blamed overmuch for this; Zoé's own mother and father neglected to see to it when she was at home.

This neglect of proper schooling is the strangest fact of Zoé's childhood. Her father and mother were, after all, persons of a certain education and culture—a point that cannot be made too much of, for it was noteworthy enough in the country provinces of early nineteenth-century France. The mother was a schoolteacher, the father had pursued the graduate studies of the seminary. Like parents the world over, they must surely have wished their children to be as well educated as themselves, or better; and they had the means. What is more, they saw to it as far as the seven oldest were concerned. Marie Louise had a thorough, well-rounded education with the Sisters of Charity at Langres. Hubert's education was such that he was fitted to make a brilliant career for himself as an officer in the French army and to marry the schoolmistress of a fashionable academy. Jacques and Antoine were trained to follow professional careers, the one in commerce and the other in pharmacy. Charles learned the catering trade. Joseph and Pierre were taken out of the village school in Fain and sent to boarding school upon the death of their mother. Only the three youngest of the family had no formal schooling. Of these, Auguste was too delicate in health for it, and Tonine at least learned from her father to read and write. Zoé alone was scarcely able to trace her name or stumble through a simple sentence.

Many excuses can be made for it: the reluctance of the ailing mother to part with her babies, the shunting about of the girls after her death, Zoé's preoccupation with the house-work when she returned home. There seems, however, only one reason: that all these human factors were permitted by God to work toward His own ends. Her lack of letters was to play an important part in both the vocation and the Marian mission of Zoé Labouré.

The stay in Saint Rémy was intended to be a temporary measure to tide everyone over the crisis caused by Madeleine Labouré's death. Like many temporary measures, however, it began to take on an air of permanency, and two years had gone by before anyone realized it.

Then two circumstances came about that made it both natural and necessary for the children to come home.

The first was the vocation of the oldest girl, Marie Louise. She had been attracted to the Sisters of Charity when they taught her at Langres, and had long ago made up her mind to join them. Her mother's death had called a halt to her plans for a time, but now she was twenty-two and anxious to get on with them again. She could make no move, however, until someone was found to take over the running of the house.

The second circumstance developed at St. Rémy. M. Jean-rot's business was flourishing to such a degree that his wife was called in more and more to assist him with it. She found herself forced to be away from Zoé and Tonine for hours at a time. The good woman herself was the first to be dissatisfied with such a state of affairs, and she solved the difficulty by hiring a nurse for the children. Even this substitution, however, could not have satisfied her wholly, and her sense of responsibility must have been uneasy and disturbed. It was probably a great relief to her when her brother proposed taking his children home again.

The pain and upset attendant on this new change were softened for the children by their father's decision to turn the house over to their charge—or, at least, to Zoé. Pierre Labouré had a great aversion to entrusting his home to a hired housekeeper, and he knew the capabilities of his favorite child.

Nevertheless, it was a hard task for a little girl—Zoé was scarcely twelve—to manage a household, and such a household! Zoé had a fair-sized family to do for: her father, Tonine, Auguste and, for a time, Joseph and Pierre, home from boarding school. Auguste was a problem all by himself, for he required the thousand extra attentions of the invalid. Then there were the hired men, a baker's dozen of them. They were part of the household, living in, their meals provided by their employer. In the middle of the day their meal had to be carried to them in the fields. A shrewd head was needed to calculate the stores and provisions to be laid in for such a hard-working, huge-eating crowd, a tireless frame to cook for them, a strong back to serve them.

The housework was enormous: beds to make, the house to sweep and dust—and it was large—piles of dishes to wash, glassware and pewter to keep bright and shining, clothes to sew and mend, launder and iron. Zoé had a servant to help her, of course, but she was a servant, and not a member of the family. The household was not hers to order; Pierre Labouré made that plain; the right and the duty belonged to Zoé.

Many a grown woman would have balked at the formidable task, but not Zoé. It was her father's wish, it would leave Marie Louise free to go to God, and that was enough for Zoé.

The Labourés had a busy round of it, that winter and spring

of 1817–18. Besides doing her housework, Marie Louise had to stop to explain the why and the wherefore and the how of it to Zoé. Zoé worked right along with her, eyes and ears alert even while her hands were occupied. It was not all new to her: she had watched her mother at work, had followed at her heels as she now followed Marie Louise, and much of it came back to her. Bringing up the rear was the little Tonine, helping when she could, mentally laying up every duty against the day when she, too, would step into the post of mistress so that Zoé in turn could follow her heart's desire. The father himself presided over all, making sure Marie Louise did not forget any least detail, noting with satisfaction how quickly Zoé caught on.

These few months were the only moments of their lives that the three Labouré sisters truly shared, knowing and sympathizing with one another as only the womenfolk of a family can. The most piteous figure of the three is Tonine, for her years of service under the parental roof were to be long and, toward the end, lonely; and, afterward, no golden religious life for her reward, but a late marriage with more than its share of heartbreaks.

With everything else, Marie Louise was making her preparations to enter the Sisters of Charity, gathering together the clothes and linens she would take with her. Naturally, her going was the household topic of the hour, a topic Zoé found fascinating, for each excited conversation fanned the flame of religious desire that was rising in her own heart.

She, too, had a work of preparation to crowd into these active days, the preparation for her first Holy Communion. She had begun it at Saint Rémy and had gotten well along in the lessons of the catechism under the constant tutelage of the village curé. It was perhaps Zoé's greatest regret in leaving her aunt's home, that she could not wait just a little, to make her first Communion. To get on with her lessons at home in

Fain was harder, because Abbé Mamer, with his three parishes to care for, was not always available; nor had she any longer the leisure she had enjoyed in Saint Rémy. Postponement was a bitter thing, for her soul was ardent and eager; yet delay was only a tool in the Hand of God to sharpen her appetite for the heavenly Bread.

The delay, actually, was longer in her heart than it was in time. It was only a few weeks after her return to her father's house, on January 25, 1818, that Zoé received her Lord for the first time, in the village church of Moutiers-Saint Jean. Doubtless this church was selected because it was the mother church of the three parishes and the seat of residence of the pastor; and the day, the feast of the Conversion of St. Paul, because it was the patronal feast of the church. Looked at in the light of Zoé's subsequent greatness, however, an even better reason for the selection is apparent. It was another of those deliberate coincidences of God. The Feast of the Conversion of St. Paul is celebrated by the Vincentian Fathers as the birthday of their Community.

The first meeting of Jesus and Zoé Labouré seemed to effect a perpetual contract of mutual love and service. Zoé, who was already good and kind and devout even to a degree of heroism, began to display more and more the outward trappings of her love for God. Tonine was quick to notice the change. Ever and again in later years she would tell her children how their Aunt Zoé had become "entirely mystic" from the time of her first Communion.

Tonine meant that, with first Communion, Zoé put aside the things of a child in piety and devotion. From this time on, she went after her spiritual advancement in dead earnest, with order and system. In spite of the mountain of duties piled upon her young shoulders, she set aside certain fixed times for prayer. The most important of these times was the early morning, and her prayer then the greatest of all, the holy Sacrifice of the Mass.

Zoé began to attend Mass daily and to receive Holy Communion frequently. Given the circumstances, these were acts of devotion approaching the heroic. There was no daily Mass in Fain; there was not always Sunday Mass. The only priest in the district said his daily Mass in the chapel of the Hôpital de Saint Sauveur in Moutiers-Saint Jean. It was not a question, therefore, of Zoé's rolling out of bed and tumbling into church. The hospital was a good, brisk half-hour's walk from Fain, and the Sisters' Mass was at six o'clock. Daily Mass for this young girl just entering her teens meant an early rising—an earlier rising even than farm life called for, because she had chores to do before she left—and a long walk in all kinds of weather and, half the year, in the dark. The youngster was determined to go, however, and she never faltered. In a sense she had to go, for she went to a daily rendezvous with God, who was her whole life. On certain mornings, frequent but not frequent enough to slake her ardor, she enjoyed complete union with her Beloved in Holy Communion. She could not have this happiness every day, for daily Communion would not be permitted the faithful for a hundred years yet.

Here in the Hôpital de Saint Sauveur, Zoé was a guest, as it were, of St. Vincent de Paul. The saint himself had founded the hospital in 1654 at the request of his friend Nicolas de Rouchechouart de Chandenier, Abbé de Moutiers-Saint Jean, and the Sisters of Charity still served it. The hospital was, therefore, another signpost placed along her way, but she failed to catch its meaning.

Zoé had decided, even at so early an age, that she was going to enter religion. Tonine says that she talked of it from the day of her first Communion. Strangely enough, however, though the Sisters of Charity were the only religious women she knew, she does not seem to have been drawn to their community in the beginning. As we shall see, it took a direct and super-natural intervention of God, a few years later, to determine her choice of the daughters of Vincent de Paul.

Attendance at daily Mass was but the start of Zoé's day-long devotion. At home she quietly began the practice of slipping away from the others to some out-of-the-way corner of the house, there to keep her numerous appointments with God. Tonine would come upon her, so often that it ceased to be a surprise, absorbed, face shining—"entirely mystic."

Zoé's great love for Our Lady came out into the open now, too. It was as if she no longer had to pretend to recognize and look up to any earthly "mother." Saint Rémy and Aunt Marguerite belonged to the past. Marie Louise—if she had ever made any pretensions toward mothering Zoé—was off in Langres, where the Sisters of Charity had received her as a postulant on June 22, 1818. The beloved servant whom Zoé had once called Mama was now subject to the authority of her former child. Zoé could acknowledge freely that she had but one Mother, without regard to the feelings of anyone.

She made the acknowledgment in a singular way.

The centuries-old village church was across the lane from the Labouré house. A few steps and Zoé could be there. How often, in her years at home, she took those few steps! There were times between tasks when she could slip over to the church for a quick prayer and, at the end of the day with her work done, a longer, quieter time.

We have spoken of the Labouré chapel in this church. The family had defrayed the cost of certain repairs in the chapel, which was separated from the nave by a low railing, and in return the villagers had given it the family name and set it aside for the family use. In the chapel was a painting of the Annunciation. This was Zoé's shrine, a fitting one for her who had been born at the ringing of the Angelus. She knew every line of the picture, every tint, every trace, every cracking and peeling of the paint. Her knees became familiar with the tiniest rise and fall of the hard stone floor, as the fingers of the blind become familiar with the feel of the objects around them. Here she knelt, before the picture of the Annunciation, day after day, year after year, in the pleasant days of spring and autumn, in the stifling heat of summer, in the freezing damp of winter. Upright she knelt, quiet and composed as a statue. All her life she feared that her attitude at prayer might not be humble enough for the house of God. Zoé was never to forget this chapel. She bore the sensible remembrance of it until the day she died, in the arthritis of the knees which she contracted from her long hours of kneeling on the stone flags of the floor.

Another favorite pastime of Zoé's was making the Stations of the Cross. According to tradition, the Stations in the village church were the gift either of Marie Louise or of Zoé herself. Zoé's devotion to Our Lord's Passion was a natural outgrowth of her early bent toward mortification.

Now, with the new burgeoning of her soul, Zoé took on a new mortification, a startling one and, in a way, frightening because it was so very adult. In spite of all the labors of her hard day, she began to fast on Fridays and Saturdays. This worried Tonine. The little sister had nothing but admiration for Zoé's intense, quickening holiness; she had even begun to imitate it: yet she felt there was a limit. Tonine knew well how work could whet the hunger of a growing girl, she knew the spells of faintness unrequited hunger could bring, and she decided there should be no more nonsense. Frowning severely on her sister, she threatened to tell their father.

"Well, then, tell him!" was Zoé's short and decided reply.

This is one of the few verbatim sentences we have from the early life of Zoé Labouré; she was not given to much talk. The very isolation of the words give them a unique significance. "Tell him!" It is amazing how much insight these two words give into the character of this remarkable youngster. The iron will, the ramrod determination, the simple directness, all are here as fullblown as they would ever be. Had they been uttered fifty years hence, they would have been no more in character. The steel scaffolding for a supreme sanctity to build upon was already up.

Somewhat taken aback by Zoé's indifference and lack of compromise, Tonine nevertheless decided to see the thing through. She told her father.

The father did not discuss the matter with Tonine. It was his way to keep his own counsel, especially where his children were concerned. He did, however, remonstrate with Zoé, pointing out to her the necessity of keeping up her strength for her arduous tasks. Zoé listened respectfully, but did not change a whit in her resolve. She went right on fasting Fridays and Saturdays. Tonine could only shrug and retire from the field. She had done her duty.

The importance of this incident lies in the fact that, wrongly interpreted, it could impugn the habitual obedience and humility of the saint. St. Catherine's obedience was her most shining virtue, and it must not be even slightly dimmed without positive proof. If we knew nothing else of Zoé Labouré but this one incident, we should put her down as a headstrong and willful child. Her entire relationship with her father, however, was one of habitual filial respect and submission. Regarding the incident in context, therefore, we come to either of two conclusions, both favorable to Zoé: either the father's admonition was of simple counsel—and there is very good evidence for this; or, if it was a command, a higher Authority overruled him. It is certain that Zoé, in disregarding her father's advice in this matter, was following God's Will.

It might be added that the incident caused little concern to the ecclesiastical judges of her sanctity. Moreover, humanly speaking, Zoé knew what she was about. She was strong and well made, and it is a matter of record that she never suffered any but the slightest indispositions in all the years that she was at home. Her frame could take the penance she imposed.

It is a sure mark of the swift progress of Zoé's sanctity, this early addiction to self-denial. Like all the saints, she seemed to recognize the importance of it by instinct. Long before Our Lady told her, she understood the necessity of prayer and penance for salvation and perfection—and this, after all, is the drift of Mary's message in her appearances at Paris, LaSalette, Lourdes and Fatima.

Instinct is a poor word to describe Zoé's way of knowing the truth. She knew it rather by the infused knowledge perseverance in prayer had brought her from God. Nor is this idle conjecture. Zoé Labouré was an untutored, unlettered girl. She could not learn, therefore, from the reading of spiritual books, but only from the sermons she heard in church; and these were the simple spiritual food of the average Christian, not the spiritual diet needed by an advanced soul like her.

There is not the slightest hint that she received any ordered spiritual direction. In her later years, she used to speak lovingly of the good advice her father always gave her, but we do not know that this advice was spiritual, and, for that matter, we know that he tried to thwart her efforts to fast. Abbé Mamer was certainly capable of directing Zoé's soul, and he was still alive at the time of her first Communion, but there is no evidence that he did. He must have been her confessor, but even confession was a haphazard thing in that district. Zoé herself used to say that when she wanted to go to confession, she had first to look for the priest.

If there was a director of Zoé's soul life at this time, we might justly expect mention of it. Tonine would have known whether or not Zoé applied to a director regularly or not, and she would have let posterity know this fact. Tonine is the source of all the information we have concerning this period

of her sister's life. Zoé, who later would confide in no one but
her director, confided wholly in Tonine during these growing-
up years. Taking Zoé's secretive nature into account, this is
highly significant. Zoé would hardly have let even Tonine
know her most intimate spiritual secrets, had there been a spiritual guide to tell them to.

Tonine fully respected Zoé's confidence: she revealed nothing of what was told her except when silence no longer mat-
tered, when Zoé was the hidden and forgotten Sister Catherine. Even then, she told only her children of their Aunt Zoé's
early steps in holiness. Nor can it be doubted that this was at
the unsuspected urging of Our Lady herself, who wanted the
whole world one day to know the greatness of her servant.

We have, then, fair assurance that, while at home in Fain,
Zoé had no authorized spiritual director. We can only conclude that God himself was her director, as He is of all the unlettered who are humble and good.

Zoé was fourteen years old now, and Tonine twelve. They
had been running the house for two years and had done surprisingly well. It was at this time that the servant who had
been part of the family for years announced that she was
leaving the household to be married. When M. Labouré offered to replace her, his two girls answered promptly:

"We have no further need of a servant. The two of us will
manage by ourselves."

It was a proud boast, but not a vain one. Zoé and Tonine
were young ladies now, quite equal to the task they had set
themselves. They were perfect teammates, who thought as one
and moved as one, without any lost motion. They differed in
temperament—Tonine was not so serious as her sister—but
they got along excellently for all that. Zoé, of course, was ever
the leader, ever the elder sister, and she kept a weather eye
open for the least impropriety or defection in Tonine. Tonine
has admitted readily enough that she was a "gamin," a mis-

chievous, carefree urchin. Actually, she had no more than her share of the average child's high spirits. It was Zoé who was different; and the early responsibilities thrust upon her had only served to deepen her natural gravity.

When Tonine got out of line, Zoé brought her back again promptly enough, and sometimes with severity. Zoé was too good-natured, however, to hold long with severity, but would endeavor to make it up to Tonine with an extra show of tenderness and affection.

The love was mutual. For her part Tonine showed it by that supreme of all flatteries, the flattery of imitation. She imitated Zoé in everything she did, even in her devotions. This latter imitation was no small act of love in one of Tonine's light-hearted temperament. She had not the fierce spiritual enthusiasm that drove Zoé to her knees. Nevertheless, she tried to follow the beloved older sister wherever she led. She knelt with her daily in the chapel of the village church. She accompanied her to every church office. This gay younger sister even stumbled along in the early morning to Mass in Moutiers-Saint Jean.

"How pious they were, those Labouré girls!" recalled an old lady of Fain many years afterward. "They never joined the other young girls at play. When church was over, they would stop for a little to pass the time of day with the young people, then hurry home to their work."

They led a true community life, Zoé and Tonine. They followed a regular order of day with fixed times for rising, Mass, prayers, meals, work—just like any religious society of the Church. They were the admiration of the village, and many a mother of Fain held them up as models to her less energetic daughters.

Zoé's limpid holiness, welling up from the springs of her soul, was bound to overflow in good deeds for others. Visiting her sick neighbors became a favorite diversion; there was no unfortunate or ailing person in the village who was not her friend. Without realizing it, she was already leading the life of a Sister of Charity, that perfect integration of body and soul, of spiritual devotion and corporeal toil, of prayer and work and outward charity.

It was a life that sat well with her father, for it was a life very like his own. Pierre Labouré was a pious man who could admire the deep piety of his daughter. Her industry and capability he could admire to the full, for they were traits she took from him, traits he taught her, by example and counsel, to marshal and use. It was no doubt his recognition of himself in Zoé that prompted Pierre Labouré to lavish upon her his special love and predilection. The boys of the family all agreed that this father, a strict and demanding taskmaster, could find little to quarrel with in Zoé, or in the way she ran his house.

Tonine has left us a charming picture of her sister caught unawares, in one of her rare, light moments. Zoé kept for herself as a daily personal duty the feeding of the hundreds of pigeons in the Labouré dovecot. It was, indeed, the one recreation of her long, hard day. The pigeons knew her and, as Tonine says, "loved her." The moment she appeared with the pan of feed, they swirled in great clouds from the dovecot windows. Swooping upon her in thick, multi-colored droves, they pecked and pulled at her hair and her clothes, completely disheveling her. What a picture she made—hair unloosened, tumbling about her shoulders, one arm upflung across her eyes to shield them from the importunities of her beloved birds! Laughing, she would scatter the grain as best she could, wholly lost in delight at the friendly onslaught.

Most remarkable of all, the birds would soar round and about her, weaving a flashing halo about her head with their wings. Surely we can be pardoned for catching here a sudden glimpse of the white wings of a cornette and the immortal aureole of canonized sanctity.

The Dream

THE MOST CONVINCING PROOF of the reality of Zoé Labouré's vocation was that she talked about it. It seems a ridiculous piece of evidence at first glance, for teen-age girls talk about everything: their technicolor dreams of the future, the type of man they mean to marry, the kind of home they plan to have. Many of them "get religion" at one time or another and vow fervently that they will go to the convent—not forgetting to let a requisite number of chums in on the exciting secret. All this is natural, normal, healthy girl talk. Zoé Labouré, however, was not given to such harmless chatter. When she said something, you could be sure that she had thought about it for a long time first.

She talked about her vocation, according to Tonine, "from the time of her first Communion." Characteristically, too, Zoé acted to further it, not in a sudden fever of activity, for hers was a long-range plan: she did not intend to leave home tomorrow or the next day; it would be years before she went. In the meantime, nevertheless, her intention one day to embrace the religious life was her chief motive for training Tonine in the role of housekeeper. When Tonine should be old enough to take over the care of the house, then, Zoé decided, she herself would go off to fulfill her vocation. In the years of waiting she would bolster it with prayer and with the intimate conversation and sympathy of her little sister and friend. Nor did she so much as mention it to anyone but her sister. Zoé went every Sunday to the hospital in Moutiers-Saint Jean to visit with the Sister Servant or Superior, Sister Catherine Soucial; but nothing was ever said on either side about vocation.

This Sister Catherine had an interesting history. As a young girl, she had been in a predicament similar to Zoé's: what to do, where to go, to find her vocation. She had the answer while praying before the famous shrine of Our Lady of Buglose, where St. Vincent de Paul had gone barefoot on pilgrimage. When her seminary in Paris was over, Sister Catherine was sent to the community house in Châtillon-sur-Seine, the very house where Zoé was to be given the final sign of her calling and where she was to serve her postulancy. The violence of the Revolution reached Châtillon in 1793, and the Sisters were driven out. Not knowing where to go, Sister Catherine was on the point of returning to her parents' home, when she heard that the Sisters of Charity were still at Moutiers-Saint Jean. She took refuge there and stayed on for sixty years.

Sister Catherine Soucial and Zoé were fast friends. That, and the religious atmosphere of the house, made it natural for Zoé to reveal her vocation; yet she kept her counsel, and Sister Catherine kept hers. The good Sister went no nearer to the heart of the matter than to encourage Zoé in her devotions and in her hard and laborious life. While it is true that the Sisters of Charity had a tradition of not seeking out vocations, yet the tradition was not ironclad; and furthermore, Sister Catherine never mentioned vocation to Zoé at all, to any religious community. It would seem that this wise woman, who had had first-hand experience of the workings of Providence, was content to let God indicate His plans for Zoé in His own good time. Besides, she must have seen that Zoé was already living the life of a Sister of Charity in the world, and that her way of life would certainly influence her choice of vocation.

As for Zoé, it was her nature to pray and to wait and to ponder and to be silent.

One night in 1824, when she was eighteen, Zoé had an extraordinary dream. She dreamed that she was in her favorite oratory, the chapel of the Labourés in the village church, assisting at the Mass of an old and venerable priest she had never seen before. Each time the priest turned from the altar for the "Dominus Vobiscum," he raised his eyes to Zoé's face and held her gaze. Each time she was forced to lower her eyes, blushing, unable to hold the steady and compelling eyes of the priest.

When Mass was over and the old man had started for the sacristy, he turned back and beckoned to Zoé to follow him. She was suddenly very frightened and, jumping to her feet, ran from the church. She glanced back over her shoulder as she ran, and the priest was still there, standing by the sacristy door, looking after her.

Then the thought came to Zoé in her dream to stop to visit a woman of the village who was sick. On entering the sickroom, she came face to face with the same venerable priest. Wild fright seized her again, and she began to back away. For the first time, then, the priest spoke directly to her:

"You do well to visit the sick, my child. You flee from me now, but one day you will be glad to come to me. God has plans for you; do not forget it."

At these words Zoé awoke and lay wondering what it could all mean; and, strangely enough, there was no more fear in her, only peace and comfort and a great happiness. Although she did not understand it then, this dream was sent Zoé by God to point out with certainty the vocation of His choice.

Zoé told no one about her dream, not even Tonine. She recounted it for the first time to her confessor in Châtillon some four years later, when she began to realize what it meant. Out of the confessional, she spoke of it only toward the end of her life nearly fifty years later, when, in a sudden transport of joy, she recounted this vivid and mysterious dream to Marie Louise, whom she had gone to visit in the infirmary of the Motherhouse of the Sisters of Charity on the rue du Bac.

Dreams and their interpretation are a slippery business, especially in spiritual matters. Everybody dreams; dreaming is a purely mechanical action of the human mind. The imagination is like a moving-picture screen upon which the films or images stored up by the memory are flashed. If the projection machine is left unguarded, as it is when the operator falls asleep, the film tends to rewind itself and get all mixed up in the process. The results are dreams. Because of their lack of intelligent control, dreams are obviously not to be trusted as guides to action. Yet the superstitious often look upon them as such guides. For this reason the Church has seen fit to condemn the interpretation of dreams generally, along with fortune telling, omens, and other occult claptrap.

Nevertheless, God has at times and for His own wise reasons made important use of dreams. There were, for example, the Old Testament dreams of Jacob and Joseph his son, and the New Testament dreams of the Foster Father of Jesus. And there was the dream of Zoé Labouré.

That God could use so perilous a means to communicate with a girl of only eighteen is eloquent testimony to Zoé's hardheaded common sense. Moreover, Zoé's ability to distinguish between this type of communication and her other supernatural illuminations makes her a most trustworthy witness. She was always precise as to whether she "dreamed" or "saw" or "heard" or "understood interiorly" whatever Heaven had to tell her.

Meanwhile, at nineteen, Zoé had her first proposal of marriage.

Zoé Labouré had certain physical, social, and housewifely graces that made her eminently desirable as a wife, especially a country wife. She was not pretty; neither was she homely. Her best physical feature was her eyes—large, solemn, wise, and blue as cornflowers. She was strong and well knit, an excellent thing in a farmer's wife. She dressed well and neatly, but not with foolish ostentation. She was innocent and good. She had already proven her ability to manage a home. With all this, she was of good family, and, since her father was prosperous, her dowry would be substantial.

The name of the young man who first proposed marriage to her has long been forgotten. He and Zoé had probably known each other from childhood, for the district was not thickly populated and everyone knew everyone else. Most likely he was one of the group of young people Zoé and Tonine stopped to chat with after church.

It is impossible to imagine Zoé encouraging this young man's attentions in any way, "dating him" as we would say today, or even going along with the ritual of courtship then in vogue. Not that she was stuffy or prudish: she was just not interested, for she had other plans; and she was too honest to waste a boy's time or ambition for nothing. She would be gentle and kind and polite with him, as she was with everyone.

Evidently this was encouragement enough for the young blade for, in accordance with custom, his father stepped in to play his part, making a call on Pierre Labouré to propose a marriage between Zoé and his son. Pierre was flattered: the boy's family was solid and respectable and ranked high in the village. He promised to speak to Zoé, to further the suit.

Zoé, of course, turned it down. Nor did her father press her to consent. Secretly, he was highly pleased. There was enormous satisfaction in the knowledge that his favorite child was desirable; it reflected favorably both on her and on him, on her good qualities and on his position. At the same time, he was more than content to have Zoé remain with him; her loss would have been a high price to pay for his social pride. The incident ended, therefore, to the satisfaction of the Labourés, father and daughter; only the young suitor was disappointed and had to look for greener pastures.

Tonine, the romantic miss of seventeen, had followed it all breathlessly. She was puzzled, to say the least, at the outcome.

"Will you never marry?" she asked her sister.

"I shall never marry," Zoé answered. "I am promised to Jesus Christ."

"Then, you haven't changed," Tonine persisted.

"I haven't changed." All her life, change would be the last thing to expect of Zoé Labouré.

There were at least two more proposals of marriage for the first lady of Fain, and they came to the same impasse. Her father smiled to himself, secure in the possession of his treasure. He slumbered on, not realizing that he was to lose her anyway. If he suspected Zoé's vocation at all—and her pious way of life certainly gave him reason enough to suspect it—he was, apparently, confident that he could deal with it.

When Zoé had reached the age of twenty-two, she sat down and took stock of her situation. She had done her duty; she had served her father faithfully and well. Tonine, at twenty, was capable of handling the household alone; and Zoé had made sure, in a long and earnest conversation, that she was not only ready but willing to do so. Satisfied, therefore, that her family responsibilities were at an end, Zoé decided to act upon her vocation. Nor would it be rash to state further that God was nudging her to action, for she never undertook anything unless she was convinced that it was the Will of God.

Nothing now stood in the way but to secure her father's consent. It would seem that Zoé had taken this for granted; otherwise she would not have waited so long to join battle with him for her rights. She would have prepared this ground as she prepared all others. As it was, she was taken by surprise.

Pierre Labouré said "No!"

Zoé's reactions to this unexpected refusal are not recorded, but they are easy to reconstruct. There would be amazement, of course; it was totally unlooked-for. There would be hurt; it was a callous display of ingratitude from the father she had loved and served so well. Especially, there would be anger.

Zoé had a will of her own and a temper to match it. She was a quiet, docile, withdrawn person, until she was crossed. Her father's refusal to consent to her vocation was probably the first time she had been crossed since childhood. She had had the ordering of the household; her father had gladly left it in her capable hands. He had given her a certain authority over Tonine and Auguste. He had left her free to follow her pious inclinations; he had not even forced her to relinquish the fasting she began when she was fourteen. It must have been like running full tilt into a stone wall for this favorite child of her father to have him refuse to grant her dearest wish.

We do not know whether a sharp exchange between father and daughter followed upon this refusal. Probably not. Zoé was too much mistress of herself to resist her father in words. She withdrew from the encounter, bewildered, hurt, angry, and heartbroken.

Until now life had been good on the Labouré farm. Pierre Labouré had basked in the mellow autumn of his days, well off, well served, respected by his fellows. Zoé had been content. She liked to manage things, and she did it well. The bright sun of her vocation had climbed steadily in the sky, promising a glorious day. Tonine had been happy also, and Auguste; but their happiness was beside the point, in a sense, since it depended greatly upon the harmony between Zoé and her father. Now that harmony had been shattered, and the former placid way of life was no more.

Things were the same on the surface. The floors were scrubbed, the woodwork dusted, the meals prepared, the livestock fed, with the same clockwork regularity; yet the life had gone out of these things. They had become routine, a way of putting in time between daybreak and sundown. Zoé's heart was no longer in them, and her heart was the heart of the home and all its works. Only her prayers kept their vitality, and they grew sad and poignant, filled with pleas and longing.

Into this house divided came a letter from Charles Labouré, Zoé's brother, who was in Paris. Years before, Charles had finished his apprenticeship in the catering trade and had gone to work for an established proprietor. Now, at twenty-eight, he had his own restaurant. Charles mentioned in this letter written to his father, that he was in need of domestic help, due apparently to the recent, untimely death of his wife. A plan took shape in the mind of Pierre Labouré. He would send Zoé to stay with her brother and help him with his business. The change would be good for everyone, because of the tension in the house. Especially—and this was Pierre's true motive—the change would serve to distract Zoé from her religious purpose. She had seen very little of the world she wished to leave, only a few straggly hamlets in fact. Paris *was* the world, a world the daughter of Pierre Labouré scarcely knew existed, save in rumor and story. Paris would knock this vocation nonsense right out of her young head. So Pierre Labouré argued. So thousands of doting fathers have argued over the centuries. To keep their daughters from the convent, to prevent them from marrying ineligible young men, these fathers have sent them traveling up and down the paths of the earth. Such plans have failed more often than they have succeeded. Certainly Pierre Labouré's plan was to fail, for, in sending Zoé to Paris, he was sending her away from him forever. She was never to return to Fain.

Zoé obeyed her father's wishes, now, as always. This obedience is the hallmark, the strength, of Zoé Labouré. No matter how fiercely the gorge of rebellion rose within her, no matter how useless she knew the command to be, Zoé always obeyed. Even at the adult age of twenty-two, even with the divine wishes crystal-clear in her own mind, Zoé felt constrained to submit to the superior God had placed over her in the person of her father. It is the only explanation for her allowing herself to be put to such torture of mind and soul during the next two years.

Zoé was quite capable of eloping to the convent; she had the courage and intrepidity for such a violent move. There can be little doubt that she would have been received, for she was of age and legally out of her father's reach. The only human motive she might have for hesitating was the lack of a dowry, but it was a lack that could be supplied, as it was eventually, without her father's help.

It is quite true, also, that Zoé loved her father and would not willfully hurt him. She knew that he doted on her, that he had always dreamed of having her near him in his declining days. She understood, as perhaps no one else did, his self-righteous excuse that, having given one daughter to the religious life, he had given all God had a right to expect of a Christian man. She understood and allowed for it.

With all this, however, her profound obedience, a virtue evident in every phase of her life, cannot be too strongly insisted upon as the mainspring of her submission, for it was ever the mainspring of all her actions.

A sparkling bauble indeed was the Paris of 1828. It shone with the brilliance of a new day. André Marie Ampère and Jean Baptiste Lamarck worked in its laboratories. Nicoló Paganini played in its concert halls. Its citizens diverted themselves with the novels of Victor Hugo and the poems of Alphonse Lamartine; they read in translation the works of Washington Irving and James Fenimore Cooper. Irving, in fact, had written his *Tales of a Traveler* in Paris only a few years before, and John Howard Payne, his immortal *Home, Sweet Home.* When Zoé arrived in the city, Cooper was actually in residence there, hard at work on his writing.

The storm of the revolution was past, the sun was out again, and Paris was back at its gay pastime of entertaining the world.

Not that Zoé could have known the social whirl and smartness of the capital. After all, her brother was only a restaurant keeper of the humblest kind. She could not miss, however, the beauty and enchantment of the lovely place. These were to be found on the boulevards and in the parks. They were the property of all and the poorest found delight in them.

Zoé did not. Pierre Labouré might have saved himself the hours of worry and scheming and the money spent on this experiment. He had miscalculated. The only effect Paris had on Zoé was to increase her misery.

Charles's restaurant was not at all what we mean by the term. It was a plainer establishment by far, more like the modern lunchroom or grille, a hole-in-the-wall on rue de l'Echiquier, where the workmen stopped for a bit of bread and cheese and a tumbler of wine. The quarter of the city was known as *Notre Dame de Bonne-Nouvelle*—Our Lady of Good News: the title was ironic, to say the least, at this lowest point of Zoé's life. Inside, the restaurant consisted of a single long, narrow room with a bare counter running from front to back on either side and plain benches set against the walls behind them. Here the rough workmen of the quarter took their daily meals, sitting all in a row like so many strange and noisy monks in their refectory, talking loudly, quarreling, laughing, raucous in their calls for service, beating with tin mugs on the scarred table-tops in deafening bids for attention.

The stale, smoke-filled air of the restaurant was a very different atmosphere from the pure country air of Zoé's home. It was an atmosphere that symbolized the completeness of the change for her, an atmosphere that choked, smothered, pressed upon her, hemmed her in with the hopeless misery of prison bars. Her brother's clients were rough, rude men who worked hard with their hands, men without culture or polish. It was not their roughness, however, that sickened Zoé; she was accustomed to roughness in the hired men of her father's farm. A crude sophistication had intruded upon the basic goodness of these city workers. Their simplicity and plainness of manner were of a very different sort from the simplicity of the farmhand. The city had peppered their talk with vulgarisms and curses and occasional obscenities; in their shouting and loud-mouth remarks they had the offensive quality of a gang of bad boys.

For all that, Zoé was not afraid of them. It would be hard to imagine her afraid of anything belonging to this earth. The only fear recorded in her life was the fear of her confessor, and that was a truly spiritual fear. Zoé was far from timid. Any insulting remarks or fresh advances—and we might surely expect them in such a place from such men—Zoé would deal with promptly and firmly. They would not happen again. And, little by little, a deep respect for this different kind of waitress, the respect of every man for a good woman, would show in the faces and the manners of the clients of Charles Labouré.

Charles himself was unhappy over his sister's lot. Knowing Zoé, he probably knew from the outset that his father's plan to distract her from her religious vocation would never work; knowing his father, Charles dared not say what he thought. He made life as tolerable for her as he could, shielding her as much as possible from the unpleasantness bound up in her work. As time went on and he saw daily the acuteness of her pain, however, he knew that something had to be done.

Zoé had accepted her fate with good grace and all the stamina of her stout spirituality, but every human being has a limit of patience and endurance. Zoé had almost reached hers. It was not only the horror of the dank, stale tavern air in her country lungs, not only the rising panic at being trapped in a tiny, hopeless cage. It was especially a spiritual desolation, for she saw the minutes and weeks and months frittering away and dissolving into nothingness like snowflakes on a wet sidewalk.

Zoé would have seen her brothers in Paris frequently enough. Besides Charles, Antoine, Joseph, and Pierre were living there. Hubert, whose home and family were in Châtillon-sur-Seine, must have come often to the capital on military affairs. He was already, at thirty-five, a member of the personal bodyguard of Charles X and a chevalier of the Legion of Honor. Each of Zoé's brothers had known and felt the iron will of his father, and therefore could understand and sympathize with Zoé in her hour of trial. Some kind of a family conspiracy was hatched to rescue her, for letters went off in the mail. The plan was for Zoé to escape to Hubert and his wife in Châtillon. Even Marie Louise, away in the convent, was taken into their confidence.

Although Marie Louise was only six years out of the novitiate, she was already superior of the house of the Sisters of Charity at Castelsarrasin. Zoé wrote to her, probably through Charles, confiding her religious desires and asking what she thought of the proposed stay in Châtillon. Marie Louise's reply is extant. It is a letter which Zoé kept and put to good use in saving her older sister from a terrible mistake years later.

Castelsarrasin
1829

My dear Zoé,

    The grace of Our Lord be with us forever.

    I cannot tell you what pleasure your dear letter gave me. I love you far too much not to congratulate you on the attraction with which God has inspired you for a community which is so dear to me. You say you wish you already possessed that happiness. Oh, if you could only realize it! If God begins to speak to your heart, no one has the right to prevent you from entering the service of so good a Master, which is the grace I beg Him to bestow on you.

We find here the first evidence that Zoé was considering the Sisters of Charity as the religious community of her choice. That she had not definitely decided, however, is apparent from a further paragraph:

It is not our custom to ask anyone to enter the community; I hope God will pardon my weakness in this regard for you. He knows that the salvation of your soul is as dear to me as that of my own, and how ardently I desire that you should be of the number of those to whom He will say one day: "Come, ye blessed of My Father, possess the kingdom prepared for you; for I was hungry and you gave me to eat, I was thirsty and you gave me to drink, I was a stranger and you took me in, naked and you clothed me, sick and you visited me, I was in prison and you came to me." That is the life of a true Daughter of Charity.

The letter is long and commonplace, filled with pious clichés the Sister Superior had heard in conferences or read in books, and needless urgings toward perfection for a soul already completely one with God. Yet it served its purpose, for it brought the sympathy and encouragement Zoé needed so badly. It reached its climax in a short, splendid sentence that must have clashed like Christmas bells in Zoé's soul: "Therefore, if God calls you, follow Him." Marie Louise, though she was to falter in serving God, will be forever blessed for that letter and that ringing sentence. In fact, as bread cast upon the waters always does, it returned its blessing to her in her lifetime. The letter concluded with complete approval of the family plans to circumvent their father.

I wish that you would pass some time with our dear sister-in-law, as she proposes, so that you can get the education which is so necessary in any state of life. You would learn there to speak French a little better than they do in our village; you could also improve yourself in your writing and arithmetic, but above everything else in piety, fervor, and love of the poor.

Everyone was in agreement. In a Catholic family, the brother or sister in religion is an oracle to be consulted in matters of moment. Marie Louise was especially an oracle to Zoé, for she had already attained the religious goal Zoé so ardently desired, and had even been chosen to direct others. Small wonder that Zoé was seized with a holy relief that this respected older sister should set her seal upon what Zoé wished to do.

The next step was to obtain Pierre Labouré's permission for the venture. It was a formidable task, and the choice for carrying it out fell unanimously upon Hubert's wife, Jeanne. Jeanne could twist her father-in-law around her little finger.

Jeanne Gontard Labouré was a cousin of Zoé's mother. Perhaps that was the basic reason why she was a favorite of Pierre's, for she seems to have been cut from the same cloth as his dead wife. She was educated, cultured, witty, and brilliant; she was also good, kind, and pious. She ran a boarding school for fashionable young ladies, and it tickled the vanity of Pierre Labouré that the noble families of the province of Barrois sent their daughters to be educated there.

This clever woman won the day. She managed to persuade her father-in-law that Zoé would profit by an extended visit with her. The old man was not altogether displeased that Zoé would mix with "young ladies of good family and receive a little education." Little did he know that he was being hoodwinked, that he was lending himself to a plan that would bring about his own ultimate defeat.

IV

The Awakening

ZOÉ'S FLIGHT to Châtillon was not exactly jumping from the frying pan into the fire, but neither was it a release into untrammeled freedom. The trials she met there were not the coarse trials of the Parisian *bistro*, but they were real trials for all that. She had traded her chains for silken strands, but silken strands, too, can bind and hurt.

The boarding school conducted by Jeanne Labouré has its modern counterparts in the ladies' seminaries of England and the finishing schools of the United States. The school was a place of elegance, done in the plush décor of the period with thick-piled carpets, velvet drapes, and full-length mirrors. It was exquisitely furnished with ornately carved tables and the tiny gilded and silk-upholstered chairs of the Age of Mozart. It was a useful and proper school for ladies of rank. They made an acquaintance with the classics; they read and composed poetry; they studied the history of France; they dabbled in astronomy; they learned to dance—in a word, they were powdered and primped for their future appearances in the flossy salons of society.

Zoé lumbered into this gilded cage like one of her own beloved pigeons among a flock of nightingales. She had never been to school before, any school. Her proper place was the first grade, not this exquisite lecture hall of refinement. She was twenty-three years old, much older than the sophisticated misses around her.

The situation was perfect material for a comic opera. Imagine a grown woman stuttering over her ABC's! Imagine the tittering and suppressed giggles of her giddy schoolmates! Imagine the blush of shame on her stricken face, the hurt in her heart, and, knowing Zoé, the quick anger rising within her and being suppressed only with heroic difficulty. Yet it was suppressed. Zoé Labouré was indeed a valiant woman. This brutal humiliation before her own sex was a far more painful trial than any broad-humored sallies of rough men.

Humanly speaking, Zoé's chief balm at Châtillon was her sister-in-law, for Jeanne Labouré proved herself a good and faithful friend. She shielded Zoé as much as possible from the ridicule of the other girls by giving her private instruction in the rudimentary knowledge she lacked. This very protection, however, was a trial in itself. It seemed that lately Zoé was always being protected from someone or something: from the vulgarity of her brother's customers, from her father, from the snobbery of the pupils of Châtillon. It is a miserable thing, to be always protected. It was especially miserable for Zoé, who had always stood on her own two feet. Had she been a weaker character, had she been less certain of what she wanted to do, she could have developed an inferiority complex of appalling magnitude. As it was, she suffered keenly beneath the indignity of it all.

Jeanne Labouré performed an even deeper service of friendship for Zoé than that of shielding and instructing her. In the Providence of God, it was Jeanne, through her piety and love of the poor, who lead Zoé to the ultimate attainment of her religious vocation. How like God and His careful, well-knit plans, to give to this second gentle Gontard the task of finishing what the first, Zoé's mother, had begun.

Jeanne set out from her lovely home on many a mission of charity. The poor of the town knew and cherished her. Her favorite charity was an institution conducted by the Sisters of St. Vincent de Paul, the Hospice de la Charité, located on the right bank of the Seine in the rue de la Haute-Juiverie. There she came and went like a member of the household, and there, naturally, she introduced Zoé with her kindred heart for the poor. It was in this house of charity at Châtillon that Zoé's vocation was determined once for all.

Some weeks after her arrival in Châtillon, Zoé stopped one day at the Hospice to speak with the Sister Superior. She had scarcely seated herself in the parlor to wait, when her eyes were caught by a portrait on the wall. It was a portrait of a venerable priest, plain-featured, even homely, but with shrewd and smiling eyes that held Zoé's gaze, even as they had done four years before. It was indeed the old priest of Zoé's youthful dream. When the first shock of recognition had subsided, Zoé was in a fever of excitement, eager to ask the question that trembled on her lips. The Sister Servant finally came. The perfunctory greetings were an agony. Then, finally, Zoé spoke the few words that were the climax to all her years of seeking.

"Sister, who is that priest?"

"Why, my child, that is our holy founder, St. Vincent de Paul."

So.

Zoé knew, and it was enough. The self-control she had long since mastered took over, and Zoé went on to speak casually of the business at hand, saying nothing of why she had asked, giving no hint of the turmoil within her.

She lost no time in seeking out her confessor, M. Vincent Prost, to tell him of her mysterious dream and its sudden unraveling. When she had finished, he said without hesitation:

"St. Vincent de Paul calls you. He wishes you to be a Sister of Charity."

The ways of God are often slow. It takes the patient temperament of the saint to wait Him out. Zoé's patience had been sorely strained: it was almost four years since the night of her dream, but its culmination was well worth waiting for. There is no greater blessing on earth than to know what God expects of you.

The extraordinary dream of Zoé Labouré and its long-delayed interpretation is surely the answer to those who claim that she meant to be a Sister of Charity from the time her thoughts turned to religion. Had she definitely decided so soon, the incident of the dream is wholly inexplicable. God is not a wastrel, lavishing the miraculous without reason. The whole tenor of the dream was to indicate to Zoé the wishes of Heaven. Had Zoé intended from the start to join the community of St. Vincent, the elaborate device of the dream as a directive loses its point.

Two stones yet lay in Zoé's path, though they worried her little, for not long ago there had not even been a path. The first of these was to obtain the consent of her father. Zoé wanted her obedience to be complete and, like any fond daughter, dreaded leaving home under the cloud of her father's displeasure. Her faithful sister-in-law again came to the rescue, counting still on Pierre Labouré's predilection for her to carry the day. We do not know whether Jeanne wrote to him or went to see him at Fain; we do not know what arguments she used, but she gained her point. The harassed old man threw down his arms. He was sick of fighting odds too great for him. Besides, during the past year he had grown used to Zoé's absence from home and had come to recognize Tonine's competence in running the house. Reluctantly, he gave his consent.

He fired one parting, ineffectual shot: he refused Zoé a dowry. It was a mean thing to do, especially to the daughter who had served him so faithfully. It could serve no point but to embarrass and hurt her, for he certainly knew that she would get the dowry somewhere. This final action of Pierre Labouré toward his daughter had the effect of casting her off without a cent. It was a despicable action, branding as entirely false the sentimental notion that he resisted Zoé's vocation because of his paternal feelings. Such feelings, naturally, were there, but even his grandchildren recognized that he had fought to hold on to Zoé "because she was of use to him." To the end he was selfish, brutal and callous.

Jeanne was ready for him. The refusal of the dowry would make no difference, she assured him, for she and Hubert would supply it. Zoé was free.

Zoé felt no glow of triumph in besting the tired old man. There was only love and compassion in her heart. She knew what he suffered, even though he had brought much of it upon himself, and she suffered too. It was her bitter price for serving God. To her eternal credit, though she must have felt keenly the shabby way he had treated her, she never spoke of her father except in the most glowing terms.

Zoé wasted no time in idle tears, but set about removing the second stone in her path, the persuading of the Superior of the Hospice at Châtillon to receive her as a postulant. This was a harder task. Zoé had profited little, if at all, from her schooling at her sister-in-law's, despite the private tutoring she had received. A girl of twenty-three has neither the aptitude nor the enthusiasm to learn what she should have mastered at seven. The Sister Superior, Sister Josephine Cany, was new; she had been in the post scarcely a year, and was timid about receiving so unprepossessing a prospect as Zoé. There would be much clucking disapproval among the mistresses of the seminary in Paris, were they to discover that

Sister Josephine had received a postulant who could neither read nor write.

Fortunately, Zoé found a champion in the Assistant of the house, Sister Françoise Victoire Séjole. It is comforting to recognize the true friends God gave Zoé when she needed them most. Sister Séjole was to be the closest friend of Zoé's religious life. This good sister was a remarkable soul, and she had the supernatural gift of discerning the souls of others.

Sister Séjole had ample opportunity to study Zoé thoroughly, for Zoé quickly fell into the habit of accompanying her on her round of visits to the sick poor. Still, it was only Sister Séjole's blessed gift of discernment that gave her deep insight into Zoé's heart, for outwardly Zoé Labouré was shy and silent, even cold, of a personality that, all her life, was to cause her to be misunderstood, slighted, and overlooked. When Sister Séjole saw that Sister Cany was hesitant about receiving Zoé, she took a hand.

"Receive her," she urged the Superior. "There is a great purity and great piety in this girl. She is out of place among all the silk dresses of Mme. Labouré's school. She is a good village girl, the kind St. Vincent loved. I will teach her her prayers and everything else she will need to enter the seminary at Paris."

Sister Cany deferred to her Assistant, and the last obstacle to Zoé's vocation was removed. After so many years of prayer and waiting and struggle against vicious odds the news, for Zoé, was easily the gladdest tidings ever brought to her.

The Sister of Charity is one of the sights of Paris, the city of her birth. She is more omnipresent than the gendarme. In her billowing blue gown and white headdress she walks the boulevards, the back streets, the alleys. She descends into the depths of the *metro* and climbs to the heights of the garret. She is never without the huge market basket slung over one arm, and packed with the foods and medicines of her trade, nor the black cotton umbrella to protect her starched white linen from the sudden rain. She moves ceaselessly, silently, seemingly unaware of the bustle and roar about her, seeking her quarry; and her quarry is always the same: the poor—the hungry poor, the sick poor, the evil poor—but always the poor.

Her convent is the house of the sick, her cell the chamber of suffering, her chapel the parish church, her cloister the streets of the city or the wards of the hospital; obedience is her enclosure, the fear of God her grate, and modesty her veil. So St. Vincent had ordained in founding the Community.

They were a startling innovation in the Church, these Sisters. Until 1633, the year of their founding, a nun was a withdrawn, secluded woman, cut off entirely from the brawling world, a cloistered maid dedicated to contemplative prayer. St. Vincent changed all that. Many a kindred soul had tried before him, men with a keen awareness of the need for a woman's touch in the active ministry of saving souls. St. Francis de Sales had tried, in founding the Visitation nuns, but his plan missed fire and the grille clanged shut on his Sisters. Where Francis failed, Vincent won out. It was to be; it was in the plan of God.

The world, the very people to be nursed and cared for, did not take kindly to the new order. They jeered, they joked, they slung Parisian mud at the Sisters who had come out to them. The Sisters did not mind. They had been splattered with cleaner, richer earth than the droppings from the streets of Paris, mud from the fertile fields of their farms at home. For they were country girls, healthy, strapping, and docile, the first Sisters of Charity.

Zoé Labouré, therefore, was to the manner born. Sister Séjole had been true to the mark when she said that Zoé was "a good village girl, the kind St. Vincent loved." Vincent de Paul's keen and fatherly eye could not have missed the marked resemblance to himself in this latest daughter of his. Of the

same peasant stock—which is a very different thing from belonging to the lower classes—she had her spiritual father's determined vigor and strength of character, his simplicity and
candor of soul, his lowliness of spirit, his penchant for obscurity. Humanly speaking, the resemblance of Vincent and
Zoé might be laid to the similarity of their origins.

Born in opposite corners of France—he was a Gascon, she
a Burgundian—both, nevertheless, sprang from the earth. Both
were children of farmers who owned their own farms. Both
had spent the years of childhood in fields and country lanes.
Both were conscious of the soil and sky, the mountains and
the plains, the lordly cedar and the common daisy. From this
intimacy with the placid development of growing things, the
unhurried pace of the changing seasons, both learned the common peasant lesson of patience. It was a lesson to stand them
in good stead in waiting out the workings of God, in acquir-
ing a surefootedness in His ways. Ultimately, it was this surefootedness that enabled them to affect so many souls for good.

The few Sisters of Charity first gathered together by Vincent de Paul have, under the divine command, increased and
multiplied and filled the earth, to the number of 43,000. There
is a story bruited abroad that, when Pope Pius XII recommended modifications in the outmoded dress of religious
women, he excepted the white headdress, the cornette, of the
Sisters of Charity—fantastic as this seventeenth-century French
peasant headgear looks to modern eyes—because "it has become the universal symbol of charity." The Sisters of Charity
have indeed become, universally, a veritable legend of charity,
and have earned the symbolic titles of folklore. The soldiers
of the Crimean War called them "Angels of the Battlefield," a
title they earned again in the American War between the
States. The Mohammedans, with an Oriental eye upon their
white wings, named them "Swallows of Allah." Anyone who
has seen one of these Sisters with four or five tiny orphans

clinging to her broad blue skirts and an infant cradled in her arms, will accord them the proudest title of all: "Mothers of the Poor." These, then, were the valiant women among whom Zoé Labouré wished to be numbered.

Humanly speaking, Zoé could have had no misgivings about the physical demands of the life. The Sisters rose at four o'clock; so had she, all her life. They cooked and scrubbed and labored hard; she had known no other way of life. They observed long silences; she was quiet and reserved by nature. The outward trappings of the rule could cause her no alarm.

Nor need she fear the long hours of required prayer. In this regard, she had served her postulancy already, in the Lady Chapel at Fain, in the hospital at Moutiers-Saint Jean, in the night watches and day-long devotions of her choosing.

It was on January 22, 1830 that Zoé Labouré quietly left the world and entered upon her religious life at the Hospice de la Charité in Châtillon-sur-Seine. True to their word, Hubert and Jeanne Labouré supplied her dowry and all the clothing of her trousseau. The dowry of 672 francs, roughly equivalent to $125 in modern money, was a notable burden of expense, especially since it was payable in gold, and this generous couple cannot be sufficiently praised for their kindness to their sister. The trousseau, which Zoé brought with her to the Hospice in a goat-skinned trunk, consisted of the following items: "four pairs of sheets; twelve worked table-napkins; linen for chemises, eleven of these to be already made up; five dresses, four of them to be of cotton and one of violet silk; four petticoats, one to be of cotton; four shawls; one white foundation of wool and three of black wool; thirteen fichus of violet silk; one bolt of cotton; thirty coifs, twenty of them to be lined; eleven pocket handkerchiefs; three pairs of pockets; five pairs of stockings; one corset; and one black robe." Zoé and her sister-in-law must have had a grand time shopping for this formidable list of things, and a busy time of fittings and sewing before she was ready to depart.

As a postulant, Zoé was not yet, of course, a Sister, not even a novice. She was an observer, come to examine the life of the Sisters at close range. She was a candidate, come to be examined in turn and passed upon. She rose with the Sisters, prayed with them, took her meals and her recreation with them. She helped in the kitchen and laundry, she sewed, she washed and dressed and supervised the foundlings of the house, she went out into the homes of the poor. And all the while she watched, and was watched.

In the short time of her postulancy, a scant three months, Zoé made a remarkable impression at Châtillon. It was not so much that she did everything she was supposed to do. Most postulants do that, both because the novelty of the life carries them along and because they are anxious to make good and be admitted to the community. It was rather the *way* she did things. She added an indescribable, intangible something to the commonest action that arrested the attention of the discerning. Whether she made beds or scrubbed floors or washed windows, she performed the duty with such care, such complete absorption, that she seemed wholly dedicated. All her life it was to be the same: she did the most ordinary things extraordinarily well.

Years later, an old woman named Mariette, who had been a servant in the Hospice of Châtillon while Zoé was living there, still remembered vividly how Zoé performed a daily act of devotion in honor of Our Lord's Passion. According to their rule, the Sisters of Charity pause in their work every afternoon at three o'clock and repair to the chapel, there to adore the dying Christ and beg Him to apply the merits of His Death to the agonizing, to poor sinners, and to the souls in purgatory. Mariette was struck by the way Zoé performed this action, more than by the veteran Sisters.

Even more illuminating was Sister Séjole's continuing discovery of new depths to the spirituality of Zoé Labouré. Although she lived with Zoé only three months, she was ready to pronounce her a soul "of surpassing candor and purity." A few months later, when the community was rife with rumors, Sister Séjole had no hesitation in saying that, "if the Blessed Virgin had appeared to a Sister of the seminary, it must be Sister Labouré. That child is destined to receive great favors from Heaven."

The days at Châtillon sped away, because they were full and busy. Here, at last, Zoé learned to write. Sister Séjole gave her the daily half hour of instruction allowed by the rule, and Zoé made notable progress in these extremely short class periods, although at her sister-in-law's fancy school she had learned nothing. Zoé's extant letters, preserved in the archives at rue du Bac, are written in a firm, plain, and legible hand, and the record book she kept at Enghien, also extant, is a model of order and neatness.

Marie Louise had written to Zoé on the day of her entrance into the religious life. This letter, which might seem tiresome to us, must have been deeply appreciated by Zoé. Certainly her family did everything possible to make up for their father's sullen behavior and to surround her departure from the world with warmth.

Zoé Labouré had come to the end of an era in her life. Her sojourn in the world, which had never held her, was over. Her campaign to fly from it, a struggle begun a dozen years before at the time of her first Communion, was successfully concluded. In the chill dawn of an April morning, she set out for Paris and the Motherhouse of the Sisters of Charity, in the company of Sister Hinaut, an old and weary servant of the poor who was going home to die.

V

The Return of St. Vincent de Paul

Zoé's arrival at the Motherhouse raised no stir. Apparently she was just another in the endless line of "good country girls" who had come to the Community since the days of St. Vincent. Few turned to give her a second glance as she entered the great wooden gate and walked for the first time down the long cobblestoned alley that led to the seminary or novitiate. A few Sisters hailed Sister Hinaut, hobbling along beside her, and Zoé stood back, silent and unnoticed, while the old friends greeted one another.

The Mistress of Novices welcomed her warmly, showed her a bed and a place at table, instructed her briefly in the rules of the house, and informed her that from now on she would be known as Sister Labouré.

Amid all this newness of scene and faces, Zoé was far from feeling strange. She was spared the lot of most newcomers to the religious life, the unreasoning panic, the sudden longing for home and familiar faces, the agonizing doubt as to whether she had made a mistake in coming. She tells us herself that, at

this crucial moment, she was so happy that she felt she was
"no longer on the earth." It is what we should expect of Zoé
Labouré, who had carefully planned this day for years, waiting, praying, removing obstacles. Now that it was here, it
brought her the same quiet sense of achievement as when she
had put the last dish on the shelf after a long, hard day in her
father's home at Fain.

Exteriorly she was calm, and it was this characteristic outward calm that caused everyone, even those who knew her
best, to put her down as cold and apathetic. Interiorly she was
a riot of ecstasy. A melting love for God, gratitude, relief,
beat and surged through her heart, tingled through her body.

The French Revolution, and in particular the Reign of
Terror of 1793, had scattered the two families of St. Vincent
de Paul, the Vincentian Fathers and the Sisters of Charity, up
and down the length and breadth of France. This, however,
had not meant the end of everything. St. Vincent had not
founded his Communities upon external trappings, such as
seminaries, churches, hospitals, and orphan asylums. He had
founded them upon a solid love for the poor. Therefore, like
all divine patriots in time of persecution, his sons and daughters had gone underground, contacting souls on street corners
and in doorways, healing bodies in cellar and garret. Apparently citizens and citizenesses in secular dress, they were
priests and Sisters of the Lord, going about His work in spite
of everything.

In 1800, Napoléon, shrewd enough to recognize that the
Sisters of Charity were the nursing corps of France, allowed
them to regroup and gave them a Motherhouse on the rue du
Vieux-Colombier. The Sisters in turn, knowing the bargain-
ing point they had in their services to the nation, pressed this
advantage upon Napoléon until he also allowed their religious
brothers to return, four years later, and take up residence on
the rue de Sèvres. In 1815, the Sisters moved to their present

quarters on the rue du Bac, the former town house of the
Comtes de La Vallière.

Recovery from the paralyzing blows of the Revolution was
slow, and when Zoé came to the Motherhouse on April 21,
1830, there were scarcely a hundred and fifty women in the
house, including the old Sisters, novices, patients, and servants.

The Sisters themselves were a raggle-taggle sight. Even
thirty years after the Revolution, they were still unable to obtain the standard blue cloth of their habits. As a result, some
wore black and some few wore blue. Zoé herself, now Sister
Labouré, dressed in the peculiar and complicated black-and-
white costume of the seminary Sisters. In cut, the costume is
very much like the "Dutch Cleanser girl" familiar to Americans. It wasn't until 1833 that the ingenious Mother-General
Boulet managed to restore the familiar blue habit to her Sisters.
The good Mother happened upon a weaver who was on the
verge of bankruptcy. She offered to advance him sufficient
funds to tide him over the crisis, provided he would contract,
in return, to weave the blue material the Sisters needed.

The upset in the Community caused by the times was, of
course, of a semi-permanent character, but Sister Labouré
came to the novitiate in the midst of a passing upset that had
the Motherhouse in a frenzy of excitement and joy. Three
days hence, the relics of St. Vincent de Paul were to be solemnly restored to the Vincentian Fathers and enthroned above
the high altar of their church, around the corner from the
Sisters in the rue de Sèvres.

During the horrors of the Revolution the precious body of
the Founder had been hidden away, safe from the hands of
desecrators. It had been a prudent step. Many incredibly foul
sacrileges had been perpetrated in the name of Freedom. A
woman of the streets had danced impurely upon the very altar
of Notre Dame. The sacrosanct body of the great Ste. Geneviève, who had saved her beloved Paris from so many evils

throughout the centuries, had been rifled from its tomb in the church built for her by Louis XV and burned ignominiously in the Place de Grève. What terrible things to come unhappy France had pulled down upon her head in that one unbelievable act! It seems hardly too much to state that she still bears the curse of it. It was most fortunate for France that it was the English strangers who burned her other noble Patroness, Jeanne d'Arc.

The third patron and hero of France alone escaped. The body of M. Vincent had happily been well hidden, and survived to honor posterity. Throughout the years of revolution the sacred relics had been moved from one hiding place to another in the Montaigne-Ste. Geneviève quarter. At length it found a resting place in the house of the lawyer of the Double Family of St. Vincent in the rue de Bourdonnais, where it stayed until the Sisters welcomed it home in 1806. On the feast of the Assumption, August 15, 1815, the Sisters brought the beloved body with them to the rue du Bac.

The body of St. Vincent has been spirited away for safekeeping, shunted about from place to place, during every war and uprising that has ripped the fabric of France. Throughout the occupation of Paris by the Nazis during World War II, it lay buried in an old packing box beneath a cellar floor. Always, however, the danger past, it has had a new resurrection, a triumphal return. Zoé Labouré, newly come to Paris, witnessed its greatest, its most triumphal return.

The Vincentian Fathers had completed the building of their mother-church of St. Vincent in 1827, but the Archbishop of Paris, Monseigneur de Quélen, long hesitated to allow them to expose the body of their Founder for public veneration. It was not that public devotion to the saint had died in France, but anti-religious sentiment was still so rife that the Archbishop feared incidents harmful to the Church. In 1830, however, when the French Army was preparing to move against

Algiers, Monseigneur de Quélen decided to brave the wrath of the godless, and publicly invoke St. Vincent de Paul, who had himself been a slave in Algeria, to bless the arms of France. To this end, with the approbation of the Holy See, he authorized the solemn Translation of the saint's relics to take place on Sunday, April 25, 1830.

In March, the body was removed from the Sisters' Motherhouse to the Cathedral of Notre Dame, where it was clothed in magnificent vestments and enshrined in an exquisite chasse of solid silver, the gift of the Archbishop. Pontifical vespers were sung at two o'clock in the afternoon, followed by the recitation of novena prayers in honor of the saint. King Charles X and the royal family attended. Then a huge procession set out from the cathedral to escort the Apostle of Charity to his own church.

It was a brilliant cortege: the elite of the army with uniforms glittering and sabres flashing in the afternoon sun; princes and nobles in velvet and lace; purple-clad bishops and ermined canons, the highest prelates in the land; a multitude of the secular clergy, dressed in the simple black soutane Vincent himself wore; the religious orders in their habits of black and white and brown; the civic officials in their robes of office; a sea of Sisters of Charity, more than a thousand, bobbing blue and black-and-white; then the sons of the saint, bearing his body joyfully in their midst; and presiding over all, His Excellency, Hyacinthe de Quélen, Archbishop of Paris.

As the splendid parade wended its way across the Petit-Pont, down the rue de la Hachette, the rue de Saint-André-des-Arts, and the rue du Four, it met with mixed reactions from the mob. By far the greater number of the common people entered wholeheartedly into the fervor of the day and packed the streets, windows, and balconies and even the roofs. Others were indifferent; some actively hostile, but these were in the minority and small attention was paid them.

Unknown and unnoted in this gorgeous equipage of a saint walked another saint named Catherine Labouré. Not entirely unknown, for Vincent de Paul knew she was there, and he found more honor to his holy remains in this one jewel than in all the proud pomp and sparkling display. He was soon to show his pleasure. He was soon to reach out and embrace this favorite daughter, to open up to her the secrets, sad and gay, of his paternal heart.

That memorable Sunday afternoon in April was but the brilliant prelude to a solemn novena of joy in honor of St. Vincent. Day after day, the Vincentian Fathers held open house for the thousands of Parisians and people from the provinces who thronged the church on rue de Sèvres to honor the Hero of France. The common people, with their unerring instinct for the right, seemed to realize that the sacred body laid out in the choir was the last holy relic of their nation left to them, and they lavished their devotion upon it. Pontifical Mass was sung every morning and a novena service held every afternoon. On the fifth day, the King himself returned. The ceremonial was an official act of reparation for the excesses of other days. The times of excess were far from over, however. The volatile temperament of her Eldest Daughter would be ever the delight and the despair of the Church of Christ.

The Sisters and the novices were present at the festivities each day. Sister Labouré was there, packed in among her companions, devout and ecstatic. She fed eagerly at the groaning table of spiritual consolation spread before her. She needed every last ounce of nourishment and strength, for each night on her return from St. Lazare, she went through a grueling experience.

Celebrations like this can be a distraction rather than a help to individual piety. There was so much to dazzle the eyes and to fascinate one: the stately and intricate movement of the pontifical Mass; the rich, glittering vestments; the gorgeous backdrop of flowers and lights; such harmony to fill the ears: the thundering of the organ; the soaring melodies of the choir; so many great personages to stimulate human curiosity. The little country girl from Fain had never seen such display. It was a far cry from the simple Mass droned in the half-dark of a winter's morning, the tentative voices of a few sleepy Sisters, the handful of worshippers in homespun. Yet, literally, it meant nothing to her, human-wise; it served only, as it was meant to serve, as a hint of Heaven. She felt, again, that she was "no longer on the earth." Earnestly, she addressed herself to prayer, and with spiritual insight, she prayed well.

She prayed, first of all, for herself, for all the graces she needed. Then, with true Christian breadth, she prayed for the "two families," the Sisters of Charity and their brothers, the Vincentian Fathers, "and the whole of France." For Charles X, the last of the Bourbons, and for the lowliest peasant in his kingdom. For Paris, the teeming mother of the land, pious and sinful, learned and flippant, beautiful and dowdy, all in turn. For Paris, sprung legendary centuries ago from the *Ile de la Cité;* for Paris, whose great bid for ultimate salvation is that the lovely Cathedral of Our Lady still marks the spot of the city's birth. For Paris, and Dijon, Orleans, and Marseilles; and for the tiny villages like Fain, that the brawling epochs have swept around and left unchanged. For Brittany and Burgundy and the Valley of the Loire. For all that sunny land, with its woods and hedgerows and vistas of landscape, cut out of some medieval tapestry. And for its puzzling people, prototypes of a puzzling race, angels of God and devils of Satan, the glory and the shame of the Most High.

Catherine was French, and we who are not cannot hope to understand. She tells us that she prayed "for the whole of France," and in that simple telling she joins hands with Geneviève and Jeanne d'Arc, with Bernard and Vincent de Paul, and with a host of others, all forming a protective cordon about their beloved country, all presenting a defiant and un-broken front to the world. Fail to understand as we may, who is to say that Catherine Labouré, and all these others, were not right in their passionate devotion to their country? Catherine was to see Our Lady herself weep over the unhappy days ahead for France, and even Christ Himself come to earth to foretell the end of the Bourbon dynasty. Catherine was French, and that meant that France was a passion with her, a thread of her life and her sanctity, weaving itself through her thoughts, her prayers, her good deeds, her visions.

Finally, with truest Christian prudence, she prayed St. Vincent to teach her what she should pray for.

Until now, Catherine's devotion to St. Vincent had been a casual thing, compared with the all-consuming thing it was henceforward to be. Not so many years ago, in her dream, she had fled from him. "You flee from me now," he had said, "but one day you will be glad to come to me." That day was here. And Catherine, with that characteristic generosity that gave everything when it was sure of the direction of its giving, came to him wholly. In these few days of novena, she told St. Vincent everything about herself, her hopes and fears, her powers and her needs. It was he she asked for the graces she required, it was to him she recommended "the two families, and the whole of France." In a word, she gave him her heart.

Now, Vincent was to give his heart to Catherine.

As the novena service ended each afternoon, the novices emerged into the spring twilight, and marched two by two around the corner to their home in the rue du Bac. There, Catherine tells us in homely fashion, she "found St. Vincent again, or at least his heart." The heart appeared to her above a little shrine containing a bone from the right arm of St. Vincent, in the chapel of the Sisters. It hovered over this precious relic, in front of St. Joseph's altar and slightly higher than the picture of St. Anne that hung on the sanctuary wall. It appeared to her on three successive evenings in three different guises. On the first evening, it was of a flesh-white color. Inwardly, Catherine understood that the color foretold peace, calm, innocence, and union for the two Communities, the priests and the Sisters of St. Vincent.

On the second evening, it was a fiery red, and Catherine again, in the depths of her own heart, understood its symbolism: charity would be enkindled in all hearts, the Community would renew its fervor and extend itself to the uttermost bounds of the earth.

The next evening was a different story. The heart of St. Vincent took on a dark red hue. On seeing it, Catherine was plunged into sadness, a sadness which presaged misfortune for herself and for the King of France. She understood by this strange, spiritual sadness that she would have much to suffer in surmounting the obstacles that would be put in her path; and she understood, without penetrating further, that there would be a change in government. Then, for the first time, Catherine heard a voice speaking to her interiorly:

"The heart of St. Vincent is deeply afflicted at the sorrows that will befall France," it said.

The apparition of St. Vincent's heart, with its various changes of color, was repeated eight or nine times, each evening when Catherine returned from St. Lazare. On the last evening, the final day of the novena, it appeared, bright vermilion, and once more Catherine heard the interior voice:

"The heart of St. Vincent is somewhat consoled because he has obtained from God, through the intercession of Mary, that his two families should not perish in the midst of these sorrows, and that God would make use of them to reanimate the Faith."

It was indeed a grueling experience for this young girl, only a few days in the novitiate. While it is a great grace to be admitted to the secrets of the saints—and Catherine recognized this grace, for she tells us that she had "consolation" from the visions—at the same time, it is a grace that does not enter easily, but rips and tears the human heart with pain. Witness the pain of the saints who have seen or heard the secrets of Heaven, who have been torn and buffeted and contradicted, from St. John the Apostle and St. Paul, the two greatest of all seers, through St. Margaret Mary, St. Bernadette, to the children of Fatima of our own day. Catherine Labouré was no exception.

"Each time that I returned from St. Lazare," she cries out, "I had such great pain!"

It is a cry of courage, for Catherine understood that, although she suffered pain, nevertheless, this oppression of her heart was a divine favor, and brought her consolation, too. She may have been a novice according to the rules of her order; she was certainly no novice in the ways of the spiritual life.

Catherine's calling as a seer, a prophet, had begun. In a few short months, history was to vindicate her forebodings of a change in government. Of her prophecies concerning the Communities of St. Vincent, her confessor, Father Jean Marie Aladel, was to speak in a conference delivered two days before his death in 1865.

"It was on the eve of the great happenings of 1830: great sorrows menaced us; our blessed Father feared for our two families, if one in Heaven can still be said to fear. He wished, at least, to rekindle fervor, to see an increase in the prayers which, each day, ascend to the throne of mercy. The saddened heart of St. Vincent appeared under a sombre aspect, it took on a hue which was not of life. But, at the close of the novena, it appeared the color of vermilion, a reflection of celestial happiness surrounded it, and he gave assurance that his prayers had been heard. The Most Holy Virgin had turned aside the evils which would have befallen us; it is to her, that is, to the August Mary, that the Company is indebted for the new graces of preservation, and the special blessings which follow Daughters of Charity worthy of their beautiful name and faithful to their holy and sublime vocation."

Father Aladel could not see a hundred years further into the future how the Sisters of Charity flourish, 43,000 strong, and fill the earth to the "uttermost bounds" predicted by Sister Labouré. He could not see the Double Family of St. Vincent, surviving two world wars and the persecution of Nazi and Communist alike, continuing and expanding their many works, dying out in one place, springing up in another. He could not see the hospitals and orphanages, schools and seminaries, mission compounds and parishes, dotting the countries of North and South America. He had seen much, but he could not see all Catherine had seen in the heart of St. Vincent.

Perhaps still prophetic of even more fruitful days for his families, the heart of St. Vincent de Paul rests today, in an exquisite reliquary of crystal and gold, on almost the exact spot where Catherine saw it in vision. Like the saint's body, this precious heart had been spirited away during the troubles of the French Revolution, and turned up unaccountably in Lyon, more than a hundred years ago, hidden in a recess cut out of the pages of a large book. Until the year 1947, it was enshrined in the Cathedral of Lyon, where Frédéric Ozanam, that man "after St. Vincent's heart," saw and venerated it in his lifetime. In 1947, Mother Blanchot, then Mother-General of the Sisters of Charity, went to Cardinal Gerlier, Archbishop of Lyon, and begged him to allow the Sisters to enshrine the heart of their Father in the chapel where it had appeared to Catherine Labouré for the duration of the festivities in honor of her canonization. The Cardinal graciously granted her request.

Whether or not Mother Blanchot had a longer range plan in mind when she first approached the Cardinal, once the heart of the Founder was safely at home in the Sister's chapel, she brought to bear on the prelate her earnest entreaties that the

Sisters be allowed to keep their borrowed treasure. The Cardinal was in sympathy with her request, nor could he gainsay the good Mother's argument that the heart of Vincent de Paul rightly belonged among his daughters, on the spot where it appeared to one of them. Braving the outcry of his own flock, the prelate finally consented—one more man to have been beaten by a woman. And who is to say whether the woman was Mother Blanchot, or Catherine Labouré?

There can be no doubt that the visions of the heart of St. Vincent were a prelude to the great apparitions of Our Lady. They hinted at what Mary was to predict and promise more fully, they foretold what Mary was to confirm: God's protection of the Double Family of St. Vincent in times of national disaster. Indeed, in a few short months, it would be St. Vincent who would obtain for Catherine the grace of seeing the Blessed Virgin.

VI

A Vision of Christ as King

WITH THE CONCLUSION of her nine days of grace, young Sister Labouré was faced with a formidable task. In spite of the reassurance of the last vision, heavy thoughts of things to come weighed her down. To make matters worse, she suffered an interior urging that could not be denied: she must tell her confessor what had happened. Her honest cry of anguish at the prospect, written down sixteen years later, gives a graphic glimpse into the torture of her soul: "I could not hold back from speaking to my confessor. . . ." She did not want to speak, but she had to.

The fact that Sister Labouré did not know the novices' confessor made the task of approaching him doubly hard. She had been to confession to him only once since her arrival, so she had no way of knowing whether he was kind or cold, whether he would receive her startling story with interest or ridicule or anger. Catherine was not stupid. In spite of her lack of education, she had native shrewdness and clear-sightedness. She knew *anyone* would shy away from and look askance at talk of visions; how would this trained priest react? She was scarcely in the novitiate a week, and here she was, babbling about "seeing things." Would he send her away, away from everything she had fought to attain? Yet it had to be done; she had to speak; there was no drawing back.

In these terrible days, it was her sound faith that sustained her, the realization that God knew what He was about. The dread moment came, and in a rush of relief, Catherine tells us that the confessor "calmed me as much as possible, turning me away from all these thoughts."

We have already mentioned this doughty opponent, Father Jean Marie Aladel. Opponent is the word, for he and Catherine were to cross swords many times before she was able to escape into the obscurity of her long life, a major part of her mission accomplished. Even then, all would not be peace between these two. He was but thirty years old when young Sister Labouré first knelt before him.

Jean Marie Aladel, like his famous penitent, was born in the Month of Mary, May 4, 1800, in the village of Ternes, near Saint-Flour, among the mountains of Cantal. He went to the college of Saint-Flour, and later to the seminary there. After two years in the diocesan seminary, he decided that his vocation lay with the Vincentian Fathers, and he was received into the novitiate on rue de Sèvres in Paris on November 12, 1821. He was ordained in 1824, the year of Catherine's dream of St. Vincent, and spent the first year of his priesthood teaching philosophy at the major seminary in Amiens. The following year he was transferred to the mission house of St. Anne in the same city. Toward the end of 1828, at the very time Catherine came to Paris to work in her brother's café, he was recalled to Paris to bolster the little staff of nine priests who were struggling to keep the headquarters of the Community going, after the disasters of the Revolution and the wars of Napoléon. There he was charged with the duties of confessor, chaplain, conference preacher, and retreat master to the community of Sisters on rue du Bac.

So much for the facts of Father Aladel's life up to his meeting with Sister Labouré in 1830. It is much harder to determine the kind of man he was. There is a *Life*, published in 1873, but it is so eulogistic that it tells us nothing of the real man; it is little more than a citing of the rules and constitutions of the Congregation with the notation that Father Aladel kept them all. The best general impression of him is that he was one of those men who are hard on themselves and on everyone else. Certainly Sister Labouré had much to suffer at his hands: there is sworn testimony that she often approached his confessional in a fit of trembling. He was cold and aloof by temperament, yet warm enough to form a deep and lasting friendship with Father Jean Baptiste Etienne, the future Superior General and "second founder" of the Congregation. Yet it must be admitted that Father Aladel leaves one with an impression of impersonality that at times approaches ruthlessness.

There can be no denying the deep piety, even holiness, of the man, nor his prudence, judgment, common sense, and administrative ability. His high posts in the Congregation and the advancement of the Sisters of Charity under his hand attest to these. Nor would it be slighting his virtues and abilities to point out that these need not have been exceptional, since there were so few men to choose from for the posts he filled, as it would not be slurring their friendship to point out that Father Etienne was particularly aware of his friend's virtues and abilities.

In the last analysis, recourse must be made to the spiritual axiom that God fits the burden to the back, and Jean Aladel's must have been a very capable back indeed, to carry the burdens God fitted to it. It was given to him not only to direct the soul of St. Catherine Labouré, and to be the external apostle of the Medal, founder of the Children of Mary, and transmitter of Catherine's divinely inspired messages of reform to the two Communities of St. Vincent; he was also given the direction of Sister Justine Bisqueyburu and her apostolate of the Green Scapular. The supreme accolade, however, was bestowed by Our Lady when she said: "He is my servant."

Sister Labouré was not to find peace in following her confessor's advice to forget what she said she had seen. She was to live in two worlds during her novitiate: the orderly world of prayer, meditation, work periods, and recreation that made up her seminary life, and that other secret, dazzling spiritual world that God let loose upon her sight. The visions of St. Vincent's heart were but the first of a train of visions.

Sister Labouré was given "another great grace," during the whole time of her novitiate: the visible presence of Our Lord in the Blessed Sacrament. She does not say whether this vision was a constant thing, that is, vouchsafed each time she entered the chapel, whether it was only during Mass, or during a certain portion of the Mass. She says only that she "saw Our Lord in the Most Holy Sacrament." She continues: "I saw Him during the whole time of my seminary, except when I doubted; the next time, I saw nothing, because I had wished to penetrate the mystery, and, believing myself deceived, had doubted."

In this straightforward statement of the saint, both her prudence and her discernment are revealed. Strangely enough, she does not seem to have had any doubts concerning the reality of the visions of St. Vincent's heart. Could it have been the sense of caution urged upon her by her confessor that caused her to examine these visions of Our Lord more closely? At any rate, she felt it prudent to doubt, not the reality of Christ's Presence in the Eucharist (she could never doubt that), but the reality of what she saw. She felt it wise to be afraid lest she suffer illusion—and not once only. Whenever she doubted, whenever she was afraid, she saw nothing. At the same time, she recognized that the withdrawal of the vision was not a punishment, but a reassurance, a proof of its reality. She understood that Jesus hid Himself when she examined the vision in order to show her that it was genuine, and that He did not want her to probe so august a mystery, but only to accept it with simple faith. When she had breathed a sigh of relief and gone back to believing and accepting with conscience clear and reassured, He showed Himself again.

This extraordinary favor speaks volumes of the way Heaven cherished this humble little novice. To see Jesus Christ once would be the supreme favor of a lifetime, but to see Him constantly throughout nine months . . . !

On Trinity Sunday, June 6, 1830, Sister Labouré was given a special vision of Jesus in the Blessed Sacrament, or more specifically of Christ as King. This time she is precise as to the moment of the vision. Our Lord appeared to her, robed as a king, with a cross at His breast, during the Gospel of the Mass. Suddenly, all His kingly ornaments fell from Him to the ground—even the cross, which tumbled beneath His feet. Immediately her thoughts and her heart fell, too, and were plunged into that chasm of gloom that she had known before, gloom that portended a change in government. This time, however, she understood clearly that the change in government involved the person of the King, and that, just as Christ was divested of His royal trappings before her, so would Charles X be divested of his throne.

It is a startling thing, this sacred vision of God Himself coming in majesty to foretell the fall of an earthly monarch, and the vision of Christ the King to Catherine Labouré seems to have had no other purpose than to foretell the fall of Charles X of France. The mystery of it will never be fully solved; yet here and there the mind may mull over certain clues.

The greatest of these clues is the nature of the French

monarchy itself, which, as Hilaire Belloc understood so well, was a holy thing, wedded to the people it ruled, and the proto- type of all the monarchies of Europe. This ancient royalty had its roots in Rome and had received its Christian mandate in the crowning of Charlemagne by the Pope on Christmas Day, 800 A.D. It had lived for more than a thousand years in one line of men. No matter how great the goodness or wickedness of these royal men—and there was an ample supply of both— the sanctity of the monarchy itself and its mystical espousal to the French people is not to be questioned. In its institutions, its duties, its relationship to those it governed, its elaborate ritual, it was an imitation on a much lower plane of the Church of God. The French, kings and subjects alike, knew this well. Jeanne d'Arc was in an agony until the Dauphin should be crowned at Rheims and his body anointed and consecrated in the sacred rite which was so essential to this kingly religion; in a sense, it was her sole mission, and it is significant that her fortunes declined afterward. Louis XI had the Ampulla of holy oil brought from Rheims that his dying eyes might rest on it. Napoleon III sought to sanctify his usurpation by hav- ing himself anointed with the small, hard lump that was all that remained of the holy oil in 1853. The Kings of France, no matter how absolute their rule, had to be born and to die, had to eat and drink, take their recreation, and pray in the sight of the people. At the birth of her ill-fated Dauphin, Marie Antoinette almost died of suffocation, because of the press of the common people in her chamber, witnessing her lying-in; only the quick-witted action of a bystander, in breaking a window to let in the fresh air, saved her.

The double religious family to which Catherine belonged had had official relationships with the French monarchy. Louis XIII had died in the arms of Vincent de Paul. The Founder continued to serve his widow, Anne of Austria, during the early part of her Regency, both as her confessor and as an important member of the royal Council of Conscience, a body established for the reform of the Church. Under Louis XV and Louis XVI, the Vincentian Fathers had been royal chaplains at Versailles, and, after the restoration, had been privileged to form a guard of honor about the bier of Louis XVIII.

That the vision of Christ the King had some intimate relationship with the end of the Bourbon dynasty seems evident, for Charles X *was* the last of the royal Bourbons; his cousin Louis Philippe, who succeeded him, belonged to a lateral line. Again we are confronted with the astonishing preoccupation of Heaven with the fortunes of France.

Before leaving this vision, we must point out the noteworthy fact that Catherine Labouré was the first saint in modern times to be vouchsafed a vision of Christ as King. In the light of the great present-day devotion to the Kingship of Christ, we would seem justified in questioning whether the vision might not have a mystical meaning. In announcing the end of the oldest of monarchies, might not Christ have meant to point up the passing quality of all earthly authority, and to foretell present-day devotion to His Kingship as the index of the eternal quality of His own Reign?

Certainly, however, Sister Labouré did not ponder thus in her heart. She knew only, as the common people know, that there was to be "a change in government," and that, as inevitably came to pass, "many miseries would follow." She knew only, as the common people know, that there had been too many changes of government in France over the last forty years, too many miseries following, and, with this instinctive knowledge of the people, she grew sad and feared.

The statesmen and politicians of the land would have laughed at the long, prophetic thoughts of the little Sister, for national order seemed well established and peace reigned. Indeed, the government was enjoying the flush of esteem that had come with the brilliant victory of the French troops in

Algiers, a victory which the nation had asked through the intercession of St. Vincent. In certain coffee houses and wine shops of Paris, however, there would have been no laughter. The brutal men assembled there would merely have smiled with grim satisfaction at this forecast of success for the revolution they were plotting.

These visions of Our Lord, like those of the heart of St. Vincent, Catherine duly reported to Father Aladel. Oddly enough, there is no record of his ever having commented on them, in public or private, during his lifetime. We can be certain that Catherine told him about them when they occurred, for it was not like her to withhold anything from her confessor; and we have the account of them written for him in her own hand in 1856. It can only be surmised that, when Father Aladel came to believe in the visions of his penitent, he did not see these visions of Our Lord as part of the series which the visions of St. Vincent's heart, and of Our Lady, constituted. He might, rightly enough, have judged in retrospect that the Eucharistic visions of Sister Labouré were for herself alone and not in the public domain, but the vision of Christ the King certainly had no personal message for her. In portending the fall of the King of France and the miseries to follow, this vision would seem to be a valid part of the general scheme of Catherine's "public" visions.

Whatever he thought, Father Aladel bade his penitent put these things out of her mind as so much nonsense.

Catherine must have found it all very confusing. She was torn between loyalties. Heaven was showering her with extraordinary favors; her confessor was telling her they were nothing of the sort. It was as if God were pulling at her one arm, while His official representative was pulling at the other. Confusing as it was, it was good for her, for it removed any least danger that she might begin to cherish her own self-importance, and it purified her soul, as trials are meant to do.

The high point of Catherine's life was fast approaching now: the great apparitions of the Virgin Mary. For these was she born, for these came she into the world, even as Christ came to bear witness to the truth. They are the reason for her being and the wellspring of her holiness. The years of sanctity that went before them, the years of sanctity that followed after, cluster about them like a setting about a gem. Not that Catherine Labouré was holy because she saw, or was to see, the Blessed Virgin; she was holy because she was faithful to the mission given her to do. God's plan for her life and sanctification was: that she should cultivate a deep devotion to the Mother of God; that she should receive, at first hand, important instructions from this great Lady; that she should carry out these instructions to the letter; and, while doing all this, she should remain hidden, living an ordinary religious life in doing ordinary religious works.

All the graces given her by God worked to this end. Catherine corresponded to every grace; she did what was expected of her and did it well. This is why she is a saint.

VII

"This is the Blessed Virgin"

ON A MIDSUMMER'S NIGHT—July 18, 1830, the eve of the
feast of St. Vincent de Paul—Our Lady came to Paris.
She came, not to the shadowy vastness of her Cathedral of
Notre Dame, but to the narrow back street called the rue du
Bac, to the Motherhouse of the Sisters of Charity.

As Sister Labouré and the other novices prepared for bed,
they were filled with happy thoughts of the morrow. They
had just left the chapel, transformed into a homely elegance of
flowers, snowy linen, and polished candelabra in preparation
for the feast-day Mass. Their Directress, the old Mother
Martha, had talked to them of devotion to the saints, and especially to their blessed Father St. Vincent, and, as a feast-day
gift, had given each of them a small piece of a surplice St.
Vincent had worn.

Tomorrow, after the glorious Mass, there would be recreation, and they would chat and laugh together and sing old
songs; and maybe they would walk over to the priests' church
in the afternoon to pray before their Holy Founder's body. . . .

St. Catherine's parents, Pierre Labouré and Madeleine Gontard. At the time of their marriage, Pierre was 26—gruff, silent, devout and authoritarian; Madeleine was 20— educated, genteel and saintly. Madeleine gave birth to 17 children, 11 of whom lived. When Madeleine died at age 42, Catherine was only 9 years old.

Upper: The Labouré farmhouse in Fain-les-moutiers, a little village of scarcely 150 inhabitants.

Lower: Catherine Labouré was born in this room on May 2, 1806 during the ringing of the Angelus. She was baptized the following day. After her mother's death, it was in this room that Catherine (age 9) chose Mary for her mother.

Upper: The Labouré parents' bedroom and the cradle in which each of their babies was placed.
Lower: Inside view of the spacious Labouré farmhouse.

Upper: Kitchen fireplace in the Labouré home. Catherine's duties when she became chief housekeeper at age 12 included seeing to the meals of five family members and 13 field hands who lived and worked on the prosperous Labouré farm.

Lower: The oven where bread was baked in the Labouré home.

80-4

Above: Catherine daily fed the hundreds of pigeons in the Labouré dovecot; this was the one recreation of her long, hard day. The birds swooped down upon her, disheveling her hair and clothes! Catherine delighted in the friendly onslaught.

Right: Tonine, Catherine's younger sister, and the sister to whom Catherine was closest. We are indebted to Tonine for information about Catherine's early life.

Above: Catherine made her First Communion at this altar rail on January 25, 1818. Years later, Catherine's sister Tonine stated that from this time Catherine became "entirely mystic"—though she remained eminently practical.

Right: The 11th-century village church of Moutiers-Saint Jean, where Catherine received her First Communion. This village is not far from where St. Bernard of Clairvaux had been born and raised centuries earlier and is only a few miles from Paray le monial, where the Sacred Heart of Jesus had unburdened Itself to St. Margaret Mary.

At age 24 Catherine was finally able to become a Sister of Charity. She had been directed to this particular community by a mysterious dream. Catherine later said that she was so happy upon joining the community that she felt she was "no longer on the earth." Here is shown the costume

of the novices as it was in Catherine's time. A professed sister stands in the foreground.

Above: The doorway of the sisters' motherhouse at 140, rue du Bac, which Catherine passed through many times.

Above: St. Vincent de Paul, the founder (along with St. Louise de Marillac) of the Sisters of Charity. Catherine was deeply devoted to this great saint, one of the patrons of France, and she received several visions of his heart. *Left:* The motherhouse of the Sisters of Charity, where Catherine made her novitiate and received the Miraculous Medal vision.

Above: St. Catherine is led by an angel to the chapel for her first vision of Our Lady. The angel appeared as a little child of four or five, of extraordinary beauty, and so surrounded with radiance that the whiteness of his gown was dazzling. He called her softly: "Sister Labouré!"
Left: The chapel of the apparitions as it appeared in the 1950s. The fresco over the altar illustrates the apparitions of St. Catherine.

The first Apparition of Our Lady to St. Catherine: "The Virgin of the Chair." (July 18, 1830). The Blessed Mother said many things to Catherine, including, "Come to the foot of the altar. There graces will be shed upon all, great and little, who ask for them. Graces will be especially shed upon those who ask for them."

The second Apparition of Our Lady: "The Virgin of the Globe." (November 27, 1830). Our Lady's hands were resplendent with rings set with precious stones which cast a brilliant cascade of light rays at her feet. Catherine heard these words: "The ball which you see represents the whole world, especially France, and each person in particular. These rays symbolize the graces I shed upon those who ask for them. The gems from which rays do not fall are the graces for which souls forget to ask."

Third apparition of Our Lady: "Our Lady of the Miraculous Medal."
(November 27, 1830). From Mary's jeweled fingers the rays of light
streamed upon the white globe at her feet. In letters of gold were the
words, "O Mary conceived without sin, pray for us who have recourse to
thee." Our Lady said to St. Catherine, "Have a medal struck after this
model. All who wear it will receive great graces; they should wear it
around the neck. Graces will abound for persons who wear it with confidence."

Apparition of the design for the back of the Miraculous Medal. (November 27, 1830).

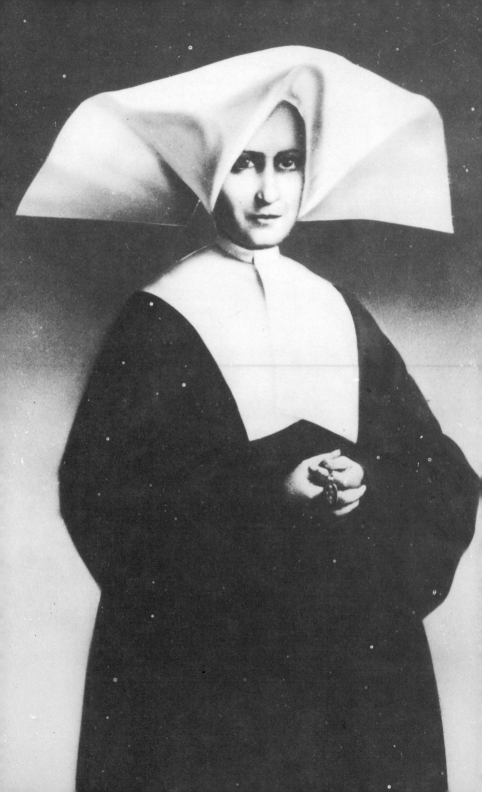

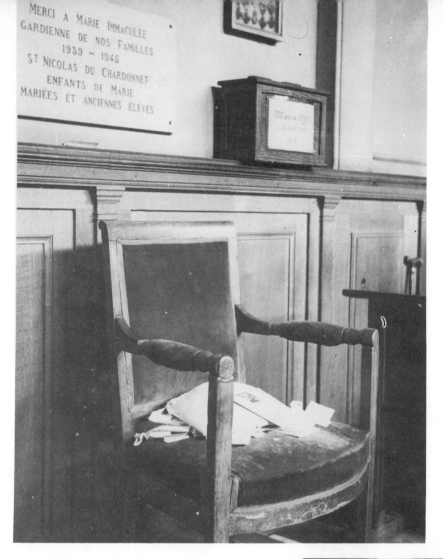

MERCI A MARIE IMMACULEE
GARDIENNE DE NOS FAMILLES
1939 – 1945
ST NICOLAS DU CHARDONNET
ENFANTS DE MARIE
MARIEES ET ANCIENNES ÉLÈVES

19
JUILLET
1830

Above: The chair in which Our Lady sat. Petitions of the faithful are placed daily on the chair.
Right: The exact spot of the Apparition of July 18-19.
Left: The official portrait of St. Catherine Labouré.

Above: The first Apparition. The little angel led Catherine to the spot with these words: "Come to the chapel. The Blessed Virgin awaits you." For two hours Sister Catherine knelt, resting her hands on Mary's lap. Our Lady told Catherine of God's plans for her and promised to confide a mission to her.

Left: A 19th-century engraving of the three Apparitions of Our Lady to St. Catherine Labouré.

The Miraculous Medal. Our Lady commissioned the medal with these words: "Have a medal struck after this model. All who wear it will receive great graces; they should wear it around the neck. Graces will abound for persons who wear it with confidence." The French words shown on the front of the medal say: "O Mary conceived without sin, pray for us who have recourse to thee." Our Lady stands with her feet crushing the serpent's head. The hearts of Jesus and Mary are depicted on the back of the medal, the one crowned with thorns, the other pierced with a sword. Twelve stars encircle the whole.

The medal was originally titled the "Medal of the Immaculate Conception," but so many miracles attended its use that people were soon calling it the "Miraculous Medal." No sacramental of the Church has had such an impact on the Catholic world since the Rosary routed the Albigensian and the Turk.

Two earlier versions of the Medal. *Above:* A commemorative medal of the dogma of the Immaculate Conception, December 8, 1854, front and back. *Below:* A medal signed by the engraver Vachette.

Upper left: Alphonse Ratisbonne, the prominent young Jewish agnostic and hater of Catholicism whose sudden conversion through the Miraculous Medal became famous all over Europe.

Upper right: Statue of Our Lady of the Rays at Ars.

Lower left: Plaque commemorating the consecration of the parish of Ars to Mary Conceived Without Sin by St. John Vianney, the Curé of Ars.

Lower right: Tabernacle at Ars engraved with the design of the Miraculous Medal.

Above: For 40 years, Catherine cared for old men such as these—serving their meals, mending their clothes, supervising their recreations, providing them with tobacco, bringing them into line when they broke her wise regulations, nursing them when they were sick, watching at their deathbeds, and having Masses said after their deaths. The Enghien buildings are in the background.
Below: The Hospice at Enghien.

Above: St. Catherine working in later years. Catherine stated to one of the sisters, "The Blessed Virgin wishes that the sister who saw her live in humility." On another occasion, upon being asked if she were not bored with her life of daily routine, Catherine answered, "One is never bored with doing the will of God."

Right: The Hospice at Enghien where Catherine served her beloved old men. During these 40 years not one died without the Last Sacraments of the Church.

Catherine Labouré

L'UNIQUE SIGNATURE
qu'on ait conservée de Catherine Labouré

Above: A page from St. Catherine's account book, and a sample of her handwriting in which she describes how she threw herself at Mary's knee on the night of the first Apparition. Below these is the only signature of St. Catherine still in existence.

Left: A statue of St. Catherine sweeping.

Above: Father Aladel, Catherine's spiritual director and the priest who arranged for the casting of the Miraculous Medal.

Left: Sister Dufès in later life. Earlier, Sister Dufès had been Catherine's superior for the last 16 years of Catherine's life. Under Sister Dufès' sometimes harsh treatment, Catherine's soul received its final, rigorous purification. Only after a silence of 46 years did Catherine reveal to her superior, Sister Dufès, that she was "the sister of the Apparitions."

Right: Painting of St. Catherine before her favorite statue. The face is taken from life.

Above: St. Catherine gives out Miraculous Medals to Communist soldiers in 1871, at the time of the *Commune.* On one occasion she was taken into custody and interrogated at Communist headquarters. Even there she pursued her apostolate of the Miraculous Medal.

Left: This is the only authentic unretouched photograph of St. Catherine Labouré taken during her life. It was taken in 1876, the year of her death.

Catherine's heart was bursting with the certainty that grew and swelled within it, the certainty that something was about to happen, something of great moment. Lying wide awake and staring up at the pale whiteness of the bed curtains, she clutched in her hand her piece of that precious surplice. She talked to St. Vincent a long time in her prayers, telling him again of her soul's dearest wish—to see with her own eyes the Blessed Virgin. It was a startling wish, a startling prayer, on the lips of this hard-headed, practical peasant girl, but it can no longer surprise us, who have seen her intense love of the Mother of God take root and burgeon and fructify; nor could it surprise her, who had witnessed the intimate wonders of Heaven, had seen the Lord Himself.

Suddenly, as if struck with an inspiration, she tore the tiny cloth in two and swallowed half of it. It was a simple act of devotion, growing out of a simple faith. Sophisticated rationalists might sniff at it as ludicrous superstition, but those whose believing mothers have signed their brows with the sacred wedding ring and given them holy water to drink will understand.

A serene peace came over Catherine. In her mind was a single, confident thought: *Tonight I shall see her. Tonight I shall see the Blessed Virgin.* She closed her eyes and slept.

She had been sleeping some two hours when a sudden light flickered in the dormitory. The light came from a candle carried by a little child of four or five, a child of extraordinary beauty and so surrounded with radiance that the whiteness of his little gown was dazzling. He approached the bed where Catherine lay. He called her softly:

"Sister Labouré!"

She did not stir. He called again, insistently:

"Sister Labouré!"

She moved a little; his voice had entered her dreams, and sleep was slipping away. Then:

"Sister Labouré!" once more, and Catherine awoke, her eyes big and staring. She turned her head in the direction of the sound. It seemed to come from near the door. Through the haze of her bed curtains she saw the brightness. She sat up quickly and drew the curtains. The child said:

"Come to the chapel. The Blessed Virgin awaits you."

Catherine was not frightened. The child had come to take her to Our Lady; it was the moment she had longed for and prayed for, the great part of her life. Only one thought leaping into her mind made her hesitate: *We shall be discovered!*

"Do not be uneasy," the radiant vision answered. "It is half past eleven; everyone is asleep. Come, I am waiting for you."

Catherine jumped out of bed and threw on her clothes. Now, the clothes of a novice Sister of Charity are a complicated bit of costume, and that Catherine could manage them in this highly excitable moment, tying every last ribbon, pinning every last pin, proves as nothing else that she was neither excited, nor upset, nor in ecstasy. She might be going to a rendezvous with Heaven, but the feet that took her there were firmly planted on the earth.

The child led the way to the door and they passed into the hallway. She was amazed to find the hall lights burning.

Down the narrow stairs they went, for the chapel was on the first floor. Catherine's wonder mounted: everywhere the lamps were lit, and yet they met no one. Once or twice, in her eagerness, she hurried ahead of her little guide, then fell back in humble confusion.

Now they were at the chapel. Catherine gasped in astonishment when the heavy door, which must be locked, swung wide at the child's mere touch. The chapel was ablaze with light! The chandeliers, the candles on the altar, all burned brightly. *Why*, she thought, *it is like a midnight Mass!*

The child moved on into the sanctuary. Obediently, Catherine followed. He stopped by the chair that the Director used when he gave conferences to the Sisters. Instinctively, Catherine knelt.

Nothing happened. The Virgin was not there. The child stood calmly waiting, as if for a cue, as if he were part of a play. The minutes were long and the stillness grew loud with noises: the scurry of a mouse, the cracking of a pew, the distant clatter of a carriage. Catherine shifted on her knees. Anxiously she glanced over her shoulder toward the gallery. The night Sisters, up with the sick, might be passing. But there was no one. Suddenly the child spoke:

"Here is the Blessed Virgin."

In the same instant Catherine heard a sound like the rustling of a silk dress, and, looking toward the direction of the sound, saw a lady descending the altar steps. The lady seated herself in the Director's chair. As she sat there, she reminded Catherine of St. Anne in the picture over the sacristy door. Catherine's eyes flew to the painting and back to the lady. But no, she was not like St. Anne. A doubt clouded the novice's mind. Was this really the Mother of God? The child reassured her:

"This is the Blessed Virgin."

Even this did not allay all her doubts. Was the whole thing a dream, a fancy of the night? She blushed. The lady was looking at her, waiting. The child spoke again, startling her, for now his voice was a man's voice, deep and commanding and stern. She held back no more, but threw herself at Our Lady's knee and rested her hands in Our Lady's lap. Then she lifted her head and looked up, up, into her Mother's eyes. Many years later she was to write with ecstatic remembrance of this moment, that it was the sweetest of her life.

"My child," said Our Lady, "the good God wishes to charge you with a mission."

But that could wait. This moment was Catherine's; and Mary went on to tell her of God's plans for her, to warn her of the trials that would come upon her, and to show her how she should bear them.

The good God wished to charge her with a mission. She would meet with many difficulties in carrying it out, but she would overcome the difficulties by thinking upon the glory of God as her reason for doing what He wanted. Most comforting of all, she would know with unerring certainty the Will of God; she would be spiritually secure, for she would recognize at all times what God wanted of her.

"You will be tormented," Our Lady continued, "until you have told him who is charged with directing you. You will be contradicted, but do not fear, you will have grace. Tell with confidence all that passes within you; tell it with simplicity. Have confidence. Do not be afraid."

"You will see certain things: give an account of what you see and hear. You will be inspired in your prayers: give an account of what I tell you and of what you will understand in your prayers."

"The times are very evil. Sorrows will come upon France; the throne will be overturned. The whole world will be upset by miseries of every kind." As she delivered herself of this ominous prophecy, pain crossed the Virgin's face. There was a remedy however:

"Come to the foot of the altar." She indicated the spot. "There graces will be shed upon all, great and little, who ask for them. Graces will be especially shed upon those who ask for them."

Then the Mother of God turned her attention to the Vincentian Fathers and the Sisters of Charity. "My child, I particularly love to shed graces upon your Community; I love it very much," she said. "It pains me that there are great abuses in regularity, that the rules are not observed, that there is much relaxation in the two Communities. Tell that to him who has charge of you, even though he is not the superior.

He will be given charge of the Community in a special way; he must do everything he can to restore the rule in vigor. Tell him for me to guard against useless reading, loss of time, and visits."

When the rule should be fully observed once more, Mary promised, another community of Sisters would ask to join the Community of rue du Bac. The prediction was fulfilled in 1849, when Father Etienne received Mother Elizabeth Seton's Sisters of Emmitsburg, Maryland, into the Paris Community. These Sisters were the foundation stone of the Sisters of Charity in the United States.

Our Lady concluded her instructions concerning the family of St. Vincent with a great promise:

"The Community will enjoy a great peace; it will become large."

Then Our Lady began to speak of the miseries to come upon France and the whole world. "There will be an abundance of sorrows; and the danger will be great. Yet do not be afraid; tell them not to be afraid. The protection of God shall be ever present in a special way—and St. Vincent will protect you. I shall be with you myself. Always, I have my eye upon you. I will grant you many graces."

The Mother of God said it all over again, emphasizing her words, lest there be any mistake. "The moment will come when the danger will be enormous; it will seem that all is lost; at that moment, I will be with you; have confidence. You will recognize my coming, you will see the protection of God upon the Community, the protection of St. Vincent upon both his Communities. Have confidence. Do not be discouraged. I shall be with you." It was a refrain of hope: *Have confidence, have confidence;* a refrain of encouragement: *Do not be afraid; God, and I, and St. Vincent will be with you.* These were words of promise, to be clung to in time of calamity, as a child clings to its mother's hand.

Then the worst: Mary began to specify the sorrows and dangers. She spoke in broken sentences, in halting phrases, fighting back the tears that stood in her eyes. "It will not be the same for other communities. There will be victims. . . . There will be victims among the clergy of Paris. Monseigneur the Archbishop . . ." She could not finish for weeping. "My child, the cross will be treated with contempt; they will hurl it to the ground. Blood will flow; they will open up again the side of Our Lord. The streets will stream with blood. Monseigneur the Archbishop will be stripped of his garments. . . ."

She could not go on. Tears choked her voice, and her lovely face twisted in pain. She could only conclude:

"My child, the whole world will be in sadness."

When will all this be? Catherine wondered, and immediately she understood: *forty years.*

The conversation was not one-sided. Catherine spoke freely, unfolding the secrets of her soul, asking questions which Mary graciously answered.

Then, like the fading of a shadow, Our Lady was gone.

Slowly, Catherine got up from her knees. The child still hovered nearby. Together they left the chapel and went back upstairs to the dormitory. The lights in the hall were still lit, but Catherine scarcely noticed them. Her heart was too filled with gladness and horror and hope and bliss, all jumbled together. The hand that had lighted them would put them out. When they got back to the side of Catherine's bed, the child, too, faded from sight as Our Lady had. Catherine felt now that she knew who he was: her guardian angel, long the confidant of her wish to see the Blessed Virgin. She climbed quickly into bed and pulled the covers around her. Just then the clock struck two. She had been with Our Lady over two hours! She slept no more that night.

This apparition of the Virgin Mary to Catherine Labouré had a personal atmosphere about it, unlike any other in history. While it announced a world mission for Catherine, that would come about in good time; the business of the moment had to deal almost entirely with her and the needs of her soul and the welfare of her beloved Community.

Even the manner of Our Lady's coming was different. In other famous appearances to chosen souls, Our Lady has burst suddenly upon their sight, as it were, from out of nowhere. Here, her coming was a calm, logical climax to years of intimacy. She arranged it with a sort of heavenly etiquette. First of all, she led Catherine, in her thoughts, to expect it. Then she sent an angel to announce her coming. When Catherine, following the angel, arrived at the chapel, she found it all in readiness for the great happening, brilliant and lighted as if for a midnight Mass. The good Sisters had unwittingly lent their hands to the preparation: spreading their best linen on the altars and decking them with flowers, scrubbing the floor until it shone, for St. Vincent's feast on the morrow. Then Catherine heard the rustle of a silken gown, and Mary came.

The crowning touch of the personal, however, was the privilege given Catherine of kneeling at Mary's knee and resting her hands in her lap. So great a favor has been granted to no other seer. Not to Bernadette of Lourdes: she was granted, once, to kiss the golden rose on Our Lady's foot. Not to the children of Fatima, not even to Lucy, upon whose shoulders the desperate message for the modern world's salvation was laid. Only to Catherine Labouré.

Catherine's subsequent visions were not like this first one. Since they were meant for the whole world, there was a certain impersonality about them, very different from the bonds of intimacy entered into on this night of July 18. In November, Mary would come suddenly, while Catherine was at prayer with her Sisters, would deliver her message and be gone. She would not even speak directly to the novice.

Here, however, there were only Mary and Catherine, and

no one else in the universe. Here they talked, the Mother and child, for two hours—a long, long time, even on the clocks of Heaven and eternity.

All too soon the prophecies of the vision were fulfilled. On July 27, 1830, just one week later, the revolution erupted in fury. Barricades were thrown up across the narrow, winding streets of the ancient capital. Boulevard and alley echoed to the rattle of musketry and the drunken cries of the looting, burning mob. The dead lay where they fell and the stink of unburied corpses made the summer air nauseating and disease-ridden.

Charles X had brought it on himself. He had failed to measure the temper of the times. It is amazing that he should have failed to realize how very deeply the ideas of the Revolution had taken root in France, that the common people had grown used to freedom in forty years, that the middle class had slowly but surely grown into a power to be reckoned with. It is amazing that he should have failed to notice the envious glances Frenchmen cast upon the growing American Republic across the water, the Republic they had helped gain and keep its independence.

Charles had seen his brother Louis XVI sacrificed in the upsurge of the new age. He had seen another brother, Louis XVIII, wisely drift with the tide, granting a constitutional charter and ruling as a constitutional monarch, even while he blustered that he held his throne by divine right. Charles X, however, was a stubborn old man of sixty-seven when he came to the throne in 1824. All his life he had fought for Bourbon absolutism, and he was not going to change in his old age. "I would rather saw wood than rule like an English king," he had said, and that about summed it up. His futile attempt to restore the "divine right" monarchy of Louis XIV came to a preposterous climax on July 26, 1830 when he dissolved the Chamber, revoked his brother's Charter, and muzzled the press. The constitutional monarchists, the middle-class shop-keepers, the extreme radicals, and the Parisian mob, all united against him. The "Glorious Three Days" of the July Revolution followed, and Charles X was toppled from his throne, the trappings of royalty falling from him as they had fallen from Our Lord in the vision of Trinity Sunday.

The Church had prospered under Charles: "For Throne and Altar" had been the motto of his reign. Unfortunately, a great number of the prelates of the land, many of them aristocrats by birth, were only too eager for the full restoration of the Bourbon dynasty, with the privileges it brought the nobles and the clergy. Now, with the fall of Charles, the Church felt the wrath of his enemies. Now it reaped the whirlwind, as it has always reaped, when certain selfish prelates have mistakenly and crassly aligned themselves with the rich and powerful against the common man and the poor. Bishops and priests, members of religious orders, guilty and innocent alike, were imprisoned and beaten and killed. Godlessness ran wild, desecrating churches, pulling down statues, trampling the cross under foot. Just as Our Lady had said.

Monseigneur de Quélen was forced into hiding. He was saved from the maelstrom, spirited away by the quick thinking of a famous Sister of Charity, Sister Rosalie Rendu, a true champion of the poor and downtrodden. During the first day of the fighting, Sister Rosalie, despite the added burden of caring for the wounded, did not neglect a certain old derelict, confined to his bed in a hovel. It was her custom to take him a daily loaf of bread. On this day, to her surprise, she found the old fellow on his feet, breathing the fire of revolution. He pushed aside the loaf she offered and told her, scornfully:

"We need charity no longer. We sack the Archbishop's palace tomorrow!"

Sister Rosalie knew her "children," and she knew this was no idle boast. She acted quickly. When the sacking came off as scheduled next day, the looters found the Archbishop and his entire household flown. Ironically, the good prelate was secreted in Sister Rosalie's own house in the midst of the Faubourg Saint Marceau, where all the looters lived!

The Vincentian Fathers and the Sisters of Charity were spared during this short but intense persecution. Our Lady had promised them her protection, and she gave it. A retreat was in progress at the Motherhouse of the Sisters when the revolution broke: the retreat went on undisturbed. Twice the mob assailed the Motherhouse of the priests; twice they went away, calmly and without incident.

Father Aladel had much to think about during these days. Sister Labouré had been to him again, with a full and explicit account of Our Lady's visit and of what she had said. The things she had foretold had come to pass. It was incredible: the short revolution was an impromptu affair; it had taken even the most informed by surprise. Sister Labouré, behind her convent walls, could have heard not a whisper of it. Then there was the incident of the attempt on the cross over the entrance to the Vincentian Motherhouse—Sister Labouré had said the attempt would be made—and the refugee bishop . . .

The novice Sister had told Father Aladel that a bishop would seek asylum at the rue de Sèvres, and that Our Lady said he could be taken in, for he would be quite safe there. Father Aladel had scarcely returned home from speaking with her when Father Salhorgne told him that Monseigneur de Frayssinous, Bishop of Hieropolis and Minister of Public Worship in the fallen government, had been there to ask whether he might not hide out among the Vincentian Fathers. Father Salhorgne was afraid the prelate might be discovered, should the mob return, and Monseigneur had left.

With all the civil and religious unrest, Father Aladel had even more important things to consider. He had to decide whether this young novice was indeed a seer, whether she had really been favored with the visions she described. The priest could not doubt her sincerity: she really *thought* she saw them. Suppose she had—what then?

As for Catherine, these terrible days were a sort of triumph, for they went a long way toward vindicating her. She was not the victim of illusions, for the prophecies of her visions had come true. It was a horrible proof, and she could not bring herself to dwell upon it. Rather, her thoughts were fixed upon the future. The Blessed Virgin had spoken of a mission. What could it be? When would she see Our Lady again? The question set up a longing in her, a longing that seized upon her soul and gave it no rest by day or night.

VIII

The Apparition of the Miraculous Medal

O UTSIDE THE CONVENT on the rue du Bac, the City of Paris
had grown quiet; people had gone back to their daily living. Charles X retreated to England, where he no longer ruled
even "like an English king." Louis Philippe came to the throne.
Although a Bourbon, he was not of the line of Bourbon kings,
but of the Orleans family, and most certainly he was not the
divine right monarch the royal Bourbons had been. Dubbed
from the start "The Citizen King," he was the figurehead the
new nation wanted.

Saturday, November 27, 1830, was just another day, busy
like all the rest with prayer and work and study of the things
of God. The next day would be the First Sunday of Advent.
At half past five, all the Sisters, professed and novices alike,
gathered in the chapel for their evening meditation. The chill
November dusk had settled outside, and the chapel was in
semi-darkness.

Catherine liked this time of evening. She had always liked
it, even at home: the laborious day was over and the tired

mind found rest in thinking of God. Tonight, the quiet voice of the Sister reading the prophecies of Christ's coming at Christmas seemed like the voice of Isaiah himself, calling down the centuries. In the darkness, time and place were no more; only the mind was alive. The voice stopped, and a great stillness followed.

Suddenly, Catherine's heart leaped. She had heard it—that rustling, that faint swish of silk she could never forget, the sound of Our Lady's gown as she walked! There it was again —and there was the Queen of Heaven, there in the sanctuary, standing upon a globe. She shone as the morning rising, a radiant vision, "in all her perfect beauty," as Catherine said later.

Catherine's eyes widened with bliss at the sight. Yet they were not so dazzled but that, womanlike, they took note of every detail of the Virgin's dress: that her robe was of silk, "of the whiteness of the dawn," that the neck of it was cut high and the sleeves plain, that she wore a white veil which fell to her feet, and beneath the veil a lace fillet binding her hair.

The Virgin held in her hands a golden ball which she seemed to offer to God, for her eyes were raised heavenward. Suddenly, her hands were resplendent with rings set with precious stones that glittered and flashed in a brilliant cascade of light. So bright was the flood of glory cast upon the globe below that Catherine could no longer see Our Lady's feet.

Mary lowered her eyes and looked full at Sister Labouré. Her lips did not move, but Catherine heard a voice.

"The ball which you see represents the whole world, especially France, and each person in particular."

These words stirred the heart of the Sister with fresh transports of joy, and the dazzling rays seemed to her to increase to blinding brilliance.

"These rays symbolize the graces I shed upon those who ask for them. The gems from which rays do not fall are the graces for which souls forget to ask."

At this moment, Catherine was so lost in delight that she scarcely knew where she was, whether she lived or died. The golden ball vanished from Mary's hands; her arms swept wide in a gesture of motherly compassion, while from her jeweled fingers the rays of light streamed upon the white globe at her feet. An oval frame formed around the Blessed Virgin, and written within it in letters of gold Catherine read the words:

O Mary, conceived without sin, pray for us who have recourse to thee.

The voice spoke again:

"Have a Medal struck after this model. All who wear it will receive great graces; they should wear it around the neck. Graces will abound for persons who wear it with confidence."

The tableau revolved, and Catherine beheld the reverse of the Medal she was to have made. It contained a large M surmounted by a bar and a cross. Beneath the M were the Hearts of Jesus and Mary, the one crowned with thorns, the other pierced with a sword. Twelve stars encircled the whole.

And then the vision was gone.

Habit is a saving thing. Certainly it saved Catherine embarrassment or discovery in the next few minutes. She must have said the closing prayers of the meditation with the others; she must have taken her place in line to go to the dining hall; she must have recited the grace and sat down at table. She did not remember. It was the chastening voice of the Mistress of Novices that brought her back to earth.

"Sister Labouré must still be in ecstasy," it said dryly.

Catherine started in confusion. Why the other novices had begun to eat!

The three great Apparitions of Our Lady to Catherine Labouré—they are designated by number for convenience—were complete. The first, the Apparition of July 18, is sometimes called "The Virgin of the Chair"; the second and third, actually two phases of the Apparition of November 27, are known by the titles: "The Virgin of the Globe" or "The Virgin Most Powerful," and "Our Lady of the Miraculous Medal."

The Medal design submitted by the engraver in 1832 and accepted by Father Aladel was the second phase of the Great Apparition of November 27, representing Our Lady bestowing her graces upon mankind through the symbolism of the rays falling from her outstretched hands upon the globe at her feet. It was not the design originally intended, which was the first phase of the Great Apparition, "The Virgin of the Globe," offering the golden ball to heaven while the rays streamed from her hands upon the large globe on which she stood. Catherine herself remarked upon this change from the original design in her account of the apparitions given to Sister Dufès, her superior, in 1876, and her words carry a tone of complaint. If she saw fit to complain, it must be that Our Lady herself had wanted the Medal to represent her in the attitude of offering the golden ball. Why, then, the change?

Father Chevalier, Catherine's last director, in his deposition before the Beatification Tribunal, expresses the opinion that the change was made because of the difficulty of representing the attitude of the first phase in metal, and also because Father Aladel thought it more prudent, in view of the anti-religious feeling at the time, to represent Our Lady in the attitude of the second phase. It is hard to see how the one attitude would have been any more acceptable to anti-religious feeling than the other. The probable reason for the change is the first point made by Father Chevalier, that M. Vachette, the engraver, saw difficulty in delineating within the limits of the engraver's art at that time, the arms and the golden ball superimposed upon the stamped image of Our Lady's body. There would have been no such problem today, when dies can be cut so deeply and etched so finely, but it was a problem in 1832. Father Aladel, with no technical knowledge of the problem, would have followed the advice of the engraver.

There is, of course, a difference of emphasis upon doctrine in the two representations, for the first phase of the Apparition, in addition to honoring the Immaculate Conception of Our Lady in the words *"conceived without sin,"* expressly demonstrates the doctrine that Mary is Mediatrix of All Graces. Very simply, this doctrine—considered by the Church to be certain although not yet solemnly defined—teaches that all prayers and petitions, whether made to God directly, to Our Lady, or to the saints, are presented to God by His Mother; and that all graces, whether answers to prayer or gratuitously bestowed by God, pass to men through the hands of His Mother. In the first phase of the Apparition, the attitude of Our Lady, eyes raised to Heaven, lips moving in prayer, and the symbolic offering of the golden ball of the world, beautifully express the intercession of Mary, while the rays from her fingers express the bestowal of God's graces through her. In the second phase of the Apparition, the bestowal of the graces alone is represented by the rays flowing from the outstretched hands.

However, while Father Aladel must have regretted the inability to present the completeness of doctrine symbolized in the first phase, he must have considered the intercessory powers of Mary as Mediatrix to be sufficiently represented by the words of the prayer on the Medal: *"Pray for us who have recourse to thee."* There is no record of dissatisfaction on Catherine's part when she saw the first Medals, fresh from the press. Her only comment was a call to arms: "Now it must be propagated." She, therefore, consented from the first to the Medal's propagation in its altered form. Moreover, as we shall see, she was in regular contact with Our Lady and would be expected to consult her on such an important change. The proof of the Medal's acceptability to Heaven is in the vast multitude of graces bestowed from the beginning on those who wore it and recited the prayer engraved on it. Catherine's complaining reference to the change, forty-four years later, may be laid to her natural anxiety, with approaching death, as to whether she had carried out her mission exactly. Such anxiety could arise easily out of her very justifiable concern, which we shall hear more of, that the *statue* of "The Virgin of the Globe," also commissioned by Our Lady, had not been made.

At the command of her director, Catherine wrote out full accounts of her visions, in 1841, in 1856, and again in 1876. It is odd that, while these accounts are minute and detailed in their descriptions, they omit two significant details of the Medal. The first of these is the serpent whose head Our Lady crushed beneath her heel, as she stood upon the white globe of the earth. This was an obvious pictorial reference to Genesis III: 15, the sole scriptural text with any reference to the doctrine of Mary's Immaculate Conception: "She (the woman) shall crush thy head (the serpent's), and thou shalt lie in wait for her heel." The second detail left out of Catherine's written accounts was the twelve stars on the back of the Medal. These stars refer probably to the Twelve Apostles, and are mentioned in the text from Apocalypse XII: 1, applied by theologians to Our Lady: "A woman clothed with the sun, and the moon under her feet, and on her head a crown of twelve stars." That Catherine transmitted the details of the serpent and the stars to her director, at least by word of mouth, is morally certain, for she approved the Medal which bore both details from the first. Besides, in 1836, when the artist LeCerf was painting canvases of the apparitions, she described the serpent to her director as "green with yellow spots"—a rather fearsome serpent, and one, certainly, to offend the sensibilities of an artist!

There was one further instruction concerning the Medal which Catherine gave Father Aladel orally. The priest was puzzled by the fact that there were no words on the back of the Medal, to balance the prayer on the front. He told Catherine to ask Our Lady what should be written there. Catherine consulted the Virgin in prayer, and returned with the verbatim reply: "The M and the two Hearts express enough."

Aside from the importance of Catherine's written accounts as religious historical documents, they are, like all such writings not meant to be published, supreme revelations of the character of the one who wrote them. If we knew nothing whatever of Catherine Labouré, we should know from these accounts that she was a practical, commonsense sort of person, not to be rattled even by the glorious visions of another world. Her first thought upon being awakened by the angel on the night of July 18 was: *We shall be discovered.* On her knees in the chapel, awaiting the arrival of the Blessed Virgin, she kept craning her neck and peering into the dim recesses of the chapel, for fear "the night Sisters, up with the sick," would see her. When Our Lady finally came, Catherine did not throw herself upon the Virgin at once in ecstasy, but wondered whether this were really the Mother of God. Certainly she had a practical prudence, much like Our Lady's when she asked the Angel Gabriel: "How shall it be done?"

Again, she is revealed as an extremely observant person, who, even in the ecstasy of her apparitions, did not miss the smallest details, and as a precise person, who did not fail to report them. Catherine tells us, for example, that Our Lady wore "three rings on each of her fingers." She tells us, further, that the rings were graduated in size, "the largest one near the base of the finger, one of medium size in the middle, the smallest one at the tip." She even noticed that the rings themselves were set with stones "of proportionate size, some larger and others smaller."

Her description of Our Lady's veil and headdress is a marvel of exactitude. "A white veil covered her head," Catherine wrote, "falling on either side to her feet. Under the veil her hair, in coils, was bound with a fillet ornamented with lace, about three centimeters in height or of two fingers' breadth, without pleats, and resting lightly on the hair."

This supreme accuracy carries over into the recording of the time and place of her visions. She saw the heart of St. Vincent "above the little shrine where the relic of St. Vincent was exposed in the chapel of the Sisters, over the picture of St. Anne and in front of St. Joseph's picture." On the night of July 18, she heard herself called by name at "eleven-thirty in the evening." She heard the noise of Our Lady's coming "from the side of the tribune near St. Joseph's picture." When she returned to her bed, "it was two o'clock in the morning, for I heard the hour strike." The opening paragraph of her account of the Great Apparition is incomparable: "On November 27, 1830, which fell upon the Saturday before the first Sunday of Advent, at five-thirty in the evening, in the deep silence after the point of the meditation had been read—that is, several minutes after the point of the meditation—I heard a sound like the rustling of a silken gown, from the tribune near the picture of St. Joseph."

The precision of these descriptions, particularly the details of the Virgin's attire, makes all the more mysterious Catherine's omission of the serpent and the twelve stars, and her failure to give us the faintest clue as to Our Lady's age or personal appearance.

Catherine had a woman's eye for color. When the heart of St. Vincent was shown her in April, 1830, she recorded that it was successively "white flesh color," "fiery red," "dark red," and "vermilion." It finally appeared "sombre, the color of dead flesh." Certainly not every woman can boast this eye for nuance and shading. Her description of the Virgin's dress in the apparition of November 27: "of the whiteness of the dawn," has ever been the despair of artists, and they have gotten around the problem by painting the dress a flat white or cream color. Catherine, who, as a farm girl had often seen the day break, meant literally that Our Lady was clothed in the color of the dawn sky: a basic white with myriad tints of red, pink, saffron, and the palest blue.

Perhaps the most surprising trait revealed by Catherine Labouré in her written accounts is her flair for the right word or phrase. Certain descriptive flashes in her story of the Apparitions would be the envy of professional writers. When she tells us that the chapel all lighted for the coming of the Blessed Virgin reminded her of "Midnight Mass," the phrase is completely evocative. As Mary came, Catherine heard "the swish of a silken gown." When the Virgin departed, "she faded away and became but a shadow, which moved toward the tribune, the way she had come." At the close of the Miraculous Medal Apparition, on the other hand, "everything disappeared from my sight, like a candle that is blown out." In describing the brilliant rays that flashed from Mary's hands, Catherine uses the word *rejaillissant*, thus suggesting a breathtaking picture of dazzling light "bursting from all sides," like a fountain. The rays grew so bright that they "flooded the base, so that I could no longer see the feet of the Blessed Virgin." Mary's hands were "bent down under the weight of the treasures of graces obtained." For an uneducated girl, Catherine's accounts are masterpieces of clarity and beauty.

As soon as possible, Catherine, with a natural fear and trepidation—she had been rebuffed so many times!—laid the whole matter of the Medal before Father Aladel. He listened patiently, but once more refused to put much stock in the visions of a novice.

The great vision of November 27, the vision of the Medal, was repeated again and again, probably five times in all. This very repetition seemed to insist on action, and each time Catherine was troubled afresh, for each time she knew that she must approach Father Aladel again, and each time she dreaded the encounter more.

These encounters of confessor and penitent had become highly excitable and unpleasant. Voices were raised and hard words uttered. The sounds of battle drifted out of the confessional to startle the ears of the Sisters waiting their turn. Although they did not know then what it all meant, Sisters later testified before the solemn tribunal convoked by Rome to investigate Catherine's sanctity, that they often overheard the voice of Father Aladel, its tone peremptorily commanding, and the voice of Sister Labouré, its tone just as peremptorily insisting. She testified herself, shortly before her death, that she once confessed to the priest that, in a moment of frustration, she had told Our Lady that she "had better appear to someone else, since no one will believe me," and that the priest in horror had called her a "wicked wasp." These pitched battles were not of her choosing, for there is further testimony of the Sisters who survived her that she approached the confessional trembling. She had a dogged and determined will, however, that would not sidestep any unpleasantness to achieve its objective, and a spirited tongue to pursue that objective against all argument and remonstrance. There is ample evidence of her tart rejoinders throughout her life.

Not that she was untractable or disobedient: that is another matter entirely. Father Aladel, who knew her soul best, never accused her of the slightest disobedience or rebellion. Quite the opposite: he called her most submissive. Therefore, when he would feel himself forced to call a halt to the discussion, his word was enough for her, no matter how sorely she might suffer in her silence. In the matter of her visions, nevertheless, she had a command from Heaven that must be obeyed, and she fought tooth and nail to obey it, to see the mission entrusted to her carried out. As always, it was her indomitable obedience that won the day.

IX

The Secret of Forty-Six Years

IN THOSE LAST WEEKS of 1830, Sister Labouré was not the only one with difficulties. Father Aladel had his own, and to spare. In a way, the difficulties of the anxious Sister were mere mental annoyances compared to the tangled skein of problems in the head of the poor priest. She, after all, had only a succession of happenings to report, happenings which she knew to be true. He had to convince himself whether they were indeed true. She had only the rather patience-trying task of pressing him to action. He had to decide whether such actions were wise. Things were crystal clear to the plain mind of the country girl from Burgundy: Our Lady had appeared to her, had ordered something to be done. All that remained was to do it; it was as simple as that.

It was certainly *not* as simple as that to Father Aladel. Our Lady had not appeared to him. All his knowledge of this wondrous thing, this Medal, was second-hand, and he had his knowledge from a simple, illiterate novice.

Her ignorance, of course, was the key to the situation. The

priest began to see that more and more as time went on. She was intellectually incapable of making up the Apparitions. Then, there were the several prophecies she had reported, some of which had already come true. Consideration of these two facts would be enough to convince him in time, especially when they were seen in the light of Catherine's character.

She was basically good and pious; she had even those flashes of spiritual intuition which God reserves for the unlettered who love Him. More to the point, she was totally unimaginative. Aside from the "visions," her thoughts were drab and colorless, even pedestrian. This much was to the good.

But, it must be remembered, everything was not so evident to Father Aladel at the moment. These dazzling events—if they were events—had happened in a bewildering rush. Scarcely a week had passed since this placid girl had first entered his confessional some nine months before, that she had not some new wonder to report. It had all come about at a most inconvenient time. Smack into the middle of his normally busy schedule had burst the disruptive forces of the celebration surrounding the Translation of St. Vincent's relics, and, when things had gotten back to normal, the surprise of the change of government with its consequent anxieties for all organizations, especially religious ones. To add to the turmoil, the reported visions of the insistent novice were tangled inextricably with these same disruptive forces. Was it any wonder the poor man's mind was in a muddle?

Father Aladel's task was made doubly difficult by Catherine's insistence that her identity remain secret. This made the task his, and his alone. He could not temper or bolster his opinion by having some trusted advisor listen to the remarkable tales of the Saint. He could not even lead her forth to testify before some competent ecclesiastical tribunal. She would have none of this. Our Lady had told her to "tell this to him who has charge of you," and Catherine would obey this instruction to the letter but not beyond. Father Aladel, then, and he alone, had to decide upon her character, her reliability, the truth of what she said. Others more skilled, Church officials trained in such matters, would handle it from there, but he had to be convinced himself before he referred the matter to them.

The fact that Catherine Labouré kept her secret for forty-six years has caught the popular fancy more than anything else about her. The secret of the Seer's identity also intrigued her contemporaries. There was a delightful sense of mystery in knowing that somewhere, maybe close by, maybe living here in this very house, there was a favored soul who had been Our Lady's messenger in delivering the Miraculous Medal to the human race. There were endless guesses, endless wonderings, endless baitings, in the hope of catching the privileged Sister off guard. It was Catherine's obscurity too, that caught the eye of Cardinal Masella, prefect of the Congregations of Rites, in 1895, and set in motion the Cause for her beatification. During the fifty years of the Process it was this obscurity that constantly impressed new prelates assigned to the Cause and won Catherine new champions. The obvious joke it suggested must have occurred to many during these years, but it was Pius XI who gave it voice at the Beatification ceremonies in 1933.

"To think of keeping a secret for forty-six years," the Holy Father is reported to have said, "—and this by a *woman*, and a *Sister!*"

Indeed, keeping her secret was the most significant act of Catherine's life after the Apparitions. It is amazing, how this habitual, heroic act runs through her remaining years like a golden thread, tying into one glorious whole all the actions and incidents of a lifetime, spiritual and temporal, important and trivial. There is literally nothing in all these forty-six years that was not touched by the influence of the secret.

Certainly, without the secret, Catherine would have been a very different person. From earliest childhood she had lived

in the back lanes and the quiet corners; she had worked behind
the closed door of her village home. She spoke little and unfolded herself less. She was withdrawn and interior, thinking
her own deep thoughts and keeping them to herself. It is appalling to think of the disastrous effects of publicity on such a
soul: how she would have shrunk in terror from the assaults
of the curious: the prying and questioning, the adulation and
praise. They would never have let her alone, and Catherine's
nature needed privacy as the lowliest creatures of the deep
need it.

It can even be questioned whether, without the secret,
Catherine would have been a saint. The secret was vital to
assure her soul of the climate in which to grow. Her sanctity
was a hidden thing, a shy blossom that bloomed unseen and
unknown, for sanctity usually follows the pattern of personality. There are saints who were born leaders and who became holy by leading, and there are saints who were born to
obscurity and who became holy by remaining obscure. Catherine Labouré was one of these latter. The world and its lime-
light were not for her. Aside from an exceptional grace of
God, she would have been as out of place as if she had been
thrust from her convent altogether.

These, of course, are only conjectures made to point up the
pervading importance of the secret. The fact is that she kept
her secret for forty-six years.

In the formal Inquiry into the origin of the Medal held at
Paris in 1836, Father Aladel testified that the very first time
Catherine told him of the Apparition of the Miraculous Medal,
she extracted from him the promise that he would never reveal her name or identity in any way. No doubt it was a
promise easily given, because at the time the priest put no
credence in her visions. He could not know then what difficulties his promise would make for him later, or he might not
have been so quick to give it. But give it he did, and Catherine

held him to it. Here again we run full tilt against the enormous strength of her will. A more pliant spirit than hers would have yielded to the importunities of high personages—the Archbishop of Paris among them—that she reveal herself to them; a weaker soul than she would have grown weary of avoiding the increasing traps set for her, and would have surrendered. But not Catherine. She was her father's daughter in obstinacy.

The question naturally arises as to whether Our Lady told Catherine that she was to remain unknown. There is no explicit indication of it in her written communications to Father Aladel. Our only *direct* knowledge is Father Aladel's assertion that Catherine made him promise not to reveal her identity. Indeed a command from Our Lady need not be posited. It is quite in character for Catherine to make the demand of secrecy without any prompting. By nature she heartily disliked publicity, and by grace she was thoroughly humble. Father Aladel has deposed under oath that the only reason he could give for her refusal to testify before the Tribunal of the Archbishop of Paris in 1836 was her profound humility and earnest wish to remain unknown.

Nevertheless, though we have no evidence from Father Aladel that Our Lady imposed silence on the Sister, we have a very definite statement from Catherine herself in the last months of her life. When she found herself bereft of her confessor in 1876, she said to Sister Dufès, her Superior:

"Since I haven't much longer to live, I feel that the moment to speak out has come. But, *as the Blessed Virgin told me to speak only to my confessor*, I shall say nothing to you until I have asked Our Lady's permission in prayer. If she tells me I may speak to you, I will do so, otherwise I will remain silent."

It is strange that in her written accounts of her conversation with the Blessed Virgin, Catherine does not say that she was charged to "speak *only* to my confessor." Yet she undoubtedly said so, forty-six years later. We must, therefore, take her at her word, for she always spoke the truth.

This final, definite declaration of Catherine's is bolstered by the testimony of Sister Tanguy, Assistant-Superior of the House at Reuilly, who relates that Catherine was one day overheard telling a servant of the house:

"The Blessed Virgin wishes that the Sister who saw her live in humility."

In the meantime, something urgent had arisen, of supreme importance to a successful solution of the whole business. Sister Labouré was nearing the end of her novitiate; she would soon be eligible for an assignment that might take her to the opposite border of France, or even to some foreign outpost. At this critical time, when he had not made up his mind about the visions, it was essential that Father Aladel keep her within easy reach. To do so was not so simple as it seemed: Father Aladel had no authority to assign the Sisters; he was not yet their director. On the other hand, at this time no one but himself knew how necessary it was for Sister Labouré not to leave Paris.

Certainly, Catherine herself was supremely interested in her appointment. In the final weeks of their spiritual apprenticeship, religious novices are naturally curious about where they shall be sent to begin their lives of active service. This curiosity gives rise to hopes and fears bandied about from one to another and forming the chief topic at recreation. It would be fascinating to have watched Catherine in these last seething weeks of her novitiate, in the midst of the banter and surmise.

As it is, we can reconstruct nothing of these days, for we have no whisper of evidence to go on. Let it not be stated flatly, however, that Catherine would have had no part of such doings. In the terse, two-sentence biography written in the seminary record book, her directress states that during her noviceship Catherine was, surprisingly enough, "gay." It is an adjective no one would have applied to her in her former life, except possibly in her earliest childhood. It is an adjective no one would ever apply to her again. Happy she was, always, but hardly gay. Yet during these short months of preparation, her directress has recorded for the ages the fact that she was gay. It is indeed a startling and provocative picture of the quietest of saints.

It must not be forgotten that Catherine Labouré had chosen and been accepted into a way of life that emphasized community living. She had weathered the period of testing successfully, the period when aspirants to this hardest of all ways of life are carefully watched to see whether they are equal to its give and take. Therefore, we must not make the mistake of considering Catherine Labouré a sort of hermit living in the midst of a bustling hive of women. She was quiet, particularly so: one who did not speak needlessly, nor waste words when she spoke. Yet she was capable of spending pleasant hours of recreation in the company of her Sisters. To say otherwise is to call her a misfit in religion; and there is the delightful evidence that, as a novice, she was gay.

Sister Labouré had, however, more motive than mere affability for her interest in her first mission. She was all too painfully aware that her business with Father Aladel was far from finished. Though she must take refuge in a firm belief that Our Lady would see things through, the young Sister can be allowed some human anxiety as to when and how.

The only glimpse we have of Catherine among her companions during the entire nine months of her novitiate concerned the keeping of her secret. Word had gotten around that one of them had seen the Blessed Virgin. The way important news "leaks out" in religious houses is something of a mystery, but it is a phenomenon common to all of them. In this case, Father Aladel was certainly the source. Apparently he had revealed the facts of the Apparitions, even though he had not yet fully made up his mind about them. At any rate, the novices were in the garden at recreation one day, when one of them, Sister Pinot, artlessly and without thought, turned to Sister Labouré, seated next to her, and asked:

"Are you the one who saw the Blessed Virgin?"

No sooner were the words out of her mouth than Sister Pinot blushed violently and turned away, ashamed of her impertinence. Catherine, however, took the affair so lightly, everyone was sure that, if one of them was the favored Sister, it was certainly not she!

However, the thought stayed with Sister Pinot to torment her, and the poor novice could find no peace of soul until she had revealed it to Father Aladel in confession. Father Aladel did nothing to disabuse her of the notion, nor did he say anything to confirm it. Nevertheless, he was so struck by the incident that he later used Sister Pinot as his secretary in matters relating to the Miraculous Medal. Sister Pinot's distress of soul ceased from the moment she unburdened herself.

How Father Aladel managed to keep Sister Labouré within reach, we do not know, but manage it he did. When the canonical time of her novitiate was over, she was missioned to the Hospice d'Enghien located at Reuilly in the environs of Paris. Father Aladel was the regular confessor at the Hospice.

The Hospice d'Enghien, in the Faubourg Saint Antoine, was far enough away from the Motherhouse on the rue du Bac, judged by the mode of transportation of those days. Today, a cab ride of approximately twenty minutes separates the two houses. The Hospice was founded by the Duchesse de Bourbon in memory of her son, the Duc d'Enghien, who had been shot in the trenches of Vincennes prison during the days of the Terror. It was intended as a haven for the faithful retainers who had grown old in the service of the Orleans family. Connected by a long mall with the House of Charity of Reuilly, it shared with the Reuilly house a common superior and chapel. This mall was to become the pathway of Sister Catherine's life, and she was to amass a tremendous mileage in forty-six years, on her errands between the two houses, and especially on her trips to the chapel which, in later years, was close by the Reuilly house.

Mother Etienne, appointed first Visitatrix of the Province of the United States when Mother Seton's Sisters joined the Community of St. Vincent, visited Enghien on May 8, 1852 and recorded the visit in her diary. The record is of interest because, unknown to Mother Etienne, the Seer of the Miraculous Medal was living in the house at the time.

> After a long ride we arrived at Enghien, a hospital and a house of mercy, founded by Mme Bourbon, a member of the royal family, in 1819. . . . Enghien is a faubourg, celebrated for its charming situation on the east side of Lake Montmorency. . . . The hospital is supported by revenues, and so liberally, that patients sometimes express the fear that they are doing no penance. Many of its inmates seem to have seen better days.
>
> The gardens of this Institute are so extensive that they send part of the fruits and vegetables to market. Mme Bourbon left this house, by will, to Mme Adelaide, sister of Louis Philippe. This lady has provided the whole establishment with linen, from the castle. She has purchased an additional asylum; it contains sixty-three girls, left orphans by the dreadful cholera of 1849. The washing and cooking are done at the hospital, and the same Sister Servant has charge of both houses. . . . This being also a house of mercy, soup, medicine, etc., are given out regularly. The church is very handsome; also, the front entrance shaded by linden trees.

Not long after she had come to stay at Enghien, probably in April 1831, on a visit to the rue du Bac, Catherine saw Our Lady for the last time. She saw her in the same beloved chapel, but not in the same spot: not on the left of the sanctuary where she had appeared before, but directly over the high altar.

Otherwise, the vision unfolded itself exactly as on the fateful evening of November 27. This last appearance of Our Lady had a special note of urgency about it, because Our Lady informed her that it *was* the last.

"You will see me no more," said the voice Catherine had come to know and to love, "but you will hear my voice in your prayers."

With this simple promise, so simple that the mind does not begin to grasp the magnitude of it, began that familiar and intimate conversation between Catherine Labouré and the Mother of God that was to last forty-six years. The two-hour conversation of these two on the night of July 18, 1830, was and remains a prodigy among heavenly favors. But it pales and becomes as nothing when measured against the lifelong communication that now began. In any perplexity great or small, Catherine had only to speak to Our Lady and Our Lady *replied.* Or the Virgin herself would begin the conversation: warning, reproving, foretelling. It was as casual and normal as the daily meeting of friends, like picking up the telephone for a chat. Catherine never referred to this promise again, except to record it in writing at the request of her director; but evidence of its fulfillment cropped up throughout her life. Father Aladel would request information about certain details of the Apparitions: Catherine would ask Our Lady and return with the answer, or, Catherine would come to him with fresh instructions from the Queen of Heaven. At the end of her life, before revealing her secret to Sister Dufès, she would "ask Our Lady" if she should do so. The very ordinariness of Sister Catherine obscures the reality of this tremendous favor.

The note of urgency, the imperious call to action, in the finality of this last appearance of Mary, together with Father Aladel's refusal to act must have produced an agony of frustration in the soul of Sister Catherine. That this was certainly so can be deduced from a later event in her life: years later she was to assert that Father Aladel's failure to carry out Our Lady's request for a statue was "the torment of my life." If his failure to fulfill one request caused her such torment, how must this failure to act at all have racked her.

Our Lady was not to be thwarted. The promised voice, the voice Catherine "would hear in her prayers," now raised itself in steady complaint that the Medal had not been struck.

"But, my good Mother," Catherine pleaded, "you see that he [Father Aladel] will not believe me."

"Never mind," the voice replied, "he is my servant, and would fear to displease me."

Sister Catherine reported this faithfully to the priest. Our Lady had touched a sore spot, and the good priest trembled in his fear. He was troubled to the depths of his soul at the veiled threat. "He would fear to displease me." God knew, it was the last thing he wanted to do! It is no small thing to displease the Queen of Heaven; it is worse to be threatened by her. And so it came about, after all the admonition and argument, all the mental wrestling, all the prudence and caution, that these few words from the lips of the Mother of God spurred Father Aladel to action.

Not that he was wholly convinced. These words had not suddenly parted the curtain and shown him the truth of Sister Catherine's claims. He had been impelled to action primarily by fear. Our Lady had said well that "he would fear to displease me." Yet this was not a superstitious fear; it was a fear born of love. He loved Our Lady dearly; he felt that he could not take the slightest chance of displeasing her. For this reason, although not completely satisfied as to the reality of Catherine's visions, the priest resolved to act.

All this is borne out by the way in which he acted. He did not, even yet, rush headlong, but waited for an opportunity to present itself.

X

The Medal and its Wonders

FATHER ALADEL had sifted the character of his penitent
quite thoroughly by now. He knew her soul, as every
priest knows the soul of a regular penitent, better than his
own. He had even acquired a special knowledge of her soul,
for she had presented a special problem and it had been necessary to give her special study. He was completely satisfied
with what he found. She was solid and trustworthy. If there
was trickery in this business, it was surely not of her making.
He had further buttressed his opinion by consulting with his
friend Father Etienne. It was proper for him to do so, for the
Medal was a matter of public concern. Not that he told his
friend the identity of the favored Sister at this time; that
would come later, at a time approved by Our Lady.

It was Father Etienne, at the time Procurator General of the
Congregation, who finally afforded Father Aladel the oppor-
tunity to act concerning the Medal. In January 1832, Father
Etienne had an official call to make upon Archbishop de
Quélen, and asked Father Aladel to accompany him. When

his friend had finished his business with the Archbishop, Father Aladel seized the occasion to tell the prelate the story of his penitent, her visions, and the request of the Blessed Virgin for a Medal to be struck. The Archbishop listened keenly and questioned him closely as to the character of the Sister and the theological details of the Medal. At length he was satisfied. He saw nothing contrary to Church teaching in the Medal. Rather, it expressed in apt and beautiful symbolism doctrines the Church had always taught. He gave his permission for the Medal to be made, and asked that some of the first ones be sent him. Monseigneur de Quélen was known for his special devotion to the Immaculate Conception of Our Lady. It is little wonder that he took to the Medal of the Immaculate Conception at once.

A glance at the character of Monseigneur de Quélen increases our admiration for God's efficiency: He lays all His plans with supreme perfection. The Archbishop of Paris was a great and good churchman in a hierarchy still mottled with prelates of a lesser stripe. An aristocrat by birth, de Quélen did not share the aristocratic passion for privilege at the expense of the poor. A priest by adoption, he did not count his priesthood a guarantee of security and comfort. A high prelate by election, he did not regard the ancient and noble See of Paris as his personal patrimony. Hyacinthe de Quélen was a true father of his people and shepherd of his flock.

Perversely enough, this good prelate had much to suffer at the hands of his people when they revolted against the oppression of selfish rulers and the pretensions of the unworthy churchmen who supported them. Like many another innocent man, he was forced to suffer with the guilty. In the revolution of 1830, he had to flee twice for his life. Each time, in a spirit of forgiveness, this great prelate returned to rule his people with love.

Shortly after Father Aladel's historic interview with Monseigneur de Quélen, a virulent epidemic of cholera broke out in Paris. Thus, ironically, after a delay at which the Queen of Heaven herself had complained, the striking of the Medal had to be delayed again, in the very moment of victory. Nursing the sick was the primary work of the Sisters of Charity; and as they moved into action in the cholera crisis, Father Aladel was wholly taken up in directing their campaign of mercy. It was the month of Mary before the busy priest made his all-important visit to the engraver, M. Vachette, at 54 Quai des Orfèvres. M. Vachette had founded his firm in 1815; the firm has long since gone out of business, but the order of 20,000 Medals given it by Father Aladel on that blessed day in May 1832 has assured it of immortality.

The first 2,000 Medals of Father Aladel's order were delivered on June 30, 1832. When Catherine received her share of these first Medals from the hands of the priest, she said:

"Now it must be propagated."

Catherine always kept some of these first Medals with her throughout her life. About ten of them survive today, jealously guarded in the archives of the Sisters of Charity in Paris. One is on exhibition in the Miraculous Medal Art Museum in Germantown, Philadelphia. They are essentially the same as the Medals we know today, except that they are not the master-pieces of artistry and engraving effected by modern crafts-men. Little, flat, oval pieces of some alloy, they are a far cry from the ravishing vision Catherine saw, yet they are the sole reason for the vision. Our Lady herself came down from Heaven to model them.

The propagation of the Medal urged by Catherine was carried out so swiftly that it was miraculous in itself. The first supply of Medals vanished in no time. Pope Gregory XVI placed one of them at the foot of the crucifix on his desk. Father Gillet, Redemptorist founder of the Sisters, Servants of the Immaculate Heart of Mary, in America, had the design of the Medal placed on his ordination card in 1836.

As soon as Archbishop de Quélen had received some of the first Medals, he put one in his pocket and went to visit Monseigneur de Pradt, former chaplain to Napoléon and unlawful Archbishop of Malines, who lay dying in Paris. This prelate had sided with Napoléon in the Emperor's quarrel with the Church, and had been excommunicated by the Holy See. He had furthered his contumacy by accepting the archbishopric of Malines from Napoléon's hands. Ousted from his illegal possession of the See at the Emperor's downfall, he now lay on his deathbed, unreconciled to the Church and defiant. He received Archbishop de Quélen, but steadfastly refused to discuss the all-important object of the visit, the abjuration of his errors. At length, Archbishop de Quélen, admitting defeat, withdrew. He had not yet left the house when the sick man suddenly called him back. In that stroke of time he had capitulated to the Queen of the Medal. Completely docile and repentant, he made his confession and was received back into the saving bosom of the Church. He died a peaceful death the next day, the first signal triumph of the Miraculous Medal.

The first order of 20,000 Medals proved to be but a small start. The new "Medals of the Immaculate Conception" began to pour from the presses in streams, spilling over France and escaping to the world beyond. Wonders sprang up in their wake, miracles of mercy and healing and grace. By December 1836, the firm of Vachette had sold several million Medals. Eleven other Parisian engravers had equaled this number, and four Lyon engravers were hard at work to meet the demand.

Excitedly, people passed the Medal from hand to hand: "Take this Miraculous Medal. . . ."

Its formal name was forgotten. It was the "Miraculous Medal" even in those first days, for the power working through it was seen to be truly miraculous. It would never be called anything else. Even the Liturgy has accorded it the proud title conferred on it by the people who accepted it with faith and love.

If the wildfire spread of the Medal was miraculous, the wonders it worked were more so. No sacramental of the Church had made such impact on the Catholic world since the Rosary had routed the Albigensian and the Turk. Its name was honestly come by, for it literally worked miracles. It seemed to specialize in the impossible, the conversion of the hardened sinner, the cure of the hopelessly ill. And yet it only *seemed* to specialize in these startling favors because they *were* startling. Actually it blanketed all the ills of daily living, if only because there were so many more of these. People came to count on this Miraculous Medal in every need. And it is this universal concern of Mary for every necessity of her children, ordinary and extraordinary alike, that has endeared the Medal to all the world.

There would be no point in cataloguing the wonders worked by the Medal in those early days, for it works the same wonders today. There are hundreds of modern conversions to match that of Monseigneur de Pradt. The hopelessly ill are still cured. And there are countless lesser favors flowing in a steady stream from the outstretched hands of the Queen of the Medal. The national Shrine of the Miraculous Medal in Germantown, Philadelphia, records 500 such favors, actually reported, every week. The favors that go unreported must be, conservatively, ten times that number. And this at but one tiny spot on the globe.

By 1833 the favors attributed to the Medal had become so numerous that Archbishop de Quélen decided to sort them out in the interest of prudence and accuracy. He confided the task to a Father Le Guillou, a noted theologian of the day. Father Le Guillou spent months in examining the origin of the Medal, and the more remarkable favors attributed to it.

His findings appeared in April 1834, in a publication called *Mois de Marie*, with an introductory letter by Father Aladel. The theologian's study had not been a canonical inquiry; that would come later. He simply reported facts, scrupulously verified. The first edition of the brochure sold out overnight; succeeding editions went as quickly. A fifth edition of 22,600 copies printed in December 1835 was gone by February 1836.

Father Le Guillou's favorable report decided Archbishop de Quélen to institute a canonical inquiry. He appointed Monseigneur Quentin, Vicar General of Paris, to conduct it. The sessions were opened on February 11, 1836, a day to be graced twenty-two years later by Our Lady's first appearance to Bernadette at Lourdes. Father Aladel and Father Etienne were the chief witnesses. Sister Catherine was called, but the court excused her upon the assurance of Father Aladel that it was morally impossible for her to testify because of an invincible repugnance on her part to reveal her identity and an apparent forgetfulness of the details of the vision.

There can be no doubt that Catherine received supernatural help in keeping her secret, not once but many times. The most startling evidence of this help occurred at the time of the Inquiry, when Archbishop de Quélen insisted that she testify in person. She might even wear a veil over her face when she did so, the kindly prelate said. In transmitting the Archbishop's wishes to her, Father Aladel had vigorously urged Catherine to accede to them. All in vain. The poor, harried Sister felt she could not go through with it. Her repugnance was so genuine that it convinced her confessor, and he defended her stand before the Court. But even he had been amazed at her assertion that it would do her no good to testify, for she had forgotten every last detail of the Apparitions!

A clinching argument in favor of the supernatural character of this forgetfulness was a parallel incident that occurred about this same time.

Plans were afoot to enlarge the chapel at rue du Bac. In order to preserve an exact record of the chapel as it was when Our Lady visited it, Father Aladel decided to have two pictures painted—of the Apparitions of July 18 and November 27. He commissioned an artist named Le Cerf for the work. At one point the artist felt it necessary to verify the color of Our Lady's veil. The priest, not wishing to prompt Catherine by asking her the specific detail, asked her to refresh his memory by relating the complete details of the Apparitions.

"I can remember no detail," Catherine answered, "except that the Blessed Virgin's veil was of the whiteness of the dawn."

The only point of information wanted!

Heaven came to Catherine's aid in guarding her secret many other times throughout her life; none, however, so patently supernatural as this period of temporary forgetfulness. It would express this heavenly aid better to say that she was given a supernatural facility in turning aside the guesses of the merely curious and the shrewd surmises of the more thoughtful. As Father Chevalier, her last director, put it:

> During her time at Enghien, it was vaguely suspected that she was the privileged Sister to whom the Blessed Virgin had revealed the Miraculous Medal. Allusions to this were made often in her presence, and indiscreet questions were even addressed to her. Some seemed to believe that she had seen the Apparition, others found it difficult to believe. Never did she appear troubled, or upset, or hard-pressed to reply: she always found the means of guarding her secret without giving anything away.
>
> You could conclude that this Sister possessed the virtue of prudence in a high degree, and you could even believe without rashness that on many of these occasions the Spirit of Wisdom helped her in a special way to guard her secret.

The findings of the Canonical Inquiry of Paris completely vindicated Catherine. The court extolled her character and virtue, and placed wholehearted credence in her visions. Two important conclusions were reached: that the Medal was of supernatural origin, and that the wonders worked through it were genuine.

The immediate significance of the Inquiry was the solemn ecclesiastical approbation it gave the Miraculous Medal. The Inquiry had a wider and even more important significance, however, for the findings of this ecclesiastical court, held within a few short years of the events it investigated and based upon first-hand testimony, were vital to the approbation of the Medal by the Holy See, to the establishment of a feast, in 1895, in honor of the Medal, and to the Beatification and Canonization of Sister Catherine herself.

Overjoyed at the findings of his court, Archbishop de Quélen now gave free rein to his lifelong devotion to the Immaculate Conception of the Blessed Virgin. In a series of pastoral letters he urged this devotion upon his people, and consecrated himself and his diocese to the Immaculate Conception. On December 15, 1836 he consecrated the church of Notre Dame de Lorette in Paris to "Mary honored in her most pure conception." Through his efforts the invocation "Queen conceived without sin" was inserted in the Litany of Loreto.

Our Lady was at work in other quarters, too. The Motherhouse of the Sisters of Charity on rue du Bac was located in the parish of a zealous priest named Father Defriche-Desgenette. The parish church was called the Church of the Missions. Father Desgenette approached Father Aladel and urged him to welcome pilgrimages to the Chapel of the Apparitions on rue du Bac. Father Aladel refused on the grounds that an influx of pilgrims would interfere with the devotions of the Sisters and destroy the recollection and interior spirit of the Community. Favorable to Father Aladel is the fact that Our

Lady did not ask for pilgrimages to rue du Bac, as she was explicitly to ask at Lourdes. Nevertheless, considered a century later, Father Aladel's refusal seems to have been shortsighted. It is to be feared that his decision actually retarded the spread of devotion to Our Lady of the Miraculous Medal. This opinion is strengthened by the tremendous strides made in devotion to Our Lady of the Medal in France since the Chapel of the Apparitions became a place of general pilgrimage several years ago. Father Aladel's decision is further to be deplored because it deprived the Sisters of Charity of presenting to the Queen of Heaven the vast devotion of the faithful who flocked to the shrine of Our Lady established by Father Desgenette some years later.

When Father Aladel turned down Father Desgenette's suggestion, he actually made the counter suggestion that the pastor make his parish church of the Missions the place of pilgrimage. Father Desgenette did nothing about it at the time, possibly because it seemed illogical to him to ask pilgrims to bypass the actual church where Our Lady had appeared in favor of another where no such supernatural event had occurred. In 1832 he was appointed pastor of the parish of Notre-Dame-des-Victoires. The parish was run down at the heels spiritually and for four years even the enormous zeal of this man of God could do nothing to reform it. He wrote of it in discouragement:

"There is in Paris a parish almost unknown, even by a large number of its parishioners. It lies in the center of the town, between the Bourse and the Palais Royale, bounded by theatres and haunts of pleasure. It is the quarter most given up to the preoccupations of moneymaking and industry, and to passions of every kind. Its church, which is dedicated to Notre-Dame-des-Victoires, is empty even on feast days. . . . No Sacraments are administered, even at the hour of death. . . . If the parish priest succeeds in gaining admission to the bedside of a dying person, it is on condition that he wait until the dying person has lost consciousness and, furthermore, that he appear only in lay dress."

As the years passed, Father Desgenette became convinced that he was wasting his time in this hell hole. And then, on December 3, 1836, he received an interior illumination during Mass: he must dedicate his church to the Immaculate Heart of Mary. A great peace flowed into his soul, but, Mass over, he began to fear that the interior voice was an illusion. He was making his thanksgiving when the same voice sounded in the depths of his soul: *You must dedicate your church to the most Holy and Immaculate Heart of Mary.* Back in his rectory, Father Desgenette determined to rid his mind of what might still be an illusion by sitting down to compose, calmly and with deep logical thought, a set of rules for an association in honor of the Immaculate Heart. Much to his amazement, he found that every last rule was already crystal clear in his mind, and, while his pen flew over the paper, the good priest trembled with the knowledge that it was not the result of his own thought that he was writing down!

On Sunday, December 11, Father Desgenette announced the formation of the new society and called a first meeting for that evening. In a burst of optimism, he counted on fifty people attending. Five hundred came, most of them men, and all of them without any clear idea of what the association was about! During the Litany of Loreto a sensible thrill of devotion ran through the congregation at the invocation "Refuge of Sinners, pray for us," which the priest recited three times, his voice charged with emotion.

Five days later, on December 16, 1836, Archbishop de Quélen canonically erected the Association of the Holy and Immaculate Heart of Mary for the Conversion of Sinners.

Thus, within two weeks, a whirlwind of grace had descended on the parish of Notre-Dame-des-Victoires. The parish was rejuvenated overnight, and the church became a place of national pilgrimage. On April 24, 1838, a brief of the Sovereign Pontiff erected the Association into an Archconfraternity with the power of affiliating similar associations throughout the Church. At the death of Father Desgenette the Archconfraternity of Notre-Dame-des-Victoires numbered twenty million associates, and 15,000 affiliated confraternities. There are many more thousands today. The center of the devotion in America is Father Baker's magnificent Basilica of Our Lady of Victory in Lackawanna, N. Y.

Thus, what Father Aladel rejected became the lifework of Father Desgenette. There can be no doubt that it was the work of Providence, but the question, whether Providence intended it originally for Father Aladel and the Sisters of Charity, will always go unanswered.

When Father Desgenette would come upon Sisters of Charity kneeling before the altar of the Archconfraternity in Notre-Dame-des-Victoires, he would say to them:

"My good Sisters, I am pleased to see you here; but your own chapel is the true pilgrim shrine. There you have the Blessed Virgin; there she manifested herself to you."

XI

The Dark Night of a Soul

WHILE ALL THIS was being done—the making of the Medal, its marvelous spread, and its official acceptance by the Church—Catherine Labouré, hidden away in Enghien, was adjusting to the routine of a lifetime.

The years 1830–36 were eventful ones for her. In no other period of her life did so many things happen in so many conflicting ways to this quiet girl from the country. It was a period of high heavenly favor in the visions vouchsafed her; and also a period of the deepest frustration in the refusal of her director to believe her. It was a period of attainment, when she laid hold at last of the quiet religious life she had always wanted; and a period of anxiety, when it seemed her serenity might be lost forever in the questioning and probing. It was above all a period of beginning, of setting forth on a new high road to sanctity with the determination to walk it to the end.

A shallow observer might see anything that would happen to Catherine after the Apparitions as an anticlimax. Such a view is understandable, but entirely shallow. It would regard the long remaining years as a gradual descent from a mountain top when they were in reality an ascent to a yet higher peak. Such a view would consider only what *happened* to Catherine, ignoring completely what she *effected* herself.

For the Apparitions in themselves added nothing to the sanctity of Catherine Labouré; it was her reaction to them that was important. She saw them in proper perspective: not as a personal favor to herself—although there was that element in them surely—but rather as a general boon to mankind. She never considered herself as anything but "an instrument," and she was right. Nor is there an exaggerated humility here; it is the hardheaded realistic insight of the saints. The mission of the Medal was but a further vocation added to the religious vocation already given her. Catherine's eternal success or failure would depend upon how she responded to both vocations, just as anyone's salvation depends upon how he lives the life ordained for him by God.

This then was the crucial period of Catherine's life, when she came to a full knowledge of what God wanted of her and set about accomplishing it. True to character, she threw herself wholeheartedly into the task. There were no half-measures with Catherine. She was a thorough workman.

The spiritual life, like any work of God, has its rules; and any saint, no matter how distinctive his holiness, must observe them. Ascetical writers define three great stages in spiritual development which they call the Purgative, Illuminative, and Unitive Ways. While these three stages are successive in general: the soul first purging itself of sins and faults and the perverse movement of the passions, then advancing to a fuller knowledge of God with the help of divine illumination, and finally uniting itself wholly to Him in faith and hope and love, there are points of contact where all three of these stages may be experienced at the same time. In fact, it is usual enough for them to be so experienced. In Catherine's life at home, for instance, we can see her absorbed in daily prayer in the Chapel of the Labourés and at the same time giving vent to occasional flashes of temper. These movements of temper endured almost to the moment of her death, when she had attained to a very high sanctity.

Th extreme instrument of purgation is contradiction, and the supreme example of contradiction is the state spiritual writers call "the dark night of the soul," a period when the soul, having abandoned the things of earth, feels itself abandoned in turn by God. It is accompanied by a horrible dryness and distaste for prayer, and a feeling very like despair; it can only be ridden out by clinging with blind faith to the hem of God's garment. St. Teresa of Avila suffered this state for twenty years. Blessed Jean Gabriel Perboyre, C.M., Catherine's religious brother, passed through it in 1840, shortly before his martyrdom in far off China. So black was his "night" that he was absolutely convinced that he would lose his soul, yet his unswerving hold on God shone out in the magnificent cry: "If I cannot love you in the next life, dear Lord, let me love you at least in this one."

Catherine, too, had her "dark night"; when, we don't know, but have it she did, for it was essential to the heroic sanctity she attained. She herself speaks, in passing, of "periods of dryness," but these may have been the ordinary trials common to all who embrace the religious life. Since contradiction often accompanies the great trial of the "dark night," we may justly look for it in the major contradictions of Catherine's life: the refusal of her father to allow her to follow her vocation and the agonizing years that followed; in the refusal of Father Aladel to believe in her visions and the mission they enjoined— her terrible suffering at this time is evident in the despairing, exasperated complaint to Our Lady that she might better appear to somebody else "since no one will believe me," or the pleading cry: "But, my good Mother, you see that he will not believe me"—and finally in the lifelong refusal of the priest to do anything about the statue of "Our Lady of the Globe," which Catherine, who never exaggerated, called "the torment of my life." It could be in one, or two, or all of these. The essential thing is to understand that she suffered interiorly, that her life was not as placid and uneventful as might seem, and that she clung to God tenaciously until He brought her into the light again.

Both God and Catherine got right down to business in this matter of sanctity. Catherine knew in theory that it would not be easy. She had learned in the seminary, from books and conferences, that it consisted essentially in the subjugation of the will, the citadel of the soul. It was a teaching she accepted without demur, a teaching indeed she actively endorsed, for she had sought the Will of God from earliest childhood. It is one thing, however, to accept a theory; it is another thing entirely to practice it. It is one thing to bow to God's Will directly; it is another thing to bow to it indirectly, hidden behind the will of a superior as human as oneself.

Until now, even in following out God's Will, Catherine had always gotten her own way. She had been the mistress of her father's house from the age of twelve; her father, who stood in the place of God, disposed it so. She had received her spiritual direction from God immediately, without the agency of human directors. Even when, in God's Providence, she had encountered human opposition, she had eventually gotten her way: she had bested her father in the matter of her vocation; she had bested Father Aladel in the matter of the Medal. Again, God had so ordered it. It would seem that He had set about bending this human will, so implacable and yet so capable of heroic submission, gradually, increasing the opposition to be overcome a little at a time. Now God changed His tactics. Catherine would never have her own way again. There would always be a superior to tell her what to do. Many times the superior would be unreasonable; sometimes she would be entirely wrong. Yet Catherine had no choice but to obey, for in making her religious profession she accepted wholeheartedly the religious axiom that the superior's will is the Will of God.

This was the essence of the holiness of Catherine Labouré: unswerving obedience to superiors, even under stress; and the stress usually lay in the fact that very often Catherine was more competent to do the work than the superior who ordered it, and both knew it. For example, Catherine was a better housekeeper than Sister Dufès, her last superior, yet she always did things the way Sister Dufès wanted them, though she knew her own way was better. Even more, the Sisters who lived with her recognized Catherine's domestic talents and were "on her side." They urged her not to defer to Sister Tanguy, the new and inexperienced Assistant placed over her in 1874, but Catherine would have none of it. The heroic victory over self, evident in these submissive actions must be fully grasped to understand the sanctity of Catherine Labouré.

But it must also be fully grasped that such a victory was not easily won. It was not always like this. The change from lay to religious life was very hard for Catherine. She who had been mistress now became a servant, or something very like it. She who had mastered every facet of keeping house was now tried at this task and that, to determine what she could do. It must have been extremely humiliating, much like the plight of a doctor of philosophy forced to return to the first grade.

Not that it was done intentionally to humiliate her. After all, her superiors did not know all her capabilities. They could discover them only by trial and error. So, when she came to Enghien she was tried first in the kitchen, and then in the laundry, and finally in the charge of caring for the old men of the house. She measured up to each task. But, ironically, the task that became her lifework was the task she was least fitted for, in the sense that it was new to her. She had had practice in cooking and washing; she had had none in taking care of old people.

The reverence for superiors that was the mark of her sanctity showed itself in the very first assignment, which was the kitchen. When she had prepared a meal, she entered upon a ritual that was, in a sense, a vignette of her life. Dishing out the first portion, she would say:

"This is for Sister Servant." She said it in the same respectful tone in which she might have said: "This is for God."

Then: "This is for the gentlemen," and "This is for the Sisters." And, what was left:

"This, if you please, is for myself."

That she did not rise above contradictions easily is perhaps best illustrated in an incident from these early days. Catherine was given a Sister to help her in the kitchen, and the two did not get along. It is probable that fault lay on both sides, for Catherine had very fixed ideas about how things should be done. As regards the chief difficulty between them, Catherine seems to have been right. Her companion insisted on doling out stingy portions to the old men, and Catherine remonstrated with her repeatedly. Finally, it reached the point where Catherine seriously considered asking for a change. She took her problem to Father Aladel, who told her to put all thoughts of a change out of her mind, and counseled her to bear this trial with patience. It was enough for Catherine. She brought all her virtue to bear on the situation, so that she was not only patient under the continued annoyances of the Sister, but even deferred to her as much as was possible and right.

There is a homely little tale of the way Catherine repaid this Sister good for evil. The bell had rung for supper one evening when the Sister discovered she had forgotten to make soup for the meal. She was in a sweat, for she would have to face the grumbling of the old men, the criticism of the Sisters, and a possible rebuke from the Superior. It was indeed a little thing, but little things can assume great proportions in community life and, at the very least, her pride was in for a tumble.

"Never mind," Catherine said, "I have just come from milking the cows, and I'm sure everyone will welcome a change to fresh milk."

And so the incident was carried off as a deliberate substitution of milk for soup, and the poor Sister's honor was saved.

This first trial of Catherine's community life might seem to have been a tempest in a teapot. It was nothing of the sort. The seriousness of it can be judged from the fact that Catherine actually sought her confessor's advice as to whether she should ask for a change. Had she gone so far as to request one, had she retreated from this first test, who knows how it would have affected her whole life and, ultimately, her sanctity?

Sanctity for a religious, after all, consists in rising above such ordinary annoyances of community life. St. John Berchmans has wisely said: "The common life is the greatest mortification." Only one who has tried to live the common life can understand how right he was. It is not so much the tiny act of annoyance in itself; it is the tiny act of annoyance repeated and repeated, day after day. Religious are human beings, and it is a commonplace that certain human beings rub other human beings the wrong way. In the roominess of the world, it is possible to avoid the people who annoy you; in the confines of the convent you are thrown together with them constantly, must even love them as sisters. The ordinary soul occasionally breaks under the strain, and charity is wounded; the heroic soul suffers in silence, and becomes a saint. St. Thérèse of Lisieux had her companion in the laundry who splashed her daily with dirty water and stretched her nerves to the breaking point. Catherine had her companion in the kitchen; and she was only the first of many. In winning this crucial victory, she set the pattern of her life. She would always accept the contradictions that came her way and make the most of them, piling up a wealth of eternal merit.

Vincent de Paul had been wonderfully wise. He had forbidden his followers bodily austerities that would sap their stamina for the unremitting physical toil of their vocation. Not that he discounted mortification. He knew well that it was the indispensable whip of sanctity. Rather, the mortifications of his followers were to be little privations, like the "holding back of a useless word." And his keen mind knew that these little privations, ceaselessly practiced, were the greatest mortification of all. So, there would be no hairshirts, no chains around the waist, no rigorous fasts, for Catherine Labouré. Her penance would be the painful bending of her stubborn will in the give and take of the common life.

XII

Three Anguished Letters

WHILE CATHERINE was in the thick of trying to convince Father Aladel to have the Medal made and of adjusting herself to her new way of life, a third cruel trial struck her unawares. Her older sister, Marie Louise, who was superior at Castelsarrasin, left the Community in a huff. There are no details of why she left, except that she was angry about something, presumably some real or fancied wrong on the part of her superiors. It must have been on this level to bring about her withdrawal from the Community.

To leave religion is a very serious thing. Vincent de Paul had some hard things to say about it. He spared no feelings in pointing out the terrible danger, even to eternal salvation, which lay in wait for him who had promised himself to God by vow and then taken it back. When all else failed, Vincent resorted to a father's tears. He was known to plead on his knees with priests who were about to leave the Community for the secular clergy or for some other order, and even to throw himself across the doorway, so that they must step across his body to depart. Such dramatics from so sensible a saint as Vincent de Paul serve to point up his horror at anyone's turning back once he had laid his hand to the plow. Vincent was on safe ground, for Christ Himself said that such a one was not worthy of the kingdom of God.

There are, of course, times when a return to the world is not only called for, but even necessary to the happiness and salvation of certain individuals, but these are the exceptional cases.

Marie Louise's return to the world seems to have been unwarranted. This judgment is made because of the haste of her departure, because she left in a fit of pique, because Catherine never viewed her sister's action as anything but wrong, and because of Marie Louise's eventual return. Marie Louise's background, also, favors such a judgment. She was obstinate by temperament, like her father and like Catherine. She had been raised by a childless uncle and aunt, who might be expected to have spoiled her to a degree, and who gave her special schooling which raised her above many of her Sisters in religion. Her rise in the Community had been fast, because of her education and the small number of Sisters at the time; she had entered the seminary in 1818 and by 1829, and possibly even before, she was already a superior. All these factors could have made her more vulnerable to contradiction.

It is not too much to say that Catherine was heartbroken at this defection of her sister. Not only had Marie Louise been Catherine's idol, but she had been her strength in the dark days when Catherine was longing to flee the world. What hurt Catherine most, however, was that she herself had tasted the joy of union with God in religion and knew with the utmost clarity what Marie Louise had thrown away. There was, also, of course, the humiliation Catherine must have felt before the other Sisters, but this was something she could offer to God against her sister's return; it must be counted but a small part of Catherine's pain. Her great agony was in the thought of

God-knew-what dangers the soul of her beloved sister might encounter in the world.

The first letter Catherine sent to Marie Louise has an undercurrent of anger, the kind of anger that comes with the first sting of pain, the first rush of tears. There is a curtness and sarcasm that borders on cruelty in this first letter, and in the action that accompanied it. Catherine sent back the letter Marie Louise had written her when Catherine was trying to escape from her brother's café in Paris. She appended to it the following blistering lines:

> Before you leave for the country of our childhood, I send you a letter that will no doubt give you pleasure, a letter you wrote me at the time I wished to enter our Community. The promises you made me, and the good counsels you gave me—apply them now to yourself. Repeat especially the words: "If at this moment someone were powerful enough to offer me the possession of, not merely a kingdom, but the whole universe, I would look upon it as the dust at my feet, knowing that I would not find in the possession of the whole world, the happiness I feel in my vocation." You once preferred this happiness to what?—I dare not say it—to a temptation: we must agree that we are very weak when we do not put all our confidence in God, who knows the depths of our hearts.
>
> I must tell you that I am very pained to see, in nearly all your letters, that you speak to me of a miracle, as if the good God performed them for no reason at all; we are poor creatures indeed, to hope that God would grant us miracles. You speak to me of one, when you have left the Community. Alas! God knows whether that is one! Have Our Lord and the Blessed Virgin and all the saints prated about their miracles? Where is your humility? It is far removed from theirs; or, to put it more precisely, you have none at all.
>
> Farewell. I advise you to go to our father's house; you will find solitude there, and it is there that God will speak to your heart. Meditate well on the death of our mother, which you

witnessed, and on that of our father, still so recent; to meditate on death is the best way of finding grace before God.

It is hard not to compare the letters of the two sisters. Catherine's direct, telling language seems to pour scorn on the fine flowing sentences of Marie Louise. This, however, is not to excuse the brutality of Catherine's words, except to repeat that they were probably a sort of blind striking back in the first flush of pain. They were certainly well-intentioned, no matter how cruel the approach. Indeed, Catherine, knowing her sister, may have felt that Marie Louise might be goaded to return by such a broadside.

The reference to "talk of miracles" is most obscure. It may have been merely a general reference to Marie Louise as one of those people who see the miraculous in everything. However, the reference seems more pointed than that. Had Marie Louise, perhaps, been exclaiming over the miraculous Apparitions of Our Lady to an unknown Sister of Charity? Were this the case, Catherine's abrupt words would be the natural reaction of one who seeks to deflect any suspicion from herself. There is a story among the members of the Labouré family that might provide a clue to the reference. According to this story, Marie Louise was at one time afflicted by a painful and disfiguring rash on her face, and Catherine cured it instantly, merely by passing her hand over the afflicted part. In this case, too, Catherine's brusque discounting of the miraculous would be a natural reaction.

The allusion to the recent death of Pierre Labouré places it in 1833 or 1834, when he would have been approximately sixty-six years old. We have no first-hand account of Catherine's reaction to his death, except that we can detect, in certain reproachful lines written by her to Marie Louise some ten years later, a daughter's pity for his bereft old age and a smoldering resentment, even after all that time, that Marie Louise had not gone to comfort him in his last days. There may be even a twinge of conscience in the picture Catherine paints, in this letter, of her old father "dying separated from his family, abandoned by his family." Such a twinge, however, could be but human regret: it would not indicate guilt on her part, for in leaving home, Catherine had left her father provided for, and had followed the clear call of God.

Since Catherine loved her father dearly, it is not hard to realize her genuine grief on hearing the sad news of his death. That she had not seen him since 1828, that their parting had been strained, would only make her grief the sharper. Never once in her entire lifetime did Catherine ever allude to the harsh way her father had treated her. Rather, especially as she grew older, she loved to speak of him to her Sisters in religion, and to recount the many wise lessons he taught her.

Strangely enough, she never mentioned her mother; although it is perhaps not so strange when we consider that Catherine was only nine when her mother died. Yet it was her mother who had given Catherine her start in sanctity, and Catherine must have realized it. Nevertheless—whether she held her relationship with her mother too sacred to discuss, or for whatever reason—when Catherine spoke of her home and her childhood, it was always of her father.

Now her father was gone, and Catherine, in the depths of her heart, mourned him sincerely.

When Catherine's first letter to Marie Louise failed of its purpose, she took a new tack. The tone of her second letter, written in 1835, is so different that one suspects the kindlier approach to have been advised, possibly by the Superior General or the Sister Superior referred to in the letter.

> I know that you want news of me. I hasten to share my happiness with you, wishing that you had the same happiness. I have just made the retreat for holy vows. I had the happiness of pro-

nouncing my vows in union with the whole Community. What good fortune for me! Tasting this good fortune, I can better understand your unhappiness at not being able to reunite yourself with the Community, in order to pronounce your vows. When I was younger, I used to dream of this beautiful day and to long for it, and I would say to myself: *My sister has the happiness of pronouncing her vows.* I wished at that time only to unite myself to you and to the whole Community; and now that I have that happiness, I search for you, in order to unite myself to you, and I find you no more, except in the midst of the world. What sorrow to my heart! This wound you have given it is very deep. You know that, my dear one; I will say no more about it.

Some time ago, I spoke to *M. le Superieure*, and I told him I had no other sorrow except that of seeing you in the world; he understood my sorrow and your misfortune. *M. le Superieure* has had the kindness and the charity to ask me to write to you for him that he offers you his services to help you return. Choose any house, it doesn't matter which one, and he himself will take the necessary steps to have them receive you. So, you see, my dear sister, the goodness of *M. le Superieure*. I can assure you of his goodness; more than anyone, I have proof of it myself. Reflect on the grace the good God still holds out to you. It is a great grace; try to profit by it.

I must tell you that it is no longer the same superior. The Community has had the misfortune of losing the former one; he died, and *M. le Directeur* also. It is M. Nozo who replaces him as superior of the Community. I think you would know him, and M. Grapien, who is the director; both of them are very good.

You can not doubt, dear sister, the goodness of Sister Superior, which she always showed you, and still she offers to render you every possible service. You were always secretive, and would not open yourself to her, a fact which caused her great pain. Since she has always shown herself to be understanding, I have spoken to her about the loss of your vocation. She always loved you, and she still loves you, as if you were her daughter. She speaks to me often of you. She would be very

happy if you wished to return to the Community. She has offered to make all the necessary arrangements. You see, my dear
sister, you cannot refuse the grace which constantly pursues
you. I think you will not resist it. I pray the good God and the
Blessed Virgin to enlighten you on the state of your salvation.

I pray you, dear one, to make your decision. We on our part
will await it with the greatest pleasure; it will give us great joy
and satisfaction. I want this with all my heart. To aid you in
making a generous sacrifice, I send you the Infant Jesus in meditation, and the Blessed Virgin, who is your patroness, and St.
Louis, who is your patron. Further, I send you the Eight Beati-
tudes, a thought which comes to me from *M. le Superieure*,
which renders it the more perfect. He gave it to me as a New
Year's present.

This long and solicitous letter was apparently written on
May 1, 1835, the day Catherine first pronounced her holy
vows, or very soon after. At the simple, private vow ceremony, she was given as her name in religion the name with
which she had been baptized, Catherine.

The Sisters of Charity take the usual religious vows of poverty, chastity, and obedience, and a fourth vow of stability, a
promise to spend their entire lives in the Community of St.
Vincent, working for the poor. These vows are not taken per-
petually, but for a year at a time, and are renewed every
twenty-fifth of March, the feast of the Annunciation of Our
Lady. Both the private nature of the vows (they are not formally received by an official representative of the Church)
and their temporary character, distinguish the Sisters of
Charity from nuns, who are *religious* properly so called. Tech-
nically, the Sisters of Charity are a group of laywomen living
in community. They are unique among women's groups in the
Church. St. Vincent established them thus to keep them from
the confines of the cloister, in order that they might move
freely among the poor and unfortunate of the world.

After all the years of striving toward her goal, Catherine must have pronounced the formula of dedication with a supreme and total abandonment. If, upon entering the gateway of rue du Bac five years before, she had felt that "she was no longer of the earth," how must she have felt now! And how heartbreaking for her to look about for her sister to share in her happiness, and not to find her "except in the midst of the world."

Unfortunately, this second letter of Catherine's had no more effect than the first. Marie Louise left her native village after a while and returned to Paris where she took a job as a schoolteacher. Although the two sisters were living in the capital, they apparently saw nothing of each other for several years: Marie Louise was too embarrassed to call on Catherine at Enghien, for she knew several of the Sisters there. However, they continued to correspond.

The last extant letter written by Catherine to her sister, probably in the year 1844, has a curiously despairing tone. Catherine seems to have given up. This, coupled with what we know of Catherine's tartness, would explain the vein of bitterness in it.

My dear sister and good friend,

I received your letter, which gave me great pleasure. It tells me that you wish to go to the country of our childhood, to care for our young brother—who lacks nothing. In buying the house, Antoine has promised to take care of him. To go to take care of a brother, that is all very well, the world would approve it; but the world would have approved also—ten years ago, when you had left the Community—if you had gone to render the last services one should render an afflicted father in his old age, afflicted as our father was in his old age, and dying separated from his family, abandoned even by his family. The world would have applauded you, had you rendered him the last duties a child should render parents at the moment of death. The mo-

ment of death is the moment of reunion, when families that
have been separated come together again, especially when they
are free to do so, as you were. Do not be surprised, then, if you
are not looked on kindly in the family, and do not expect to be
well received. . . .

Have you forgotten the wonderful religion of the country?
One Mass on Sunday, and it is still necessary for a pastor from
a neighboring parish to come to say it. Vespers are chanted by
the schoolmaster, so there is no benediction. To go to confession, you must first look for a confessor. Have you considered
whether so little religion can be safe enough? Judge for yourself. . . . As for me, to the little that can be gotten there, I say
farewell. . . . What will the world say? . . . Ah, it will say—
we must let the world say it, for it is not for a Sister of Charity
who belongs to God to say it. . . . We must leave it to the
judgment of God.

My dear friend, as for your project of coming to see me, there
would be much inconvenience, since you are known to most of
the persons in the house. I do not urge you to come. You tell me
that you made a sacrifice in leaving me. I believe you made your
sacrifice ten years ago, and I believe you made it gaily. I do not
believe you can make further sacrifice. I have made my sacrifice, which has cost me very dear. The good God knows the
sorrow I have had; yes, God and Mary our good Mother alone
know it; and now this sorrow is renewed. Up until now, I had
thought you would return to the Community, but I see the time
pass, and it has already passed. . . . Time past is no longer in
our power; the present is in our power, but the future is not. Let
us profit by it, let us give ourselves to God without reserve. I
recall the letter I wrote you six years ago: I made you the best
offers . . .

It was the dark before the dawn; Catherine's hope for her
Sister was at its lowest ebb. After all her letters—and it must
be remembered how laborious it was for this poorly educated
girl to write a letter—after all her prayers, it must have
seemed to Catherine that this resolve of Marie Louise to re-

turn to Fain, away from the religious advantages of Paris and the daily sight of Sisters of Charity on their missions of mercy, was the end. Once gone, she would never return. Certainly Catherine invoked the power of the Medal to bring her sister back. It must have been bitter as wormwood for her to hear of famous conversions, like those of Archbishop de Pradt and Alphonse Ratisbonne, to hear of the countless daily wonders worked through the Medal, and to have her own most important prayer go unanswered. It would not be surprising had she felt that the Medal was not for her, as Bernadette was later to feel that the miraculous healing of the spring at Lourdes was not for her.

Yet Heaven was only waiting out Catherine. Her tears for her sister were, in the end, as effective as the tears of Monica for her son, Augustine. Shortly after this last letter of Catherine's, Marie Louise returned to the Community, probably in 1844 or 1845. Marie Louise had been about thirty-eight years old when she left; she was nearly fifty when she returned. Although eleven years older than Catherine, she was to outlive her, confined the last ten or fifteen years of her life to the infirmary at rue du Bac.

XIII

The Old Men of Enghien

ABOUT A YEAR before pronouncing her vows, Catherine had been removed from the kitchen and given charge of the laundry and clothes room. The change was not necessarily a reflection on her ability as a cook. In religious life, such changes are a matter of course, made at times for the sake of variety, at times to fill a vacancy, at times to make room for someone else, and, it must be confessed, at times for no conceivable reason at all.

There is but one tale told of these months in the laundry. Seeing a Sister emerge soaking wet from her duty at the wash tub, Catherine went immediately to the Superior and saw to it that the Sister got warm flannel to wear, so as not to catch cold. It is heartwarming to know that the Sister remembered this little act of kindness for sixty years, and came forward to recount it to the Beatification Commission in 1895.

The incident serves to show the balanced judgment of the saint. No one had a deeper spirit of poverty than she; indeed, with herself, she carried poverty to the extreme of rigor. After her death, the Sister Servant was amazed and humiliated at the few belongings, the absolute minimum of Catherine's possessions, and kept saying over and over to herself in reproach: "I didn't know, I didn't know." Catherine herself expressed her accurate concept of religious poverty more than once, in speaking to the young Sisters.

"It is necessary to preserve things, and not to abuse them. They are not really ours, for we have nothing of our own, but we must manage with the greatest care, for we have an account to render to God."

This, without a doubt, would be the principle she observed in distributing clothes and caring for them, as it was with everything else. But she struck the proper balance in that she was generous with what was needed. She never stinted; she never deprived others in the name of poverty. Her common sense was truly remarkable.

In 1836, Sister Catherine Labouré was thirty years old. Now she took up a pattern of life that was to change very little throughout forty years: she was given charge of the old men who had come to Enghien to end their days. The little farm attached to the house was also given into her keeping; it was a charge she enjoyed, for it reminded her of home and she found relaxation in feeding the chickens and milking the cows.

As mentioned before, the Hospice d'Enghien was administered by the Superior of the House of Reuilly. Since Reuilly was the distance of a long city block from Enghien, the Sister who had charge of the old men inmates of Enghien virtually ruled the house. She directed the daily duties of the Sisters working there; she had custody of all the keys of the house; she took her place beside the Sister Servant in chapel, at meals, and at recreation. She was, without the title, Assistant Superior of both houses.

It speaks volumes for the capability of Catherine Labouré that she was assigned to this important post at the age of thirty.

No one who has never cared for old people can fully appreciate the difficulty of the task. When people grow old, the powers of the body break down and, often as well, the powers of the mind. It is this latter affliction that causes people to say that the old are like children. But it is not so. There is a vast difference between the thoughts and actions of children whose minds have not yet developed and the thoughts and actions of adults whose once vigorous and crowded minds have failed. The failure to realize this difference and, as a consequence, to treat old people as children, has caused many a deep hurt and resentment in the old. To care for the aged with true understanding, therefore, demands not only great patience and indulgence, but especially great delicacy. Not to treat them as adults, allowance being made for their sickness of mind or body, is to alienate them, perhaps forever.

Sister Catherine's task was made doubly hard by the fact that her charges were all men. The only man she had ever known with any degree of intimacy was her father, and he had been in the full vigor of his powers. With her native shrewdness, it could not have taken her long to realize that men were much easier to understand than women, that they were on the whole simpler, more honest and direct. At the start, however, they were a new species to Catherine. Besides, not all of her charges were of the good moral fibre of Pierre Labouré. The only requirement for entry into the Hospice d'Enghien was that the men should have served the Bourbon family for a requisite number of years; it was inevitable that there would be a quorum of villains among them. Catherine had met the type at her brother's *bistro* in Paris; now it was her duty to care for them and do her best to reform them.

The strange Sister who had asked Catherine whether she was bored with her work among her old men had a keen appreciation of the nature of the work. Catherine's day changed very little over forty years; only the faces of her charges changed as new inmates came to take the places of those who had died. Her order of day was substantially the same in 1876 as it was in 1836. The story of how she cared for her beloved old men is, exteriorly, the story of her life: serving their meals, mending their clothes, supervising their recreations, providing them with snuff and smoking tobacco, bringing them into line when they broke her wise regulations, nursing them in their illnesses, watching at their deathbeds. Select any year of the forty, and the results are plain to see: her old men were perfectly cared for in body and soul. Catherine was completely devoted to them, even jealously so. She was rarely off duty, and then only for the good of her own soul.

When the Sisters of a neighboring house in the Faubourg Saint Antoine would invite the Sisters of Reuilly and Enghien to the plays enacted by the children of the house, Catherine would always send her regrets.

"These festivals are good for the young Sisters," she would say, "but I have to care for my old men."

She refused every such invitation. But, when it was her turn to go to the rue du Bac for a conference, that was a different matter; she was never known to cede her turn to anyone.

In the matter of food for her old fellows, Catherine was a stickler. She insisted that it be the best the Hospice could provide, and that there be plenty of it. Once, on her feast day, she received a touching compliment, the more touching because the old fellow who delivered it slyly timed it for a moment when Sister Tanguy, at the time Catherine's immediate, and rather waspish, superior was present. As the meal ended, the old veteran selected by his comrades for the honor arose with all the courtliness he could muster, and said:

"Sister Catherine, you are very good to us, and at table you always ask us: 'Have you had enough?' "

A short speech, but complete, with very practical proof for

what he had to say! Catherine must have been embarrassed at this unexpected eulogy, but she would not have been human had she not felt a warm glow of pleasure.

A Sister remembered watching Catherine gather peaches in the garden one day. Remarking on the ripeness of the fruit, the Sister asked if she might have some.

"No, Sister," Catherine said firmly. "I'm sorry, but these are for the old men. Later, if there are any left, you may have what you want." Relating the incident, the Sister would add wryly that none were left.

With Catherine, even religious exercises must give way to the service of her old men. Sister Jeanne Maurel, whose task it was to carry the trays to the sick, grew very angry at the kitchen Sister one morning. It was a "last straw" occasion, for the kitchen Sister was one of those people who are never on time for anything and she had kept Sister Maurel late for Mass habitually by her leisurely methods at the stove. Sister Maurel was in fine fettle, grumbling away to herself, when she finally reached the sick ward.

"Sister," Catherine admonished her, "you must give everything to God, and never complain."

Nor did she let it go at that, but made poor Sister Maurel promise to follow her advice. At first glance, it might seem strange for a saint to place work before so holy a thing as the Mass; but Catherine was following the lead of St. Vincent himself, who constantly told his Sisters that they must forego any religious exercise, even the Holy Sacrifice, if the sick or the poor needed them. In such cases, St. Vincent would say, "You are leaving God for God."

That Catherine's unflagging devotion paid off is proven by the fact that the old men were never known to complain. This is truly remarkable when we consider the many different personalities she served and the usual cantankerousness of old people; it is even more remarkable when we remember that

Catherine's old men were used to the comforts and fine food of great houses.

It must not be thought, however, that Catherine was over-indulgent toward her charges. When they stepped out of line, she had her own methods of correction, and they were right in character: eminently practical and so simple and direct as to provoke a smile. Her cure for drunkenness is a case in point. The old fellows had a day out each week, and, of course, there was always that hard core of high livers who would head straight for their favorite bar. Now Catherine had nothing against drink: she was born in the heart of the Burgundian vineyards. In fact, as a European, Catherine would be hard put to understand the uneasiness of Americans, still scarred with the excesses of Prohibition, toward what she accepted as part of God's everyday gifts. There was a long period in her religious life when she did not touch wine, but this was from a sense of uniformity rather than distaste: by a somewhat distorted sense of caution, wine was allowed at first only to the sick Sisters, then later to the teachers and the older Sisters; but Catherine would not touch it until its use was extended to all. Drunkenness, however, was another matter entirely and, once in a while, some of Catherine's more reprobate charges would stagger home tipsy. Punishment was inexorable and swift. The culprit was put right to bed; and there is something intensely human in the picture of this holy Sister struggling up the stairs with a drunken old man, and the old fellow splitting the air with a few raucous bars of a tavern ballad or a couple of well-used oaths. Once the offender was safely in bed, Catherine would carry off his clothes and hide them, and there he would stay for three whole days—and there would be no day out for him the next week!

On one occasion, a couple of the Sisters, fairly outraged at a long-time offender who had come home in a particularly obnoxious condition, reproached Catherine for not having been more severe with him.

"I can't help it," Catherine answered simply. "I keep seeing Christ in him." This was Christianity in its perfection, but it was also, as the Sisters came to realize later, wholly sensible: there is nothing to be gained by expostulating with a drunken man, and Catherine knew it. The unhappy fellow got his tongue-lashing the next morning.

The occasional drunkenness of her charges, however, was, in a sense, the least of Catherine's worries. There were certain of them who were impure, and it is a soberly attested fact that Catherine had the supernatural gift of discerning which ones they were. "That man is not good," she would observe with great delicacy, pointing him out to her Superior.

It was an act of utmost heroism for Catherine to look after these unhappy victims of vice. She herself was the soul of chastity. Her sister Tonine had graphically described Catherine's innocence as a young girl by saying that "she did not know evil." Sister Sèjole had said that she "had never known a young girl more pure or candid." And several of the Sisters with whom she lived concluded upon reflection that it was Catherine's shining chastity that led Our Lady to grant her the Apparitions of the Medal. This last is a singular judgment, for it suggests that there was something arresting, something almost visible, about the chastity of Catherine Labouré. She was, after all, an old lady when these Sisters who made the judgment knew her, and chastity is the common ornament of nuns; surely there is question of an extraordinary depth of purity in her when people were especially struck by the chastity of an old nun. Catherine's purity was evident in the clear and honest glance of her eye and the shining brightness of her face. It can be imagined with what repugnance this pure woman went to care for men whom she knew to be dirty and foul in mind and body.

Her repugnance was so great that it swept over her in waves of disgust and, try as she might, even with her great strength of will and self-control, she could not prevent it from showing in her face. It was only prayer and her magnificent faith that enabled her to withstand the first shock of revulsion and to recognize, even behind the mask of sin, Christ in the sinner. It is the measure of her sanctity that she ministered to the impure as tenderly as to the others.

The other spiritual problem Catherine had with her charges was attendance at Sunday Mass. It was not the problem that secret sins of impurity were because, while her old men shared the disinclination of many French males to attend Mass, they were more or less trapped into attendance by the fact of living in a Catholic institution. Sister Catherine saw to it that they were at Mass every Sunday, at any rate, and some of them, whether from native piety or the discovery that going to Mass was not so humiliating or distasteful as they had imagined, actually went during the week.

Of course, there was the usual quota of rebels who held out against the most eloquent exhortations to virtue or the practice of religion. Against these Catherine used the ultimate weapons of prayer and charity. In such capable hands as hers these weapons were absolutely invincible, and even the most hardened sinner was eventually brought humbly to heel.

She had a quaint spiritual medicine for some of the most rebellious. She would prepare some drink, a glass of milk or wine, and before handing it to the sinner steep in it a copy of the *Memorare*. It was a simple, childlike act of faith and devotion, one perhaps that she had learned in the Christian household at Fain, like the act of swallowing the tiny piece of St. Vincent's surplice on the night of the first vision of Our Lady.

One old fellow in particular was a challenge to Catherine. He was wicked in the literal sense of the word, believing in nothing and loud and shocking in his disbelief, cantankerous and disagreeable. He was the scandal of the house. Even the dedicated Sisters would expostulate with Catherine (as if she could help it!):

"Sister Catherine, how wicked your old devil Marcel is!"

Catherine's eyes would fill with tears and she would reply only: "Pray for him." It was what she did most fervently—that, and turning upon him the full force of her attention and charm. She won him over and he died in the grace of God. They all did, even the most abandoned of them. During the long span of forty years not one of Sister Catherine's old men died without the Last Sacraments of the Church.

Nor did Catherine's sense of responsibility to her charges end with their deaths. She had Masses offered for the repose of their souls, and the offerings for these Masses came from her own personal resources. By the vow of poverty, Sisters of Charity may possess money of their own and use it, with permission, for pious works. This was one of the ways Catherine used the money given her by her family.

It is one thing to care for old men, however faithfully and meticulously, solely from duty; it is quite another to supplement duty with the true love of a woman's heart and the true sublimity of Christian charity. This latter was Catherine's way. Many, even among her daily companions, have stopped at the cold, reserved outer shell of Catherine Labouré, and failed to penetrate to the inner fire. Not so her old men; they knew her and loved her. Not so her family, especially those like her sister Tonine or her nephew and niece, Father Meugniot and Mme Duhamel, who knew her best. She took knowing, did Catherine, but it was worth the effort. Certain of her nephews and nieces enjoyed visiting their Aunt Marie Louise better than their Aunt Catherine, because Marie Louise was easier to know, livelier and more appealing, especially to children. Indeed, Catherine's love of family was so controlled that it has gone largely unnoticed, and yet it showed itself in such deep concern for her family's welfare that one is led to suspect her tenderness toward her family as the source of her tenderness toward her old men.

Love of home and family was deep in her. It showed itself in the long hard years of caring for her father at Fain, in the sense of outrage that made her accuse Marie Louise of not easing their father's last days. It showed itself in the things about her father she chose to remember: not the harshness, but the solid piety and the shrewd lessons of life he taught her. And who is to deny that she found it easier to be patient with the truculence of some obstinate old fellow because she saw in his features the face of her father? Or that her fingers were quicker to soothe because she felt beneath them, not the fevered wrinkled brow of a dying old man but, in retrospect, the smoother brow of her invalid brother Auguste?

When Catherine left the world, she did not cut herself off from her family. She was no monster of mortification, coldly turning from the warm human relationships God had given her. She never saw her father again, because he was hundreds of miles away in Fain; but her brothers were in Paris—Hubert, Jacques, Antoine, Charles, Joseph, and Pierre—and she saw them and their families as often as time and travel would permit. If they were sick and could not come to visit her, she went to visit them.

In 1858, Tonine moved with her family to Paris and took a house in the Boulevard Pereire, not far from the Hospice d'Enghien, and the old intimacy with Catherine was renewed. After her father and brother Auguste died, Tonine was finally free to marry Claude Meugniot, in 1838, and they settled in the village of Vizerny. Here were born their children, Marie and Philippe, who were to be closest to Catherine of all her nephews and nieces.

At the age of fourteen Philippe began to read Latin with the village curé and his Aunt Catherine wrote immediately to ask him whether he intended to become a priest. Her action was not prompted by the exaggerated zeal for family vocation characteristic of certain religious, but by true prophetic sight. The boy replied that he was thinking of the priesthood, but could promise nothing. His reply, vague as it was, prompted Catherine to action: she brought Philippe to Paris and personally conveyed him to the College of Montdidier, conducted by the Vincentian Fathers. Philippe spent several years there preparing for the secular clergy, and his aunt hovered over his vocation anxiously, asking him at every opportunity whether he meant to persevere. Philippe himself says that her anxiety was dictated not by zeal for his vocation alone, but also by a sense of justice, for Catherine and one of her companions had undertaken to pay for his schooling and she impressed upon him constantly that such money was not to be wasted.

The boy saw his aunt frequently during his vacations and on one of these occasions Catherine decided to speak to him about entering the Community of St. Vincent. Once more it was not a question of catering to a selfish wish on her part, but a true vein of prophecy. She had been showing Philippe a piece of the cassock of Jean Gabriel Perboyre, the Vincentian priest who had been martyred in China in 1840. Suddenly she said to Philippe:

"If you wish to enter the Community, our priests will receive you." She went on immediately, smiling as if it were all an elaborate joke:

"They might even make you a superior and then you would be more free." Surprising bait for a saint to dangle before a young man, but Catherine knew whereof she spoke. She went on to tell of Father Perboyre and his life in China, almost as if changing the subject, but it was actually a preface to her final suggestion:

"You, too, might go to China."

Without any further pressure from his aunt, Philippe did enter the Vincentian Fathers and his life after ordination fell out exactly as Catherine had suggested it might: he was appointed Superior when quite young and later served as procurator of the foreign missions in Hong Kong.

This was but one of the many casual prophecies Catherine made in her lifetime, so casual that they went unnoticed, not only at the time they were uttered, but even after they had been fulfilled.

Catherine also came to the aid of Philippe's sister Marie. Marie had married Eugène Duhamel and borne him two little girls. One day M. Duhamel walked out, never to be heard from again until word of his death reached the deserted wife. Catherine used her influence to have the little girls educated at the House of Reuilly under her watchful eye.

Indeed, over the years, Catherine had enough family troubles to occupy all her prayers. There was Marie Louise and her flight from religion. There was one of her brothers—we do not know which one—who did not practice his religion. Catherine arranged for a niece, Léonie Labouré, to keep an eye on him so that, should he fall ill, he would not die without the Sacraments. There was her brother-in-law, Tonine's husband, who was also indifferent to his faith. Catherine kept after him herself, visiting him often—he was a chronic invalid—and each time urging him to make his peace with God.

"I pray for you," she would remind him, "but you must pray also." He was a cavalier sort of person for, after Catherine had gone, he would say to his family:

"Zoé wishes to convert me, but she hasn't managed it yet." Then he would add, with a chuckle: "A fine girl, all the same."

There came a time when the doctors gave him up, and he surrendered to the prayers and pleading of his sister-in-law. God and Catherine had a little joke at his expense, however. After receiving the Sacraments, he suddenly grew better:

"Somebody has won me a year's delay," he said. He must have known who. He continued faithful to his conversion and died peacefully, with the Sacraments, just a year later.

Tonine herself lingered for fifteen months with a painful illness before her death. Catherine was a frequent visitor, and constantly sustained her sister, helping her to bear her sufferings and to keep up her flagging spirit. Life had not been overly kind to poor Tonine. Once she said to Catherine:

"Had I known what would happen to me, I would have been a religious like you."

"Each to her own vocation," Catherine replied. "You would not, then, have had the consolation of giving a son to God."

At the end, Tonine fell into a coma, lasting several days, during which time she neither spoke nor recognized anyone. One day Catherine came, and putting everyone out of the room, closeted herself with this dearest sister and companion. A long time passed. When Catherine finally emerged she summoned her niece, Mme Duhamel, and her children.

"Go to your mother," she said, "she wants to speak to you." Without another word, Catherine left the house. Rushing to Tonine's bedside, her daughter and grandchildren were amazed to find her wide awake and smiling. Completely alert, she gave them her final instructions, and died the next morning, serene and happy.

Aimée Labouré, widow of Catherine's brother Jacques, testified in 1907 that she and her husband would go to visit Catherine two or three times a year during the twenty years of their marriage. "When I went to see her, she always received me cordially," the sister-in-law said, "reproaching me for not coming more often, and never failing to exhort me to fulfill my religious duties. She especially interested herself in the salvation of my husband, who could not go to see her as often as I, because of his work. When my husband grew gravely ill, she came to see him, made sure he had received the Last Sacraments, and gave him the Miraculous Medal, which she herself put around his neck."

This short testimony gives the pattern of Catherine's relations with her family: cordiality, warmth, human love, constant thought for the things of God—and the Miraculous Medal. There is something especially warm and moving in the picture of this humble Sister, who gave the Medal to the world, hanging it around the neck of her own brother.

XIV

The Medal and Ratisbonne

SOON AFTER THE APPARITION of July 18, 1830, Catherine had told her director:

"The Blessed Virgin asks another mission of you. She wishes you to establish an order of which you will be the founder and director. It is a Confraternity of Children of Mary. Many graces, many indulgences, will be granted to it. The month of Mary will be celebrated with great solemnity. Mary loves these festivals. She will reward their observance with abundant graces."

Father Aladel took no action on this request until 1835, five years after it had been made. Even then, the first group of Children of Mary did not come into existence until 1838, at Beune, in the district where Catherine Labouré was born.

In his first audience with Pius IX, after the Pontiff's accession to the throne, Father Etienne petitioned for the formal establishment of the Children of Mary as a Pontifical Association. The Holy Father granted this request in a rescript dated June 20, 1847, which granted to the new Association all the indulgences already enjoyed by the *Prima Primaria*, the Sodality in honor of Our Lady set up by the Jesuits in 1584. Thus the Children of Mary came into official being seventeen years after the request of Our Lady.

The Children of Mary is a religious society—of girls primarily, although there are some boys in the group—whose members have banded together to do particular honor to Our Lady, through acts of devotion, but especially in imitating her virtues of purity, humility, obedience, and charity. In other words, like any religious society of the Church properly so called, it has for its chief end the perfection of its members, and there can be little doubt that, over the years, countless young souls have become heroically holy through the Association of the Children of Mary.

After its official foundation the Association sprang up all over the face of the globe, in every country and among every people. Its present-day membership may be guessed from the fact that, in 1948 when a centenary celebration was held in Paris, 10,000 delegates from every country in the world attended.

Catherine never connected herself with the Association in any official way, but she always went out of her way to show her pleasure when any child of her acquaintance was inducted into the society. Each new member of the group established at the Sisters' house in Reuilly always had a few words of welcome and counsel from her lips. She could be said, in fact, to have had a special zeal for the salvation of youth. She was deeply concerned with the temptations surrounding the children of the neighborhood, for the quarter where the houses of Reuilly and Enghien were located was rough and crime-ridden. Whenever her duties would allow, she would cross the yard to the Reuilly house and spend some time among the neighborhood children who had gathered there. Whether due to her influence or not, these street waifs were later admitted to the classes held for the orphans of the house.

An interesting exchange took place one day between Catherine and one of the Sisters of the house, which indirectly affected these children. The Sister, Sister Fouquet, was walking in the garden, when Catherine approached her.

"Little one," Catherine said gently, "little one, you are pondering somthing evil in your head." When the young Sister had recovered from the shock of having her thoughts read so clearly, she blurted out her troubles all in a rush:

"I entered the Community to care for the sick. They have put me with the orphans—and now children from the neighborhood have joined the classes. I shall never be able to teach, especially before so many!" And she finished defiantly: "I would rather return to my family."

"Be brave," Catherine admonished her gently. "I will pray to the Blessed Virgin for you. Promise me that you will stick at it for a year, and I promise you that you will pass your school examinations and will persevere in your vocation."

When Sister Fouquet told this story, she was already forty-two years in the Community.

Some years later, in 1873 or 1874, Catherine was involved in another incident concerning this clash of hospital and orphanage work, which had been the Sisters' main work, and teaching, which was becoming a principal work of the Community at that time. Many of the older Sisters looked with distaste on the work of teaching, as a departure from their primitive rule. It even got abroad that Catherine herself preferred the work of the hospital Sisters to that of the school Sisters, and feared that the second work might eclipse the first. How definite were her views in this matter will never be known. It could well be that some chance remark on her part was exaggerated out of all proportion because of the suspicions that she was the Sister of the Visions. At the Beatification process, the matter was mentioned only as hearsay.

At any rate, Catherine had gone to the Motherhouse one

day with a group of Sisters from Enghien to visit several of the novices who had postulated there. A young teaching Sister, Sister Darlin, was serving her turn as portress that day. Observing the group from Enghien her eyes rested especially on Catherine:

"I had been told that she was the Sister who had been favored with the Apparitions of the Most Holy Virgin," Sister Darlin states. "I looked upon her with respect, thinking to myself sadly that this worthy Sister did not appreciate the school Sisters, and I liked school work a great deal. I said to myself: *Is it possible for her to love the Most Holy Virgin so much, and not to care for an office in which it is possible to inspire the children with great devotion for Mary?* "I wished to speak to her very much, but did not dare."

At that same moment, Catherine left the group and approached Sister Darlin.

"Come with me, Sister," Catherine said smiling pleasantly, "we shall go to the 'Holy Mary' class and say an *Ave Maria* together."

Sister Darlin stared in amazement; then flushed with pleasure. This was precisely the class of which she had particular charge. More than that, Catherine had never, until that moment, laid eyes on her.

Catherine's efforts to reassure Sister Darlin of her good will were not at an end. After they had recited the *Ave Maria*, Catherine took out her purse and gave the delighted Sister one of the first Miraculous Medals; then she invited her to accompany her to the infirmary to visit Marie Louise, who was ending her days there.

So great a show of favor on Catherine's part was too much for the poor Sister. She lost her head. On the way to the infirmary and during the visit she showered Catherine with attention, running ahead to open doors, getting her a chair, bowing and scraping in every way.

On the instant, Catherine changed from the smiling Sister of a few minutes before. Her face froze in stern lines, her whole body stiffened. "She looked at me coldly," Sister Darlin lamented, "as if to say: 'Are you finished with your attentions and reverences?' She practically turned her back on me. Knowing I had offended her, fearing I had offended the Blessed Virgin, I burst into tears and fled from the room."

The incident, with its mixture of the supernatural and the human, is a graphic picture of the personality of a saint, a scant two years before her death.

Meanwhile in 1841, Catherine had complied with the wishes of Father Aladel, and written out her first complete account of the Apparitions. Hard on the heels of this document, she sent him an insistent note (unsigned, as were all her communications to him; Catherine took no chances of some other eye than Father Aladel's falling upon her name).

> For ten years, I have felt myself driven to tell you to have an altar erected to the Blessed Virgin on the spot where she appeared. At this moment, more than ever, I feel myself pressed to tell you this, and to ask of you a Communion, by the entire Community, every year. Every indulgence will be granted. Ask, ask; everything you ask will be granted.
>
> I ask you to do the same in memory of the heart of St. Vincent. I have spoken of this to you several times, and now I remind you again—a Communion please.
>
> I believe that the good God will be glorified and the Blessed Virgin honored; it will give new fervor to all hearts.
>
> I beg you to request this of our Most Honored Father. I am, in the Sacred Hearts of Jesus and Mary, your faithful and submissive daughter.

There could be no more agonized cry of Catherine's heart than this letter. It becomes the more poignant, to know that it went unheeded. Catherine was extremely naïve, to look for the erection of the altar by the "Saturday before the first Sunday of Advent." She desired this with special fervor, because the year 1841 was the first since 1830 when the anniversary of the great Apparition of November 27 would fall on the very day it had occurred, the Saturday before the beginning of Advent. The altar Catherine pleaded for was not erected until 1880, four years after her death.

At this same time, Catherine reminded her confessor by word of mouth that the Blessed Virgin had asked for a commemorative statue of the first phase of the Great Apparition depicting Our Lady with the golden globe in her hands, and offering it to God. Father Aladel made some start on this project in 1841, for certain tentative designs for the statue were found among his papers. The project was abandoned, however, for reasons which are not very clear; one reason given was that "the origin of the statue would have to be explained"—a preposterous excuse indeed! Catherine was to call the failure to make this statue "the torment of my life," and had actually to break her silence of forty-six years to have the statue made. It was not completed until after her death.

To make matters worse, in 1854 the French Government made a present to the Community of two magnificent blocks of marble, in gratitude for the nursing services of the Sisters during the cholera and the Crimean War. It was noised abroad that Father Etienne, the Superior General—certainly in consultation with Father Aladel, who was then Director of the Sisters of Charity—had decided to use the marble for an altar and statue to be placed in the chapel of the rue du Bac. Catherine, hearing of it, must have felt that, at last, her desires would be realized. Her hopes were soon dashed. The altar erected was a new high altar for the chapel—not the altar "on the spot where she appeared," which Our Lady had asked for. The statue made, and placed over this new high altar, was of Our Lady as she appears on the Medal—not the "Virgin of the Globe" which, again, Our Lady had asked for.

Catherine was dead many years when the commemorative Communions she asked for in 1841 were finally decreed by the Superior General.

It is hard not to blame Father Aladel in all this. In fairness it must be admitted that he was not a free agent, that he, too, had superiors, both in the Community and in the larger world of the Church. On the other hand, the requests were from the lips of the Mother of God. Catherine did all in her power to have them fulfilled. It was very unpleasant for her to dun her confessor so constantly, to battle with him, for their fulfillment. The question may be justly asked whether Father Aladel, for his part, did all in *his* power to move his superiors toward fulfilling exactly the requests of the Mother of God.

Father Aladel had been hard at work, however, in spreading the story of the Miraculous Medal, and the wonders it had worked. In 1834 he published an account of ninety pages, which he called *The Miraculous Medal*. The book went into four editions before the year was out, and had grown to 270 pages. New editions appeared in 1835, 1836, and 1837. The eighth edition, of 608 pages in length, was published in 1842. When this eighth edition was being readied for the printer, Catherine told Father Aladel she would not see another edition. Her prophecy came true. The ninth edition of *The Miraculous Medal* was not published until 1878, and Father Chevalier, Catherine's last confessor, was its editor. Catherine renewed her prophecy in 1876, telling Father Chevalier that she would not see his edition in print. He laughed at her, saying that it was ready for the press.

"You will see," she replied, smiling back.

The edition was not published until 1878 and was the first to contain a biography of Catherine, who had died on December 31, 1876.

Not the slightest hint of the turmoil and frustration in Catherine's life showed to others. She went about her duties quietly and methodically; interiorly she continued to grow in the love of God. The Sisters who lived with her noted her piety, but failed to see in it anything but the holy life of an especially good religious. Only after her death would they remember things that should have given them clues to her identity and her heroic sanctity.

In chapel, she always knelt up straight, completely absorbed, her fingertips scarcely touching the pew in front of her, certainly not enough to give her any support. So absorbed was she, indeed, that from time to time, other Sisters would turn toward her to bolster their own devotion by the sight of one so lost in prayer—but these were intimate, unconscious actions that they would not speak about among themselves. Years later, when the Sisters had heard that she had enjoyed the vision of Christ in the Blessed Sacrament throughout her seminary, they would remember her habitual attitude in chapel, and several of them were led to wonder, very seriously, whether she had not enjoyed this privilege throughout her entire lifetime.

The Sisters were permitted, at this time, to receive Holy Communion only three times a week. Catherine would prepare for each Communion by endeavoring to perform each action of the day before as perfectly as possible. As she grew older, she enjoined this practice on the younger Sisters.

She made visits to the Blessed Sacrament as often as her duties allowed her, even as she had slipped away between household tasks in Fain to pray in the village church. Sister Cosnard had a fond recollection of these visits:

"Whenever possible, she would go to the chapel and, having removed her white apron before entering, make a profound and respectful bow to the tabernacle (women did not genuflect at this time). Then she would cast a look of filial devotion toward the statue of the Blessed Virgin, and kneel to pray. After a moment she would leave, her face radiant, and don her apron and return to her work. It was most impressive. Several times I have seen her enter the chapel with tears in her eyes. When she left, the tears were gone, and her face was shining."

Catherine's act of turning toward the statue was so habitual that the Superior got to wondering whether it were indeed an act of devotion, or merely a habit. To satisfy her curiosity, she had the statue moved one day to another position in the chapel. She watched carefully as Catherine entered. Catherine made her usual profound reverence to the Blessed Sacrament, then turned her gaze on the statue of Our Lady in its new position. There was no fooling her; her relationship with Mary was genuine and deep.

In 1840, Our Lady came again to the house on the rue du Bac, to reveal her Immaculate Heart to a novice named Justine Bisqueyburu. Sister Justine had entered the novitiate on November 27, 1839, the ninth anniversary of the Apparition of the Medal. Toward the end of January she entered upon her retreat in a prayer hall, behind the Chapel of the Apparitions. This prayer hall contained a miraculous statue of the Blessed Virgin, which was very old and which had figured several times in the supernatural protection of the Sisters and their house. During the exercises of retreat, the Blessed Virgin appeared suddenly to Sister Justine, on January 28, 1840. She wore a long white dress and a blue mantle. She was barefooted and bareheaded, her hair falling free to the shoulders. In her hand she held her Immaculate Heart, pierced with a sword, and surrounded with flames. This vision was repeated several times as the retreat continued, and later on the principal feasts of the Blessed Virgin. On September 8, 1840, the feast of Our Lady's Nativity, the vision took on an added detail. The Virgin carried the Immaculate Heart in her right hand, and, suspended from her left hand, a kind of scapular of green cloth. On the face of the scapular was a representation of Mary as she had appeared in the preceding apparitions, and on the back "a heart all burning with rays more brilliant than the sun, and as transparent as crystal; this heart, surmounted by a cross, was pierced with a sword, and around it were the words: "Immaculate Heart of Mary, pray for us now and at the hour of our death." The Green Scapular, as this sacramental is popularly called, is not really a scapular, but rather a "cloth medal," for it consists of only one piece of material, and is worn about the neck as a medal would be worn. Sister Justine confided her vision to Father Aladel, as Catherine Labouré had done, and she found the same difficulty in having the scapular made as Catherine had encountered with the Medal. It was not until 1846, after Our Lady had complained several times that her gift to the Community was not appreciated, that the approbation of Monseigneur Affré, Archbishop of Paris, was finally sought and obtained for the distribution of the scapular.

In spite of the slowness of the authorities to act, heaven continued to lavish its treasures on the Community of St. Vincent. Throughout the year 1845, another Sister of Charity, Sister Appolline Andreveux, stationed at the Hospice de Saint Jean in Troyes, received several visions of Our Lord in His Passion. On July 26, 1846, Christ appeared to Sister Appolline, holding in His hand a red scapular. One piece of the scapular bore the image of Christ on the Cross, surrounded by the instruments of the Passion, and the words: "Holy Passion of Our Lord Jesus Christ, save us." The other piece bore representations of the Hearts of Jesus and Mary, surmounted by a cross, and the words: "Sacred Hearts of Jesus and Mary, protect us."

Sister Appolline was to meet with prompter action than either Sister Catherine or Sister Justine. Sister Appolline had confided her visions, in writing, to Father Etienne, and the Superior General sought and obtained approbation for the making of the scapular from Pius IX in 1847, during the same audience in which the Pontiff approved the Children of Mary.

Strangely enough, there is no record of what Catherine had to say about these visions. Certainly she recognized in them a connection with her own, in the Hearts of Jesus and Mary and the Cross.

The year 1842 had scarcely begun when an event occurred which brought the Miraculous Medal to the notice of the world outside the Church and resulted in the official recognition of the Medal by Rome itself. The event was the Conversion of Alphonse Tobie Ratisbonne. Ratisbonne was a citizen of the world in every respect. Scion of an old and wealthy Jewish family of Strasbourg, he was a lawyer by education and a banker by trade. At twenty-eight, he was in the prime of life, good-looking, good-humored, a man of charm and of countless friends. His friends included even many Christians, of the Protestant persuasion, however, for he had an almost uncontrollable hatred of Catholicism. This hatred had been increased by the conversion and subsequent ordination to the priesthood of his older brother, Théodore. Alphonse had never known Théodore very well—but, as a proud Jew, Alphonse could not forgive the older brother's defection to the camp of the enemy.

In 1841, Ratisbonne became engaged to an aristocratic Jewish girl of seventeen. Since the marriage was not to be celebrated immediately, he decided to while away his last months of bachelor freedom by wintering in Malta. He left Strasbourg on November 17th and, traveling in slow stages, arrived in Naples in December where he was warmly received in Jewish circles, especially by the Rothschilds.

The *Mongibello*, the ship on which Ratisbonne was to sail for Malta, kept delaying her departure from day to day. In a fit of restlessness, Alphonse decided to go a different route, by way of Palermo, and set off for the ticket office. By mistake, he found himself at the window for the Rome coach. Now one boast Ratisbonne had made before leaving home, was that under no condition would he so much as pass through Rome, the center of Christendom. Finding himself at the Rome ticket window proved to be the last straw piled on top of his restlessness and the delay of the ship. In a fit of temper he booked passage on the Rome coach and sent a message to friends that he would return to Naples on January 20th.

Ratisbonne arrived in Rome on January 6, 1842 and checked in at the Hotel de Londres. By chance he met an old friend, Gustave Bussières. Through his friend, Ratisbonne met his brother, Baron Bussières, a recent convert to Catholicism, who was to change Ratisbonne's whole life.

Ratisbonne proceeded to "do" Rome, like any tourist: St. Peter's, The Coliseum, the Forum, and so on. He soon became bored, the more so because, just as he had anticipated, the Eternal City filled him with even deeper disgust with the Church, and he booked passage on the Naples Coach for January 17.

Ratisbonne was a punctilious man, and returned the visits and kindness shown him by calling at his friends' houses, as the custom was, and leaving his card. His courtesy was his undoing, for, at the home of Baron Bussières, the Italian footman misunderstood his intention and ushered him into the presence of his master. The Baron, learning of his imminent departure, with all the over-zealous aplomb of certain new converts, launched into a last-stand effort to bring Ratisbonne to the knowledge of the truth. Ratisbonne was speechless with rage, and threw back in Bussières's face the treatment of the Jews in the Ghetto of Rome, which misery Ratisbonne blamed on the Church.

At the height of the argument, the Baron produced a Miraculous Medal. Here was one of those Roman superstitions Ratisbonne ranted about. Did he dare to wear it and to recite the Catholic prayer to Our Lady known as the *Memorare?* If it were all mere superstition, it could do him no harm. Driven into a corner and appalled at the "ridiculous" turn of events, Ratisbonne acquiesced and even allowed Bussières's little daughter to place the Medal on a ribbon around his neck. Bussières further asked Ratisbonne to copy the prayer out and return it to him, since it was the only copy he had. This was probably a delaying tactic, for certainly the Baron could have easily come by another copy of so familiar a prayer as the *Memorare.* Ratisbonne was a man of his word. He copied out the prayer in his own hand. No sooner had he done so than the words continued to ring in his head, as he later said, "like one of those airs from an opera which you sing without thinking of them, and then feel annoyed at yourself for singing it."

In the meantime, the Baron had met an old friend, the Comte de la Ferronnays, at a dinner at the Palazzo Borghese, and told him of giving the Medal and prayer to Ratisbonne. De la Ferronnays, who had been a diplomat under the Bourbons but now lived in retirement in Rome, promised to pray for Ratisbonne. True to his word, he went to the basilica of S. Maria Maggióre, where, he told his wife, he recited more than twenty *Memorares.* Shortly after returning home, he suffered a heart attack and died.

All was prepared. The conversion of Alphonse Ratisbonne had begun. During the night of January 19–20, Ratisbonne was confronted with a vision of a plain, bare cross, which gave him no peace. On the afternoon of the following day, Ratisbonne set out to finish up his farewell calls, in an effort to shake off the disturbing vision. He met Baron Bussières, who was on his way to the church of S. Andrea delle Fratte to make final arrangement for the funeral of his friend Comte de la Ferronnays. When he had told Ratisbonne of the Comte's promise to pray for him, Ratisbonne agreed to accompany him to the church. Arriving at S. Andrea's, shortly after noon, Bussières asked Alphonse to wait for him in the carriage, but Ratisbonne said he would go inside and look around. The Baron went directly to the sacristy, and Ratisbonne began idly to examine the architecture of the place, when suddenly a huge black dog appeared from out of nowhere and began to frisk in front of him, but in a menacing way, as if to bar his path. The dog disappeared as suddenly as it had come and Ratisbonne's eyes were drawn by a great burst of light, streaming from the little chapel of the Guardian Angels on the left-hand side of the nave. He raised his eyes and gazed into the calm and compelling eyes of the Virgin Mary. She appeared exactly as she was represented on the Medal, arms extended and hands bent down with the rays of grace which streamed from them. Ratisbonne saw her face for only a moment, for it was of such blinding beauty that he could not bear to look on it, but could raise his eyes only to the level of her hands, which, he said "expressed all the secrets of the divine pity." Our Lady did not speak, but Ratisbonne "understood all."

It was over in a moment. Like that fire-breathing Jew, Saul of Tarsus, Ratisbonne was struck to his knees and converted on the instant. Returning from the sacristy, Bussières found Ratisbonne on his knees, and as he raised him up, Alphonse whispered:

"Oh, how that gentleman has prayed for me!"

Back in his hotel, Ratisbonne sent for a priest, told him all that had happened, and begged for immediate baptism. That night he kept vigil by the body of Comte de la Ferronnays in the church of S. Andrea della Fratte. Immediately after the funeral, Ratisbonne entered upon a ten-day period of retreat with the Jesuits and received instructions in the faith from Father de Villeforte.

Ratisbonne's reception into the Church at the Gesú was a

ceremony of international significance. Everyone who was anyone in Rome attended. Cardinal Patrizi, the Vicar of Rome, received Ratisbonne's abjuration of his errors, baptized him, confirmed him, and gave him his first Communion.

News of the "Madonna del Ratisbonne" and his miraculous conversion had Rome agog, and quickly fanned out through all Europe, especially in diplomatic and financial circles, where Ratisbonne and Bussières and De la Ferronnays were widely known. Interest centered especially on the Medal which, until this time, had only the approbation of the Archbishop of Paris. Rome immediately instituted an official inquiry into the circumstances of Ratisbonne's conversion. Cardinal Patrizi was put in charge of the inquiry, and twenty-five sessions were held between February 17 and June 3, 1842. The findings of the court "fully recognized the signal miracle wrought by God through the intercession of the Blessed Virgin Mary, in the spontaneous and complete conversion of Marie Alphonse Ratisbonne from Judaism to Catholicism." It was a major triumph of the Miraculous Medal.

Ratisbonne entered with the Jesuit Fathers to study for the priesthood and spent ten years in the bosom of the Society. When, however, his superiors repeatedly turned down his request to go to China, he left, for, as he put it, his true vocation was to be an apostle, "not a sixth-form master." He joined his brother, Théodore, who had founded the Congregation of Our Lady of Sion for the evangelization of the Jews, and spent more than thirty years in the Holy Land as a missionary to his own people.

Ratisbonne made several attempts to converse with the unknown Sister who had been given the Miraculous Medal in 1830, but he never got beyond Father Aladel, who told him regretfully that the Seer insisted on remaining unknown. The Holy Father himself, Gregory XVI, became intensely interested, and wanted to converse with the Sister, but Catherine was adamant. Had the Pope commanded her to come forward, there would have been an interesting development, for it would seem that she would have had to obey the Vicar of Christ. As it was, Gregory did not insist, but he left her in her silence.

XV

The "Cross of Victory" Vision

ON FEBRUARY 22, 1848, there erupted the first of the bloody Parisian battles that marked that year of Revolutions. Louis Philippe had grown bored with being a figurehead king and his Bourbon blood had begun to show in a series of high-handed actions that smacked of a return to absolutism. He overplayed his hand, however, by refusing to allow the middle class to hold political rallies, or even a banquet, and the revolution was on. Barricades were thrown up in the streets while the royal soldiers stood by. In a few short hours "The Citizen King" was on his way to exile in England. A provisional government was set up the next day, manned by two parties: the Republicans, who wanted political reform, and the Socialists, who wanted a reform of society itself.

This February revolt was not directed in any way toward the Church. During the years of Louis Philippe's reign the Catholic Party had aligned itself more and more with the forces of democracy, and the hatred of the Church so rampant in 1789 and 1830 had waned.

Indeed, the Paris mob carried the cross in procession from the Tuilleries to the Church of St. Roch, while cries of *Vive le Christ* resounded on all sides. Further, the mob treated priests with great respect and invited them to bless the symbolic "trees of liberty." The Church responded to this show of good will by supporting the provisional government.

The *rapprochement* was shortlived. The Socialists of Louis Blanc, who detested the Church, soon got the upper hand in the government. They were aided in their bitter attacks on religion by the renegade Abbé de Lammenais, who accused the Catholic Party of being monarchists. Although the Catholics answered the charges, the clergy were set upon in some of the provinces.

A new Assembly was elected on April 23. It was overwhelmingly anti-socialist, and when the noted Dominican preacher and spiritual writer, Lacordaire, arrived in his white robes to take his seat in the Assembly, he received an ovation from the Paris mob. The Assembly suppressed the National Workshops set up at the demand of the Socialists to employ 100,000 jobless workingmen, and, in retaliation Blanc stirred up a fresh revolt. Workingmen threw up new barricades and a bloody, three days' battle was fought, June 24–26. The revolt was finally put down by General Cavaignac, but not before Monseigneur Affré, Archbishop of Paris, died by an assassin's bullet on the barricades.

With true heroism, the Archbishop had resolved to plead with his children to stop the carnage, had resolved to offer his life, if need be. All fighting ceased as he appeared atop a barricade, his arms raised for silence. A shot rang out, and he fell mortally wounded. Thinking themselves duped, the revolutionists resumed firing and the bloodshed went on for another day. Although he died in vain, it must have consoled the prelate, in his last moments, to hear leaders of both sides disavow his murder. They spoke the truth; Monseigneur Affré had been respected by all. The man who killed him was himself shot down the next day, and died confessing his crime, in the saving arms of the Church.

Sister Rosalie, the redoubtable Sister of Charity who had saved the life of Monseigneur de Quélen in 1830, repeated Monseigneur Affré's heroic attempt on June 26. She was more successful than he. Climbing upon a barricade in the Faubourg Saint Marceau, she literally brought the Revolution to an end in that Quarter by commanding a cease fire.

When peace and stability were restored, a general election was held, and Prince Louis Napoléon, nephew of Napoléon Bonaparte, was chosen President of the Second French Republic. The constitution was solemnly proclaimed in the Place de la Concorde. Before the ceremony, the crowd intoned the *Veni Sancte Spiritus*, and Monseigneur Sibour, the successor of the martyred Archbishop Affré, blessed the assemblage. Catholicism was still the heritage of the French people.

Catherine was not involved in any direct way in the Revolution of 1848, as she would be in the Communist uprising of 1871. However, at the end of July, Father Aladel received an urgent note. It had to do with a new vision, a vision of a mysterious cross which Catherine had seen earlier in 1848, or perhaps even in 1847.

A cross, covered with a black veil or crape, appeared in the air, passing over a section of Paris and casting terror into hearts [she wrote]. It was carried by men of angry visage, who, stopping suddenly in front of Notre Dame, let the cross fall into the mire, and, seized with fright themselves, ran off at full speed.

At the same instant, an outstretched arm appeared which pointed to blood, and a voice was heard, saying: "Blood flows, the innocent dies, the pastor gives his life for his sheep."

She went on to recount how the cross was lifted up anew with respect and placed upon a base some ten or twelve feet square, where it stood to a height of fifteen or twenty feet.

Around it were carried some of the dead and wounded who had suffered "in the grave events which transpired." The cross was then held in great reverence and was called the "Cross of Victory." People came to see it from all parts of France and even from foreign lands, led both by devotion, since many miracles of protection were attributed to this cross, and by curiosity, because it was also a great work of art.

Catherine described this mysterious cross as made of some precious, exotic wood, and ornamented with golden bands, a thing of marvelous beauty. Upon it hung the figure of Christ, and with her usual precision Catherine described this figure "with the crown of thorns on His head, the hair entangled among the thorns of the crown, the head drooping upon the side of the heart; the wound in His side, about three fingers in breadth, open and blood flowing from it drop by drop."

Catherine concluded the letter thus:

> Father, this is the third time I have spoken to you of this cross, after having consulted the good God, the Blessed Virgin, and our good father St. Vincent, on his feast day and every day of the octave.
>
> I abandoned myself entirely to him, and asked him to take away from me every extraordinary thought either on this subject or any other. Instead of finding peace after this prayer, I found myself the more pressed to give you the whole thing in writing. I do it by obedience and I hope afterward to be no longer disturbed.
>
> I am with the most profound respect, your entirely devoted daughter in the Sacred Hearts of Jesus and Mary.
>
> July 30, 1848.

The conclusion of this letter gives us some hint of the agony of soul this mysterious vision of the cross caused Catherine. So great was her agitation that she was driven to ask St. Vincent to wipe out of her mind all memory of this singular vision "and any other extraordinary thought." Certainly, all the visions of Catherine Labouré caused her great pain and harassment of soul, and, at this point, she seemed to want no further part of that miraculous supernatural world in which she constantly lived.

After Catherine's death, another note concerning this "Cross of Victory" was found among her effects, but this note throws no more light on the vision than did the first:

> The enemies of religion carry a cross, covered with a black veil, which casts terror into souls; the cross triumphs. It is called the Cross of Victory, and wears the livery of the nation. It is set up alongside Notre Dame, in the place of Victories.
>
> It is made of a strange precious wood, magnificently ornamented, with golden apples at its extremities; the great Christ nailed to it leans His head to the right side [sic] and there streams from the wound on his right side a great deal of blood.
>
> The badge of the nation is fixed at the height of the great beam of the cross; white, symbol of innocence, "flickers" upon the crown of thorns, the red symbolizes blood, the blue is the livery of the Blessed Virgin.

Heaven—and Catherine—were still preoccupied with France. What nation has been given to see its colors part of a miraculous vision, or explained in such mystic symbolism?

This strange vision of Catherine's has been all but forgotten. Of her biographers, only Lucien Misermont so much as mentions it. Neither she, nor Father Aladel, ever referred to it again. No doubt the obscurity of its meaning has discouraged anyone who stumbled upon it. It would seem to have a very limited significance, directed only to France and her throes of 1848. "The pastor who gave his life for his sheep" certainly could refer to Monseigneur Affré, who perished while on a peace mission in the Revolution of 1848. So, too, however, did Monseigneur Darboy, in 1871. Nor should it be forgotten that, in 1830, Our Lady predicted that "the cross will be cast down, blood will flow, they will open up again the side of Our Lord.

. . . Monseigneur the Archbishop will be stripped of his garments. . . . The whole world will be in sadness"; and when Catherine wondered, *When will this be?* she understood clearly *Forty years*—that is, in 1870 or 1871.

A moment's thought will show that the cross played a prominent part in most of Catherine Labouré's visions. Christ wore it on His breast in the vision of Trinity Sunday, 1830, and it fell to the ground at His feet; it appeared atop the golden ball Our Lady held in her hands in the first phase of the great vision of November 27, 1830, and in the second phase of the vision it appeared again, on the reverse of the Miraculous Medal. On the night before his conversion, Ratisbonne was haunted by the vision of a mysterious cross, a cross which he recognized, once converted, on the back of the Miraculous Medal given him by Baron Bussières. It is the "Cross of Victory" specifically set up before the Cathedral of Notre Dame and the pilgrims flocking to it from all parts of France and outside of France, that make this vision so mysterious. The prophecy seems not to have been fulfilled. Was it only an allegory, or is its fulfillment yet to come? Could the cross and the "trees of liberty" carried by the Parisian mob in the recent Revolution have been part of its fulfillment?

Whatever the vision's meaning, or its outcome, Catherine unburdened herself of it and life went on. Despite her prayers to St. Vincent, she was not to know release from the miraculous.

On a certain morning about the year 1850 when the rising bell rang at 4 o'clock, the Sister who slept in the bed alongside Catherine's noticed with alarm that Catherine was missing. Worse, her bed had not been slept in. Dressing quickly, the Sister ran to the Superior with the disturbing news. Other Sisters noticed the commotion and joined the search. Catherine was found in the garden, on her knees before the statue of Our Lady, hands joined in prayer. Apparently she had been there all night. She was in a state of trance, or more properly, of ecstasy, for she heard no one approach her, nor did she rouse when they spoke to her. Even as the Sisters watched, she extended her arms wide as if in complete acceptance or submission. Then she came to herself, visibly embarrassed at discovering her audience. She got to her feet without a word of explanation and went to the chapel for the morning meditation. Although she showed signs of great fatigue from the night-long vigil she knelt up straight as ever at her prayers, heard Mass, and began the day's duties, as if nothing had happened. That afternoon she asked permission to go to the rue du Bac to consult with Father Aladel.

This garden statue of Our Lady was a favorite of Catherine's. It was her custom—and the whole house was aware of it —to pray before it often. It got to be a sort of game with the orphans of the house, to hide in the bushes and watch the holy Sister at her prayers. Not many years after the incident the statue was replaced by a new one. This replacement was shattered by the Communists in 1871, and the old statue restored to its place of honor, to the evident joy of Sister Catherine.

In 1854, Pius IX made the momentous pronouncement that, beyond any shadow of a doubt, Our Blessed Lady was "preserved and exempt from all stain of original sin, from the first instant of her conception." Pius himself recognized that the impetus of devotion to the Immaculate Conception that led to this definition had come from France. Indeed, it is certain that the Apparitions of the Miraculous Medal to Catherine Labouré in 1830 hastened the solemn declaration of the doctrine of the Immaculate Conception in 1854, just as the Apparitions of Lourdes, wherein Our Lady declared: "I am the Immaculate Conception," set the seal of Heaven's approval on it.

There was great joy in France in 1858 when it became known that Mary had appeared to Bernadette Soubirous, a peasant girl of the French Pyrenees. No one was happier than Catherine Labouré. "You see," she exclaimed, "it is our own Blessed Mother, the Immaculate!"

On the day of the first national pilgrimage of France to the grotto at Lourdes, a group of the Sisters of Enghien were standing at the front door of the house, deep in conversation. Catherine joined them, and, before they knew what was happening, she had launched into a detailed description of the ceremony taking place at that moment at Lourdes. Several days later, the Parisian papers verified everything she had said.

It is interesting to conjecture whether Catherine had her knowledge of an event occurring several hundred miles away by clairvoyance or whether she was bilocated, being actually present at Lourdes and Enghien at one and the same time. There are several well-authenticated cases of bilocation in religious history, notably those of St. Catherine of Siena, St. Alphonsus Ligouri, and, more recently, of the English lay apostle, Teresa Higginson. Whatever the way in which Catherine Labouré came to a knowledge of this distant event, her knowledge was definitely of supernatural origin.

A tangible reminder of the very real connection between the Apparitions of Paris and Lourdes was the medal Bernadette wore about her neck during her meetings with the Mother of God. It was not a Miraculous Medal, but a sort of hybrid: the face of the medal was an exact copy of the front of the Miraculous Medal, but the back was devoted to St. Teresa of Avila. This medal was given by Bernadette to a parish priest of St.-Thomas-d'Aquin in Paris, who was on pilgrimage to Lourdes, and eventually it found its way to the rue du Bac, where it now reposes in the archives.

The incidents of Catherine's ecstasy in the garden and clairvoyance concerning Lourdes help to explain the increasing suspicions that she was the Sister of the Apparitions of 1830.

It is a vexing thing, the way these rumors concerning Catherine got around, and they must have annoyed her a great deal. They were a threat to her security and, in a very real sense, a danger to her peace of soul. Always to be on one's guard can be very unnerving, and the sly allusions, the open questions, plagued Catherine all her life. She had to have heavenly aid to turn them aside so often and so well. Indeed the fact that she managed to go along so placid and serene, seemingly unconcerned, demonstrates a great trust in the power of Heaven to protect her. It was not herself that she had to fear, for she had the shields of a strong will and a deep humility. Her danger lay from others, and she had to rely on Heaven to divert their thoughts and stop their mouths or, in the breach, to give her the means of baffling them.

As is so often the case, it would seem that Catherine was most often betrayed by well-meaning persons, persons who truly admired her and wished her well. The chief culprits seem to be Sister Séjole, her one close friend, and Father Etienne.

Sister Séjole will be remembered as the young Assistant at Châtillon who perceived from the first the greatness of Catherine's soul and urged the Superior to accept her as a postulant. When it became known that the Blessed Virgin had appeared to one of the novices, Sister Séjole exclaimed:

"If it is true, it must be Sister Labouré. That child is destined to receive the greatest graces from Heaven."

Sister Séjole always held this conviction and, although she never questioned Catherine about the Apparitions, she lost no opportunity, when in Paris, to visit her. What is more to the point, she urged others to do the same.

"Later on, when they speak of her who saw the Blessed Virgin," she told them, "you will be happy to have known this beautiful soul, living such an ordinary life and keeping herself hidden behind her duties." This is but one example of what was a practice with Sister Séjole.

Father Villette, Procurator General at the time of the Ordinary Process in the opening years of the present century, states boldly in his deposition that "if at the end of Sister Catherine's life, only a few persons doubted that she was the Sister favored with the Apparitions, it was because Father Aladel and Father Etienne, Superior General of the Sisters of Charity and confidant of Father Aladel, departed a little from the silence they had guarded up until this time."

Issue can be taken with Father Villette on two points: it is certain that Catherine's identity was not so widely known, even at the end of her life, as Father Villette indicates; and it would seem that Father Aladel must be exonerated of the charge that he had broken faith with his penitent. To begin with, Father Aladel died in 1865, eleven years before Catherine, and therefore was not alive to depart from his customary silence, even a little, "at the end of Sister Catherine's life." Furthermore, there can be found no slightest trace of evidence that Father Aladel ever revealed Catherine's identity to anyone, except perhaps to Father Etienne and, as shall be seen, this can be justified.

Father Villette is right, however, in saying that Father Etienne revealed Sister Catherine's identity, at least by indirection, to Sister Dufès when he sent her to the house at Enghien as Superior in 1860.

Aside from working closely with Father Aladel in the affairs of the Community, Father Etienne was his most intimate friend. However, it would be most unjust to Father Aladel to suggest that it was through their friendship that Father Etienne came to know that Catherine was the Sister of the visions. It would be wholly wicked to suggest that so good a priest as Father Aladel would have sacrificed a priestly confidence to friendship.

The more sensible explanation of Father Etienne's knowledge is that he was told the identity of the Sister, with her permission, because of the nature of the offices he held in the

Community. We have, in fact, the evidence of Father Chevalier and Father Chinchon, both confessors of the saint in their turn, of Father Villette and others that Father Aladel did at some time during Catherine's life reveal her identity to Father Etienne. Further, there is found among Catherine's writings, in her own hand, a casual reference to a conversation that she had with Father Etienne concerning certain specific requests of the Blessed Virgin, and the whole tone of the reference indicates that this was not the first such conversation.

As both Procurator General and Superior General, Etienne was of the first rank in the hierarchy of both the Vincentian Fathers and Sisters of Charity. Added to this, the Double Family of St. Vincent was under process of reformation at the time, and this reformation stemmed directly from the admonitions of Our Lady given during the Apparition of July 18, 1830 and through interior communications granted Sister Catherine at various times in the years that followed it.

When Father Etienne was elected Superior General in 1843, he set about initiating so faithfully and energetically the reform demanded by Our Lady that he earned the title of second founder of the Double Family. The reform was not a work of days, or even months, but of years, and throughout the years Catherine continued to convey the express wishes of the Blessed Virgin to her Superiors. Sometimes she sent these messages through Father Aladel, who had been elected Third Assistant to the Superior General in 1834 and Director of the Sisters in 1846, but it is conceivable that she also at times delivered her messages to Father Etienne in person; indeed, on the strength of the written memorandum found among her papers, it is practically certain.

There is every indication, therefore, that Father Etienne came by his knowledge of Sister Catherine legitimately and with justification. There can be no quarrel with him, or with Father Aladel, on this point. Fault can be found only with the

fact that he passed his knowledge on. It may be argued that
the Superior General would have felt himself justified in iden-
tifying Sister Catherine to Sister Dufès since the latter was to
be Catherine's Superior, but at the same time the necessity of
doing so can be justly questioned. None of Catherine's previ-
ous Superiors seems to have known she was the Sister of the
Apparitions, nor does there seem to have been any particular
inconvenience to anyone because of the lack of this knowledge. Moreover, Catherine was strongly insistent upon remaining unknown, even to her Superiors.

This is the only occasion of which we have definite knowledge of Father Étienne's breaking silence. There may have
been others; but a secret needs to be let out only once in order
for it to spread.

At any rate, whether through Sister Séjole or Father Etienne or the guesses and deductions of the Sisters themselves,
there was a steady undercurrent of rumors to the effect that
Sister Catherine Labouré was the one favored by Our Lady.
The remarkable thing, remarkable enough to indicate the
protection of Heaven in the matter, was that the rumors never
got out of hand. Although they persisted for years, they never
seem to have been taken very seriously.

Sister Henriot, for example, told the Tribunal of Beatification:

"I entered the house of Reuilly in 1861 as an 'orphan.'
[She was twenty-one years old at the time!] Several times my
companions, pointing out Sister Catherine, said to me: 'There
is the Sister who saw the Blessed Virgin.' *I must say that we
did not attach great importance to these words.*"

Sister Tanguy, sent to Enghien in 1863, was told she was
going to the house of the Seer of the Medal, but she, too,
testified that the information made no great impression on her.

Even more remarkable, Catherine prophesied many events
in her lifetime, and her prophecies all came true, yet no one

seems to have been particularly struck by her miraculous gifts.

There are many examples of the dexterity with which Catherine avoided the pitfalls laid for her, examples revealing her consummate prudence.

At times Catherine adopted the simple expedient of ignoring the questions put to her.

The Sister pharmacist at Reuilly used often to cross the hall from the pharmacy to the portress's lodge to say her chaplet with Catherine. There was an uncommonly ugly statue of Our Lady in the portress's lodge and one day the pharmacist thought to use it as bait in drawing out Catherine.

"Don't you think, Sister Catherine, when the Blessed Virgin appeared to one of our Sisters, as they say, she could not have been as homely as that?"

Catherine smiled, but never answered her.

On another occasion, a young Sister who was showing a gentleman and a lady through the convent saw Catherine approaching down the corridor.

"Here comes the Sister who had the vision," she whispered to her visitors.

Much to her dismay, the gentleman immediately went up to Catherine with outstretched hand.

"Oh, Sister," he cried, "how happy I am to meet the Sister of the Medal!" Sister Catherine merely simulated surprise. The young Sister, sorely embarrassed, rushed to make her apologies to Catherine when the visitors had gone.

"They told me in the seminary that it was the Sister of the poultry yard at Enghien who had seen the Blessed Virgin," she explained, "and I repeated it."

Catherine was very good about it. "Little one, you shouldn't speak out at random like that," was all she said.

When she felt the circumstances warranted it she could be curt, especially in the case of those who took for granted that their assumptions were wholly valid. Two postulants were leaving Enghien to make their seminary at the Motherhouse, and they induced one of the Sisters to take them to Sister Catherine before they left. They found her at recreation in the garden, close by a statue of Our Lady. The scene was well set for their desires.

"Go quickly now," the Sister said, pushing them forward, "for you know that Sister Catherine hates to waste time."

The girls ran and threw themselves on their knees before the astonished Catherine.

"We are leaving for the seminary, Sister; tell us something of the Blessed Virgin."

"Mademoiselles, make your seminary well," Catherine replied. That was all.

And there is always the resolute character with the direct approach, who rides roughshod over all convention and human feeling. One day a Sister came expressly to seek Catherine out. Sister Dufès summoned Sister Henriot, the former "orphan" now back at Enghien as a professed Sister, to conduct the visitor to Catherine. They came upon the saint hard at work.

"Did you postulate at Châtillon?" the visitor asked abruptly, without introduction.

"Yes," Catherine answered mildly.

"In what year and during what months?"

Catherine told her. And then the broadside:

"Are you the Sister favored with the visions of Our Lady?"

Catherine bent to her work, without deigning a reply.

Sister Catherine was not the only one constantly on her guard. Father Aladel had to step carefully, too. Once, when he was visiting a certain Community house in Paris, the Sisters crowded around him, begging for a "first-hand" account of the Apparitions. He was about to launch into his story when his eye caught Catherine among the Sisters. He flushed and stammered. Then he became frightened for fear his embarrassment had been noticed and would be rightly taken as a sign that the Sister of the Apparitions was present. Swiftly he breathed a prayer to Mary for help. To his amazement Catherine was smiling and pressing him with questions along with the others, as if she had never heard the tale before. He carried on easily from there.

Some years later Father Aladel found himself in a situation even more perilous to the secret. When the paintings of the Apparitions commissioned from the artist LeCerf were completed and hung in the Motherhouse, Father Aladel was anxious for Catherine to see them, not alone from reasons of sentiment, but in order to check on their authenticity. He arranged to meet her casually in the hall where the pictures hung. While examining the pictures, they were surprised by a certain Sister who advanced upon them like a schoolmistress who has caught the culprits she was laying for. Seemingly certain of her quarry, the Sister rather brutally ignored Catherine and threw her triumphant statement at the priest:

"This must be the Sister of the Apparitions."

Although startled, Father Aladel was sure of himself and of Catherine this time.

"Tell her, Sister," he said.

Catherine merely laughed, as if the idea were completely ridiculous.

"Oh, I see she is not," the baffled Sister said, "or you would not have told her to answer."

And so it went, the guarding of the secret, through the years, almost like a game with its set of rules for ducking and dodging and stepping aside. Catherine acquired a great facility at it as time went on; indeed, she would hardly have been human had she not found a certain enjoyment in the cat-and-mouse contest. While the well-timed smile or laugh or shrug of the shoulders was all-important in turning aside her pursuers, it is hard not to see in them flashes of her country wit and the human satisfaction that, in this serious guessing game, she held the key.

It was in a sense a lifework to guard her secret, but she was willing to endanger even this in the interest of the truth.

In the last year of her life, Catherine sat sewing at recreation, listening to the small talk but saying little herself, as was her wont, when suddenly she was shocked to hear one of the young Sisters advance, in scoffing tone, the opinion that the Sister who saw Our Lady saw only a picture.

Swiftly Catherine raised her head and fixed the thoughtless Sister with stern, compelling eyes.

"Sister," she said slowly and clearly and in a tone of voice that caused everyone to turn and listen, "the Sister who saw the Blessed Virgin, saw her in flesh and bone, even as you and I see each other now."

XVI

The Commune and Communists

ON MAY 1, 1860, Catherine celebrated the twenty-fifth anniversary of her vows. There was no great to-do over the event, for she was not an important personage in the eyes of men, but there would be the little intimate celebration in the bosom of her Sisters, with the feast-day dinner and the presentation of holy cards and homely gifts. She was fifty-four years old now, a senior Sister in the house, revered and respected by all the rest. At recreation, she took her place by the side of the Superior, intent on her sewing, saying very little unless she were spoken to. Once, one of the Sisters teased her about her quietness.

"Sister Catherine, you sit sewing and say nothing."

"Why should I say anything," Catherine replied, smiling, "I know nothing."

Catherine took advantage of her age, now, to admonish the younger Sisters gently, in the way of teaching them lessons of holiness.

"My little ones," she would say, "do not murmur, do not

seek to turn aside from the orders of our Superiors, for they represent God."

The same spirit of faith she exercised toward Superiors, she exercised as well toward public events. "Let us allow the good God to work," was her credo. "He knows better than we what is needed."

Catherine was shocked one day to notice a young Sister saying her beads, while she carefully examined the pictures on the wall. As gently as she could, but with the Labouré firmness, she reminded the Sister that she should always say her beads with fervor. Lack of fervor in saying the chaplet, according to Catherine, was one of the things Our Lady had complained of. Catherine herself always said her beads with great reverence, pronouncing the words slowly.

"Be calm, do not be so disturbed," was her advice to one of the children of the house. It was advice she herself followed faithfully. Not that she was never upset, indeed extremely so, at times; but she always took immediate steps to repress any agitation of soul. "Come to the foot of the altar," Our Lady had said. In taking this invitation literally to heart, Catherine always found solace and peace for her soul.

In 1860, Sister Jeanne Dufès was appointed Superior of the houses of Reuilly and Enghien. Her arrival marked the last phase of Catherine's life, a period of sixteen years during which Catherine's soul was to receive its final, rigorous purification—a purification to which Sister Dufès contributed often—and during which the threads of Catherine's life were to be gathered together and neatly tied before her holy and peaceful death.

Sister Dufès was born on May 24, 1823, in the little village of St. Victor de Malcap, not far from Nîmes. She entered the community in 1839, and was, thus, only thirty-seven years old when she was placed over Catherine Labouré in 1860.

Sister Dufès was to prove the perfect wheel upon which

every last vestige of self-love and self-will in Catherine—and traces of both remained until the end—was to be broken. From their first encounter, these two women felt a natural antipathy to each other. The basis of it lay in the fact that they were very much alike. Both were practical, competent women of irascible temperament. Sister Dufès put it very well when she said, quite humbly:

"There is this difference between Sister Catherine and myself that, while we are both very quick, she conquers her quickness at once, but with me it is hard and long." Should Catherine bristle when crossed by the little difficulties of the common life, Sister Dufès would say, in the peasant idiom: "*C'est la soupe au lait,*" which means roughly: "She is as hot, or quick-tempered, as milk-soup"; but would immediately add, rather wistfully:

"I do not know how she is able on the instant to capture such absolute calm."

Sister Dufès has testified that, from the time she entered the Community, she had heard of Sister Catherine Labouré, and that some connected her with the Apparitions of 1830. When Father Etienne appointed her as Superior in 1860, he told her: "I am sending you into the house of Sister Catherine Labouré, where she leads a hidden life." It could very well be that the vague adulation of Sister Catherine in certain quarters had unconsciously prejudiced Sister Dufès against her, so that, when she was appointed as Catherine's Superior, she was determined to keep the saint in her place.

Whatever the reason, Sister Dufès neglected Catherine from the first. It was a new experience for Catherine, who, as custodian of the aged inmates of Enghien, had been virtual Superior of that house. Sister Dufès's neglect became even more apparent when Sister Tanguy was appointed Assistant Superior and took over the Enghien house in 1874. In the intervening years Catherine remained in charge of Enghien but Sister

Dufès showed small interest and smaller appreciation of what she did.

Sister Desmoulins, who was a close friend of Sister Dufès, testified on this point:

"I recall that her [Catherine's] last Superior, Sister Dufès, told me: 'It is a unique thing, that I never felt drawn to avail myself of Sister Catherine. I never asked a service of her. I liked her well enough, but I left her in her corner.' "

Sister Desmoulins went on to proffer an explanation:

"Sister Dufès and I came to the conclusion that Sister Catherine must have asked of God that she be treated so, and that God had granted this request as He granted her others.

"Sister Dufès had great intelligence, spirit of organization and exceptional *savoir faire*. She was accustomed to make the fullest use of all her subjects, even the mediocre ones.

"It is impossible, therefore, that, without the express will of God of which she was a worthy instrument, she should do as the former Superiors and leave Sister Catherine in the works she had always performed, when without a doubt she was capable of rendering more important services to the Community."

It may very well be as Sister Desmoulins said, that God had ordered things so. At the same time, both she and Sister Dufès would seem to be too quick to shift the blame for the latter's neglect of Catherine on to God. It must be remembered that all this was hindsight, manufactured after Catherine's death when everyone was acclaiming her.

As a matter of fact, Catherine's capabilities were quite obvious to the other Sisters of the house. One Sister has stated bluntly, in referring to Catherine's talent for housekeeping: "She was even more competent than our Superior." Even complete strangers were impressed by Catherine. A visiting Sister, meeting her for the first time, was so struck by her dignity and simplicity that the thought came to her, significantly enough, that Sister Catherine was perhaps not in her rightful place and was capable of filling a higher position in the Community. This Sister even asked the saint whether she was bored with what she was doing. Catherine answered:

"One is never bored with doing the Will of God."

The major Superiors, who saw Catherine only from time to time, seemed to have had a truer picture of her than Sister Dufès had. Mother Devos, then Mother General of the Community, summoned Catherine one day in 1870, and told her that she was being considered for a Superior's post. Catherine became very upset at the news, and protested her unworthiness and lack of ability. At length, her protestations prevailed, and Catherine finished the story by saying:

"And she sent me back to Enghien," in a tone that implied: "And she did the proper thing!"

It was bad enough for Sister Dufès to neglect Catherine, but she took to reprimanding her beyond her deserts, and, what is against the spirit of the rule, in the presence of others.

"She was sometimes reprimanded by the Superior, severely, and for things of trivial importance," Sister Cosnard testified. "I felt bound to tell Sister Dufès my astonishment at seeing her scold a venerable Sister so vehemently for the smallest things.

" 'Let me be,' she replied, 'I feel compelled to do it.'

"On the occasion I refer to, Sister Catherine knelt at the feet of Sister Dufès, humbly and without saying a word."

Sister Cosnard added that, at the time, she was struck by Sister Dufès's asserting that she felt compelled to give these reprimands. It would seem that Sister Dufès herself recognized the injustice of them, and the theory that Heaven forced her to these severe measures for the good of Catherine's soul cannot be discounted. At the same time, the question may be justly raised, how much may be attributed to the Will of God, and how much to Sister Dufès's temper.

Sister Charvier bolstered the testimony of Sister Cosnard:

"I must say that Catherine's Superior humiliated her more than once; we were sure that she received these mortifications of self-love in silence and that she never showed anything but respect and devotion to this Superior [Sister Dufès].

"Several times I observed Sister Catherine, after having been humiliated before several of us, go to the chapel, then return to knock at the door of the Sister Superior, and ask some permission or other.

" 'Sister,' she would say in a very pleasant tone, 'would you be good enough to grant me such a permission?'

"I felt that she did this to show the Sister Superior that she bore no grudge because of the reprimand she had received. I was always edified."

At the first inquiry into Catherine's virtues, Sister Dufès had forgotten her treatment of Catherine, for she testified that she had never had the least occasion to reprimand her.

During recreation one day a young Sister expressed an opinion which Catherine contradicted.

"I notice that you hold your own opinion most emphatically," the Superior said to her, laughingly.

Immediately Catherine got painfully to her knees and begged pardon before all.

"I am nothing but a haughty woman," she said.

The sight of this old Sister humiliating herself brought tears to the eyes of her companions.

At the Wednesday conference, when it was the custom for each Sister to accuse herself of some fault in the little chapter ceremony common to all religious communities, Catherine almost always accused herself of the same thing:

"I accuse myself of having failed several times to make acts of the Presence of God." According to the rule, the Sisters were to recite a set prayer each hour at the striking of the clock. It was her occasional failure to do this that Catherine confessed.

In 1863, a terrible fire broke out in the paper and paint factory which was next door to the Reuilly orphanage. The contents of the building were, of course, highly combustible and huge flames shot into the air. The Sisters' house was in great danger; flames actually licked at the roof, and it seemed impossible that the house should escape. The Sisters and children milled around in confusion. Catherine alone was calm.

"Don't be frightened," she said, "it will stop."

In spite of all human prevision, the Sisters' house was spared.

Across the sea, America was in the throes of the terrible Civil War, and, hearing of the carnage made all the more frightful because brother was killing brother, Catherine must have realized more and more the devastating truth of Mary's prophecy that "The whole world will be in sadness."

The year 1865 brought a profound change in Catherine's life, with the sudden death of Father Aladel.

On Sunday, April 23, Father Aladel gave his last conference to the Sisters at rue du Bac. It was a conference strangely prophetic, in the light of what was to happen. He chose his text from the Epistle of St. Paul to the Hebrews, Chapter XIII, verse 7: "Remember your superiors who spoke to you the word of God." The very next sentence in the text reads: "Consider how they ended their lives, and imitate their faith." Actually, the priest spoke not of himself, but of the Blessed Virgin and St. Vincent. The conference itself was a summing up of the glorious events which had cast their greatness over his own life, for he spoke at length of the visions of the heart of St. Vincent and of the promises Our Lady had made, both to the Community and to individuals.

He finished in these words:

"Everything has been given us by Mary Immaculate. To her we owe our vocation, our progress, our perseverance. Every good has come to us with her love, and on our last day when, after the *Consummatum Est* of our final sufferings, our

soul shall quit the body which held it captive, if our blessed
father St. Vincent finds in us a great spirit of faith, a great
charity, a tender love for the Immaculate Virgin, he will present us to her, and Mary Immaculate, leading us to Jesus, the
divine Spouse of pure and devout souls, will give us the dia-
dem of a glorious immortality."

At the end of this last conference, the director's voice grew
so weak that his final words were lost to his hearers. The next
day, he was at his desk as usual. Toward evening, disquieting
news reached Paris. Father Etienne, in Dax to bless a monu-
ment to St. Vincent, had been stricken and was in critical
condition. The news was a sore blow to Father Aladel, for,
aside from the universal veneration he shared with the Community for a beloved Superior General, Father Etienne was
his closest personal friend. His pain was the deeper because
the General was hundreds of miles away and Father Aladel
could not hope to go to his side. From certain words that
escaped him, later reported by the Mother General of the
Sisters, who was with him when the news came, it would seem
that on the spot Father Aladel offered his own life to God in
exchange for the life of his friend. It was a curious repetition
of history. Vincent de Paul had fallen gravely ill some twenty
years before his death, and a young confrère, M. Dufour by
name, had offered his life for the saint's and God had accepted
the bargain. He was to accept this one also.

The next morning, Father Aladel rose with the Community
at four o'clock, dressed, and was leaving his room to go to the
Community meditation, when he suffered a stroke and fell to
the floor, unconscious. He died that afternoon at two o'clock.
It was April 25, 1865, the thirty-fifth anniversary of the
Translation of St. Vincent's relics and of the first miraculous
vision of Catherine Labouré. Father Etienne passed through
the crisis of his illness and recovered to rule the Community
for nine more years.

Father Aladel's funeral was held on Thursday. Father Meugniot, Catherine's nephew, relates a curious incident that took place, respecting his aunt.

"It was at the burial of Father Aladel, during the first years of my vocation as a missioner. I had the office of thurifer. At the cemetery, in turning around to carry out a certain function, my gaze fell on Sister Catherine who was in the first row with her Superior. I was struck by the radiance of her face. I could not understand it. Reflecting today upon the circumstances of this death [Father Aladel's], upon the thoughts which must have occupied Sister Catherine at this moment, I cannot doubt that her show of happiness was the result of recalling the rapport she had had with the venerable dead."

Catherine's rapport with Father Aladel had not always been a relationship of joy. Often it had been stormy and painful. Nevertheless, out of it had come major fulfillment: the spread of devotion to the Miraculous Medal, the Children of Mary, the reform of the Double Family of St. Vincent, Catherine's own growth in sanctity. She had every reason to be happy that this co-worker in the things of Mary had come to his reward. She had not heard the last conference of this good priest, but surely a conference so prophetic had been spoken of and had come to her ears. She would have no difficulty in seeing in her mind's eye the soul of her director conducted by St. Vincent to Our Lady and to the throne of Jesus Christ: she and Father Aladel had spoken of these three great Personages many times. Was her knowledge of his beatitude more sure than that? Several days after the death of St. Jane Frances de Chantal, Vincent de Paul, who had been her director, saw the soul of the saint join that of St. Francis de Sales and the two of them absorbed into the bosom of God. Was the radiance of Catherine's face an outward sign of some interior certainty such as this? Did she actually see her director in glory?

In 1865, also, Catherine made a prediction concerning her beloved old men.

"We shall leave Enghien," she said one day to Sister Cosnard.

"Who told you that?" asked the Sister in astonishment.

Catherine made no direct reply, but her face lighted up, and gazing into space, she continued:

"Yes, I see a grand château, and written over the doorway the words 'Hospice d'Enghien.' " She repeated it several times. She went on to say that the château was situated near running water, and that the old men would be transferred there, and would be dressed in uniforms.

It all came about as she said—in 1896, twenty years after her death. The Orleans family, who were the patrons of Enghien, decided to turn over their ancestral home to their old servants, who had resided for many years at Enghien. The château was grand and impressive and sat in a beautiful landscape on the banks of the Loire. When the old men and the Sisters were moved there in 1896, it was decided that henceforth the men should dress in blue uniforms. Over the door was placed the inscription *Hospice d'Enghien-Orleans,* just as Catherine had seen it. What distinguishes this supernatural knowledge of Catherine's from the other visions and prophecies is the fact that, in this case, she *saw* a future event. The letters she read to Sister Cosnard in 1865 were not erected until 1896.

Politically, conditions in France were extremely restless and the pot that would boil over in the miserable events of 1870–71—and Catherine Labouré would be in the thick of them—was already on the stove. At the close of 1848, Louis Napoléon had been elected President of the Second Republic. He had nailed down his position by the incredible *coup d'etat* of December 1851, in which the French people, by plebiscite, gave into his hand the drafting of a constitution. A second *coup d'etat* in December 1852, made him, again by popular vote, Emperor of the Second French Empire. The honeymoon lasted until 1860: peace reigned and the prestige and popularity of Napoléon III waxed strong. Then the people began to see through this astute politician. The next ten years were years of one desperate gamble after another on the part of Louis Napoléon to regain his popularity and establish a firm Bonaparte dynasty. Unfortunately for him, they were also years when Prussia was on the rise, and Prince Otto von Bismarck had dreams of empire himself. In the last years of the decade the ambitions of both were at stake. The fight came in the Franco-Prussian War of 1870, and Louis Napoléon lost.

It was a humiliating day for France when the German troops occupied Paris and King Wilhelm of Prussia was declared German Emperor in the Palace of Versailles. The city had gone through a long seige and the people had frozen and starved by turns and sometimes both together. True to tradition, the Sisters of Charity had nursed and fed them and given them blankets to shut out the cold. The Houses of Reuilly and Enghien had done their share.

The Third French Republic, which had taken over after the fall of Louis Napoléon in September 1870, had a shaky hold at best on the reins of government. Divided inwardly, it was forced to fight an outward enemy in the vicious revolution which exploded on March 18, and which called itself the *Commune* of Paris. The men of the *Commune* were the dregs, not only of France, but of Italy, Germany, Russia, and America. Paris had become the rendezvous of all wickedness. While many historians hold that these men were not Communists, as we know the word today—pointing out that *communes* were the names given to the districts of Paris—there can be little doubt that Karl Marx, Pierre Proudhon, and other anarchists had tremendous influence over this mob. Carleton Hayes, the eminent historian, has testified that half the mob were direct descendants of the bourgeois Radicals of 1793, while the other was divided equally among the followers of Marx and the Anarchist disciples of Proudhon. M. Bourgoin, in an official finding of the Third French Republic commission, instituted after the uprising had been put down, stated: "It appears to me that three elements impeded the national defense from the very beginning and finally prepared the events of March 18. These three elements were the Masonic Lodges of Paris, the Socialists, known as Positivists, and the International." It is also significant that Marx had been in France during the Revolution of 1830 and 1848, to study these uprisings at first hand. As a matter of fact, the revolutionists were popularly known as "Reds" (*Les Rouges*), from the red sash they wore as a badge, and it is stated in the *Annales de la Congregation de la Mission* for 1871 that Paris was "in the grip of a secret society known as the International."

Whatever the differences of ideology among the parties that united in this violent and lawless *Commune* of 1871, there can be no doubt that the spirit of communism permeated the union. Catherine Labouré was thus the first saint in modern times to be caught up in a Communist rebellion.

The sympathies of the French people were not anti-Catholic in 1871 any more than they had been in 1848, but the ideologies of the group behind the *Commune* included hatred of religion. Before the terrible weeks were over, the churches of Paris would be desecrated, profanation of things sacred would be a commonplace, the clergy would be arrested by the dozen, and thirty priests, including the Archbishop would die.

This time the houses of Reuilly and Enghien were plunged into the maelstrom. That they emerged unscathed was due to the personal protection of the Mother of God, a protection she had promised forty years before.

On a day shortly after the outbreak of the *Commune*, the Sisters were at recreation in the community room. Sister Catherine, who sat in her accustomed place beside Sister Dufès, turned to the Superior and said:

"I had a dream last night."

"What was it?" Sister Dufès asked.

"I dreamed that the Blessed Virgin came to the Community room, looking for you. You were not here. She then went to your cell, but you were not there either. She seated herself in your chair, and said to me: 'Tell Sister Dufès that she will have to leave, but that I will guard her house. She will go to the Midi with Sister Claire, and she will return on May 31.'"

The effect of this news was something less than sensational: no one paid any attention to it, least of all Sister Dufès, and, having accorded Sister Catherine the hearing that common politeness demanded, everyone returned to her own conversation.

Meeting Sister Dufès by chance the next day, Catherine ventured to say to her:

"Do not pay too much attention to what I told you yesterday, Sister. It was a dream."

"Don't worry, Sister Catherine," the Superior replied, airily, "I never gave it a second thought."

Scarcely two weeks later, on Good Friday, April 7, the Sisters of Reuilly and Enghien came to grips with the *Commune*. Two gendarmes, loyal to the government and cut off from their companions, thought to hide out in a detachment of national guardsmen who had espoused the cause of the Revolution and had set up a medical supply station in the rue de Reuilly, not far from the Sisters' house. An informer, learning their identity, went to headquarters to denounce them. The frightened men fled to the Sisters for protection. Hot on their trail, a detachment of Communists demanded entrance to the orphanage, and even laid violent hands on Sister Dufès when she blocked their path. There had not been time to hide the gendarmes, so they were easily taken.

The forceful character of Sister Dufès now showed itself in an admirable courage. Knowing that the poor gendarmes would be summarily shot, she followed their captors to the medical station and pleaded for their lives, pointing out that they had done nothing against the interests of the people, but had only cared for the sick and wounded. Her defense was telling, for the Communist chief released the men in her custody, after she had promised to be responsible for them.

Two days later, on Easter Sunday, repenting of their good deed, the Communists were back at Reuilly, an aroused mob at their heels, demanding the return of the prisoners. Sister Dufès refused to hand them over, and a violent scene ensued. In the midst of the shouting and recriminations, one of the Sisters of the house recognized in the crowd a man of the neighborhood whom she had fed, together with his family, during the months when the Germans had besieged the city. The tongue-lashing she gave the man for his ingratitude did nothing to soothe the heated tempers of the Communists. They finally forced their way into the house and made a thorough search for the men. This time, however, the delaying tactics of the Sisters had given the gendarmes time to hide. One of them had taken refuge among Catherine's old men and climbed into a bed in the dormitory. By a stroke of miraculous luck, the searchers passed him by with scarcely a glance. Father Chinchon, successor to Father Aladel as confessor to the house, had returned to the Motherhouse not long before the Communists arrived, but his companion, a subdeacon, had been left behind. With true feminine ingenuity, the Sisters had provided him with an old pair of trousers and a blouse, and a cap to cover his tonsure; a large loaf of bread which they thrust under his arm was the crowning touch, and thus disguised as a workingman come to the Sisters for food for his family, the young cleric passed through the mob.

Thoroughly enraged at not finding their quarry, the Communists turned on the Sisters, and their chief ordered Sister Dufès seized as a hostage. Immediately the forty Sisters of the house, Catherine among them, surrounded their Superior.

"We shall go with her," they said. The chief had not been prepared for this; it was one thing to take a lone Sister into custody; to take forty of them was quite another matter. Throwing up his hands in exasperation, he cried:

"What shall I do with these frightened swallows!" referring to their huge headdresses, which fluttered and bobbed in the gleam of the torches. If they were frightened—and they would scarcely have been human if they were not—their words and actions did not show it. In an attempt to recover his prestige as he led his band of cut-throats away, the Communist chief called back:

"You will hear more of me tomorrow."

The encounter had lasted several hours, and it was now ten o'clock at night. Fearing the Communists might return the next day to carry out their threat against the Superior, the Sisters prevailed on Sister Dufès to leave for Versailles the next morning at 11 o'clock. She took Sister Tanguy with her. Throughout the next week, Sister Dufès worried over the welfare of the Sisters left behind. At length she sent Sister Tanguy back to Paris, requesting that Sister Claire be sent in her stead. When Sister Claire arrived she and the Sister Superior went into temporary exile in the Midi, exactly as Catherine had said she would in her account of the dream of Our Lady. The strangest thing about these troubled days was that no one remembered Catherine's prophecy.

The days of harassment were not over for the Sisters of Reuilly and Enghien. Two women arrived one day, dispatched by the Communists to "replace the Sisters." The revolutionaries were evidently having their little joke: how could two women replace forty? After a carefully polite argument, the women left and were not seen again. It was a bit of comic relief, but the poor Sisters were not in the mood for jokes.

On the evening of April 23, Father Mailly, from the Vincentian Motherhouse, went to see how the Sisters were faring. He discovered that Catherine and her companions in the Hospice d'Enghien had been separated from the Sisters of Reuilly and had not had Mass or Communion for two weeks. He heard their confessions and promised to return and say Mass for them the next morning. The deprivation of these essentials of Catholic life must have been a sore trial to the Sisters and have caused a special anguish in the soul of one so holy as Catherine. Father Mailly came back the next morning, disguised as an itinerant painter, with his cassock concealed in a package under his arm, and the Sisters possessed their Blessed Lord once more. He had barely left when a band of Communists arrived "to search the house," an annoyance they had inflicted upon the Sisters with regularity since the departure of Sister Dufès. On these occasions, it was Catherine who had to meet and expostulate with the revolutionaries. In the absence of the Superior, the responsibility of the house was hers. On one occasion she was actually taken into custody and subjected to an interrogation at Communist headquarters. She answered firmly and calmly. Throughout all these trying days, in fact, she never departed in the least from her customary calm, and the Sisters clung to her as their tower of strength. Though all others had forgotten, she knew that Our Lady was guarding the house, so that nothing could happen to any of them. Catherine even pursued her apostolate of the Medal among the Communists, and many of them, seeing the Medals she had given their companions, asked for medals themselves.

When the Communists came on April 24, the Sisters were engaged in dispensing food and clothing which the people of England had sent for the relief of the poor. More than two hundred women were queued up in the street outside the house. The Communists decided to commandeer the supplies for their own uses.

"You must tell the women what you are doing, sir," warned the Sisters, "for they will tear out our eyes if they are forced to go home empty-handed."

The words were hardly spoken when the women, sensing what was taking place, advanced on the Communists in a menacing mob, shouting curses and threats. The chief hurriedly summoned the national guard billeted nearby, but the guardsmen lived in the neighborhood and were unwilling to antagonize their friends and acquaintances. Admitting defeat, the Communists returned the supplies, and watched in amazement as the Sisters quickly restored order and went on with their work of mercy.

Not many days after, the Communists returned, this time to stay. They occupied the first floor of the house and ordered the Sisters upstairs. Before complying, the Sisters hurriedly removed the ciborium from the Tabernacle and took it with them. Several days and nights of horror followed. The nerves of the Sisters grew taut with fear as the hours slowly went by. Downstairs they could hear the Communists stomping about in their hobnailed boots, barking orders, quarreling with one another, laughing uproariously. From outside came the ceaseless boom of cannon and rattle of gunfire, now near, now farther away, as the struggle for control of the capital surged back and forth. The nights were worst of all, for the men took to drinking, and their voices became louder and rougher, and all sorts of obscene language and filthy humor assailed the ears of the poor Sisters. Catherine's serene courage never wavered and she spent the long hours calming the others, leading them in prayer, reminding them that God and Our Lady would protect them. The one great fear in the minds of all the Sisters was that, during their drinking bouts, the Communists would remember the women upstairs and break in to force themselves upon them. The night came when it seemed this fear would be realized. The revolutionists had drunk more than usual and were particularly loud and raucous. At length there was a muffled shout, and a noisy scramble for the stairs leading to the room where the Sisters were huddled together. Hurriedly the good women distributed the Sacred Hosts among themselves and consumed them, so that the Blessed Sacrament, at least, would not be profaned. Then they turned to meet the rabble.

The leader hammered loudly on the door, demanding that it be opened. At the sight of the Sisters, standing calm and unflinching in their path, the Communists fell silent. The blue eyes that had looked on the Mother of God blazed at them, and their own drunken gaze faltered. With an oath, and an amazing about-face, the leader turned on his companions.

"These ladies are under my protection," he cried. "I will throw myself across this doorway; to reach them you will have to kill me first!" The heroics were not needed. The announcement was excuse enough for the shamefaced men to retreat, and they fell all over themselves getting down the stairs.

The Sisters were safe for the moment, but they well knew that they might not be so fortunate the next time. Therefore they resolved to quit the house. Next morning they took their leave, traveling in small groups so as not to attract undue attention. Sister Catherine and Sister Tanguy were the last to go. It is not clear what became of the children and the old men during the few weeks the Sisters were gone. Apparently the Communists had provided for them in some rude way before the Sisters were imprisoned in the house. Certainly the Sisters, and Catherine least of all, would not have abandoned them. The two Sisters, the old and the young—Catherine was sixty-five, Sister Tanguy thirty-four—gathered together a few belongings and started for the door. They were not to leave, however, without a final insult. The Communist sentry demanded that they open their parcels. Kicking Catherine's few clothes about with his foot, the guard uncovered a little circlet of gilt metal. It was the crown from Our Lady's statue in the chapel. In removing it, Catherine had promised the Mother of God that she would return to crown her before the Month of May was gone. Satisfied that the trinket was of no value, the guard ordered the Sisters to gather up their scattered effects and be off. Catherine's control was magnificent. She might have felt justified in giving vent to her natural feelings in order to rebuke wickedness, but, although the gorge of anger must have risen fiercely in her, she held her tongue.

An omnibus took the refugees out of the city. On all sides they were insulted. Stones were hurled at the bus when roving bands of rebels caught sight of the white cornettes. Mothers even taught their children to call them coarse names.

It was dark when the weary travelers reached Saint-Denis, the burial place of the old Kings of France. The Superior of the Sisters' house there, rather stuffily in a time of such crisis, held to the rule that only one traveling Sister could be received, and offered Sister Catherine hospitality, as the older. Catherine, with her large charity and common sense, would not forsake her companion, and the two of them went on further to Boulainvilliers, where Sister Mettavent took them in.

From Boulainvilliers Catherine wrote a long letter to Sister Dufès—the length of the letter was a feat in itself for Catherine, who wrote so laboriously—reminding her again that the Sisters would be back at Reuilly and Enghien by May 31.

At this moment, Father Chinchon, who had gone to Dax to prepare the Vincentian seminarians for a return to Paris once hostilities ceased, was reading a prophecy to the young men, made by a Sister of Charity forty years before. According to this prophecy, he told them, the church's troubles were not over yet: "Monseigneur Darboy, the Archbishop of Paris, will die a violent death."

Back in Paris, the entire prophecy was coming to a final,

flaring fulfillment. On Ascension Thursday, May 18, a mob broke into the church of Notre-Dame-des-Victoires, so intimately connected with the Miraculous Medal, and perpetrated terrible sacrileges. Even the graves were pried open. The remains of the saintly Father Desgenette were scattered over the pavement, and his head paraded around on a pike. When Catherine heard this sickening news, her brow darkened and her lips tightened in the familiar way:

"They have touched Our Lady," she said. "They will go no farther." Did Catherine mean by these words, an oblique reference to the preservation of the Motherhouses of the Vincentian Fathers and the Sisters of Charity, which were not far from Notre-Dame-des-Victoires? Twelve years before, St. John Mary Vianney, the Curé of Ars, predicting the horrors of the *Commune,* had said to a Vincentian lay brother: "They will wish to destroy both your houses, but they will not have the time."

On May 21, the Republican troops, under the command of Marshal MacMahon, broke through and pentrated into the city. The days of the *Commune* were numbered. The Communists did not give up easily, however. In bitter retaliation for the break-through, they executed the hostages held in the prison of La Rouquette: two secular priests, two Jesuits, one layman, and Monseigneur Darboy himself. The martyred Archbishop has been accused of being too subservient to the wishes of Louis Napoléon, and it must be admitted that there are grounds for the accusation. Whatever went before, in these days of stress he showed himself a hero. Refusing to flee when his people were in agony, he suffered a cruel imprisonment, during which every indignity was heaped upon his person, and he met his death with a calm and holy courage.

With the death of Monseigneur Darboy and those of the other seventy hostages: secular priests, religious priests, and laymen—all killed between May 24–26—the depths of Our

Lady's prophecy were plumbed. These deaths marked also the
end of the *Commune*. When passions had died down, the
Third French Republic was proclaimed and Marshal Mac-
Mahon elected its first President.

Sister Dufès began the journey home, stopping on the way
to collect Sister Catherine and Sister Tanguy. They arrived in
Paris on May 30, and after Sister Mauche, who was to become
Mother General of the Community in 1910, had pronounced
her vows at Mass on the morning of May 31, Sister Catherine
carried out the little crowning ceremony she had promised the
Mother of God.

"I told you, my good Mother, that I should return to crown
you on the thirty-first of May," she said, with great satisfaction and love.

Another of Catherine's prophecies had been fulfilled, without attracting particular notice. How many others have shared
the same fate? In 1856, for instance, she wrote to Father
Aladel that a month would be set aside to honor St. Joseph.
This was done by Pius IX in 1864. At the end of one of her
accounts, Catherine made an especially fascinating prophecy:
"Oh, how wonderful it will be to hear, 'Mary is Queen of
the Universe. . . .' It will be a time of peace, joy and good
fortune that will last long; she will be carried as a banner and
she will make a tour of the world." Are these words being
fulfilled in our day? Do they refer to the universal acceptance
of the Miraculous Medal? to the constant references of Pius
XII to Mary as, "Queen of the World"? to the recent tour of
the Pilgrim Virgin? to the "battle" standard of the Legion
of Mary which carries the Miraculous Medal? If so, our age
shall see "the time of peace, joy and good fortune that will
last long." It is a reassuring thought.

XVII

Death and Glory

WITH THE END of the *Commune*, a peace descended upon
France. For the time, at least, the nation seemed to want
to forget the past. Under the personal religious impetus of
Marshal MacMahon, national pilgrimages set out for the
sacred shrines of the land: Chartres, Paray-le-monial, and
Lourdes, and work on Sacré Coeur, the basilica of reparation,
high above Paris on the hill of Montmartre, was begun. Cath-
erine had predicted a resurgence of devotion to the Sacred
Heart of Jesus: this was a tangible beginning. The Miraculous
Medal was as familiar in the daily life of the people as the com-
monest household utensil. Literally hundreds of millions of
Medals had been stamped and diffused in the forty years since
Our Lady had given it. An English bishop had written in 1855:

> Except for the Holy Cross, no other Christian symbol was
> ever so widely multiplied, or was ever the instrument of so
> many marvelous results. . . .

These years of external peace were the sunset years for
Catherine Labouré. Life at Enghien went back smoothly and

quickly to its accustomed round, and it was as if there had been no wars or revolutions. Religious houses are run by an ancient rule, and the greatest cataclysms are mere interruptions of its flow. Catherine's soul had a new peace within it, for the terrible events foretold by the Mother of God were over and done with. She could not but have felt relieved at the knowledge, for anticipation of the worst, anticipation based as hers was on certainty, must have been a cross, which she had borne silently for forty years. Back in 1830, Father Aladel had asked her:

"Will you and I be alive when these terrible things come to pass?" And she had answered in a phrase of simplicity reminiscent of Jeanne d'Arc before the judges:

"If we are not, others will be."

On the surface, it would seem there was nothing more for Catherine to do but to die. There were many things to do. There were many more nights and days of caring for her old men, of answering the door, of feeding the chickens and the cows; many more Masses to be heard and prayers to be said; unlike other saints, Catherine seems not to have yearned for death. It is one of the appealing things about her, because it is something she shares with the common run of men: no one is in a hurry to die. She looked forward to death with a happy equanimity when she knew it was on the way, but she never strained at the bonds of flesh. Such a straining was not in harmony with her practical common sense and peasant patience. She would wait calmly until God was ready.

Old age was telling on her. The arthritis of the knees she had contracted, kneeling on the cold flags of the chapel in Fain, was becoming more general. She hobbled about with greater difficulty than before, and the tall, strong figure had grown bent. She refused to take notice, however. Every morning she walked the long path between Enghien and Reuilly, and invariably was the first in chapel for morning prayers. Even snow did not deter her; she floundered through it somehow, before anyone appeared to shovel a path. She worked as hard as the youngest Sister in the house, and asked no quarter. If there was a floor to be scrubbed, Catherine went down on her poor old swollen knees and scrubbed it, despite the pleas of other Sisters to let them do it for her. In chapel, she still knelt without any support, as she had always done. During her last retreat at the Motherhouse, only a few months before her death, she was offered a cushion to relieve the pain of kneeling for many hours throughout eight long days, but she refused it.

These last years are an excellent source for the student of her sanctity. Her secret lay in the fact that she did what she was supposed to do, as well as she could, and for God. It was as simple as that. There can be no doubt that she did not do a particular work as well at sixty-eight as she had done it at twenty-eight. She did it as well as she could—that was the point—and it was just as pleasing to God, for her heart and soul were in it, and He was both. God is the only master Who rewards effort rather than result.

Actually, her Superiors could see that she was unable to do what she formerly did, and little by little they relieved her. At first, it was in the form of extra assistants to help her care for the old men: Catherine had grown older and more crippled than some of her patients. Then they would take her away from the work for longer and longer periods, and put her to minding the door. In the portress's lodge she had not so much moving about to do, and could sit at her sewing. She was a famous seamstress in the house, and could mend so finely and invisibly that everyone brought work to her. There was always a fresh pile to start on. In her last year, she was confined to the portress's lodge exclusively.

The help given Catherine made for new problems in her life. Catherine was never lucky in her assistants. A lay helper was given her at this time who proved a sore trial indeed. She was actually a cast-off, for one Sister has stated quite frankly that "they could not employ her any place else, so they gave her to Sister Catherine." This poor creature was mentally deranged, and of a personality so fearsome that the Sisters nicknamed her *La Noire*, "The Black One." She was very cruel and ugly to Catherine, but the saint bore it all with patience. Things got so bad at times that the Sisters would threaten to go to Sister Dufès and have the woman removed from the house; but Catherine would not allow it. She knew that the poor woman could not support herself elsewhere, and so continued to suffer her.

Abuse from such a person was bad enough, but Catherine had also a tormentor among her own Sisters. The other Sisters found this one "entirely insupportable." She had a nasty disposition and took fiendish delight in venting it upon Catherine. She made jokes at Catherine's expense, and treated the saint as if she were stupid. Catherine seemed not to notice. Never did she answer back, although she would have had the support of the whole house. Sister Maurel has said, indeed, that Catherine "was humble enough to believe that she was truly stupid."

By 1874, Catherine's health had greatly deteriorated. They began to bleed her in both arms from time to time because she complained that she was smothering. Catherine seems to have had an asthmatic condition, and her heart was involved. Bloodletting was an old-fashioned remedy, much in vogue then. The Mother General decided, at this juncture, to relieve Catherine from her charge as custodian of the house of Enghien and of the old men. Sister Tanguy, who was thirty-seven at the time, was appointed Assistant-Superior of both Reuilly and Enghien and given special charge of Enghien. Catherine had been Assistant-Superior, in fact, for thirty-eight years, but she had never held the title.

It was a hard blow to Catherine. Not that she failed to realize that her powers were on the wane. No one, however, especially one of Catherine's temperament, likes to give up;

and the old have a particular aversion to being supplanted by the young. The blow was all the harder to Catherine, because Sister Tanguy was to be her successor. She had lived with Sister Tanguy for eleven years, and she did not particularly like her. Sister Tanguy was one of those women with an efficient mind and a sharp tongue. It is true that she did Catherine a great service in her copious and eulogistic testimony at the Beatification Inquiry, but she owed it to the saint for her treatment of Catherine when she was alive. Sister Levacher has stated in a blunt and detached manner:

"She [Catherine] had a great love for her Superiors. She loved perhaps less than the others our Sister Assistant, who was rather harsh of character, but she loved her sufficiently that you could say she practiced charity towards her."

This is damning Sister Tanguy with faint praise indeed! It also shows that Catherine's lack of warmth toward the Sister Assistant was apparent to the others. Nonetheless, Catherine did not let her human dislike get in the way of charity; we have the word of Sister Tanguy herself for it:

"There is a custom in our Community that, at night after the doors are locked, the keys are brought to the bedside of the Superior. At Enghien, they were left with Sister Catherine, who was the oldest in the house, for it was impossible to carry them across to Reuilly, where Sister Dufès slept.

"When I arrived to take over the house of Enghien, I overheard a conversation. Some Sisters were counseling Sister Catherine to hold on to the keys. Sister Catherine replied that they should be handed over to her who represented the Superior, and that she would hand them over."

There is something humorous, and at the same time moving, in this very human scene of Catherine poised between the new Superior and the resentful Sisters. Of course, the Sisters were actually fomenting mutiny, and Catherine would have none of that. It is heartwarming, however, to know that Catherine was so close to her companions that they could even make the suggestion, knowing it would go no further. It is to be hoped, for their sakes, that Sister Tanguy did not know for sure the identity of the rebellious Sisters.

Catherine's reaction to the new order of things, moreover, was not mere passive submission. She showed an active good will toward her successor. Even after the change had been effected, Sister Dufès kept Catherine in her accustomed place beside her at table; there was no point in pushing the tired old lady completely aside. Catherine, however, had too much self-respect and virtue to accept a place that was not rightfully hers. Casually, she asked the Sister who had charge of the dining room:

"Would you change my napkin, and give my place to Sister Assistant? It tires me to cross over to that side of the table."

The distance involved was so negligible as to leave no doubt about Catherine's motive, and the Sister was touched by the saint's spirit of deference and humility.

Sister Dufès, who liked things cut and dried, was determined to have a statement from Catherine's own lips, and so asked her bluntly whether she was upset at Sister Tanguy's appointment.

"Have no fear," Catherine answered, just as bluntly. "Our Superiors have spoken, and that should be sufficient for us to receive Sister Tanguy as an angel from heaven."

Catherine spent most of her days in the portress's lodge now, praying, sewing, chatting with the young Sisters who stopped to visit with her, never failing to give them some word of spiritual advice.

One day, Abbé Omer, who had charge of a chapel of convenience in the neighborhood called St. Ratagunde, knocked at the door of the lodge. In greeting the priest, Catherine addressed him as "M. le Curé" or pastor.

"You are mistaken, Sister," he said, smiling. "Of what church am I pastor?"

"Of the Church of the Immaculate Conception."

"No, no. I am chaplain of St. Ratagunde."

"True," the old lady's eyes twinkled, "but you will be pastor of the Immaculate Conception."

The naming of the chapel of St. Ratagunde was a sore point with Catherine. When the chapel was built in 1873, she greatly desired that it be dedicated to Our Lady conceived without sin. When it was not, she confided her disappointment to Sister Cosnard, but added:

"All the same, they will call it after the Immaculate Conception in the end."

In 1877, after Catherine's death, Cardinal Guilbert established the chapel as a parish church, gave it the title of the Immaculate Conception, and appointed Father Omer as its first pastor.

On another day, Catherine was besieged in her portress's lodge by two clerics who came from Cardinal Richard, the Coadjutor of Paris, to determine once and for all whether she was the Sister of the Apparitions. Politely but firmly, she brushed them aside.

"I do not know what you are talking about, Messieurs," she said. "It is the Sister Superior you want." And she left them standing in the middle of the parlor completely baffled.

According to Father Chevalier, her last confessor, Catherine underwent an interrogation concerning the visions by the major Superiors of the Community in 1874, after Father Boré had succeeded Father Etienne as Superior General. The results were wholly unsatisfactory, for Catherine could remember nothing. It was but one more example of the supernatural loss of memory by which Heaven protected her secret. Lest there be any suspicion that it was otherwise—the natural forgetfulness of old age, for example—it must be stated emphatically that, in Catherine's last years, there is no evidence whatever of senility. Quite the contrary. Her speech and mode of action were as sensible and clearheaded in her last days.

This was especially apparent in the way she handled the crisis precipitated in the last year of her life, like a surprise ending to a play. It concerned the making of the statue of "Our Lady of the Globe." Forty-five years had passed, and the statue had not been made, despite Catherine's dunning notes to Father Aladel and her periodic reminders in the confessional. Father Aladel was ten years dead, and Father Chinchon had taken his place as Catherine's director. She must have told him of the statue but, like Father Aladel, he had done nothing. There seems to be more of an excuse for Father Chinchon's failure to act: he may have felt that Father Aladel had very good reasons for not acting, reasons that Father Chinchon himself could not know. In such a situation, so many years after the visions, a sensible man can be allowed a certain sense of caution. There can be no doubt, either, that Catherine herself had grown used to things as they were, even as an invalid grows used to pain, for it was a question of pain: Catherine said frankly that the failure to make the statue was "the torment of my life." At any rate in May of 1876, Catherine was spurred to action with dramatic suddenness.

There were two things which prompted her to act. The first was the unexpected transfer of Father Chinchon to other duties: after ten years, Catherine found herself suddenly bereft of her confessor. The second was a supernatural conviction that she would die before the end of the year. In a flash, she saw time running out, and trembled when she thought of appearing before Our Lady, with the mission entrusted to her not completed.

The day of decision must have been for her a day of terrible anguish. Where should she turn? To whom could she go? If she had not been able to prod Father Aladel to action in thirty-

five years or Father Chinchon in ten, how could she succeed
with a new confessor in a few months? In her anxiety, only
one course was plain: Father Chinchon, no matter what his new
duties, must continue as her confessor; and she must make him
see that the statue had to be carved. There was only one person
who could restore Father Chinchon to her, and that was the
Superior General, Father Boré. She would go to him.

Of course it was a mad thing to do, and the plan was
doomed to failure from the start. That Catherine, with her supreme common sense, should even attempt it, is sufficient index
of how very upset she was. She was certainly not thinking
straight. With all that, there is a heroism in the sight of this
determined old lady, completely reckless of the consequences
to herself, of the peril to her secret, marching right to the top,
to the General himself, that brings a cheer to the lips.

Father Boré was a kindly man, and so he received her
kindly. She was a faithful old servant of the poor who de-
served his kindness. Besides, he remembered her as the Sister
who, rumor said, had seen Our Blessed Lady. He had even
questioned her himself, but had learned nothing. The interview might have gone smoothly enough, except for the fact
that Catherine had not thought things out to the end; she had
not seen that, in order for the statue to be made, drastic steps
had to be taken. Someone besides Father Chinchon had to
know her secret, someone who could do something about it—
and who better than Father Boré himself? Due to age and her
habitual guarding of the secret, however, Catherine had not
seen that far, and so, in the presence of the Superior General,
she failed completely. She was able only to falter out the request that Father Chinchon be restored to her as her confessor.
She could say no more. No reason for the wild request. No
hint of her true identity. Nothing.

Father Boré felt for her, but he could do nothing. He could
not appoint a special confessor for one lone Sister. He saw she

was upset. It was her age—the poor thing was in her dotage. What else could he think? Very gently, he refused her.

Catherine returned home in tears. Sister Dufès was shocked. She had never before seen Catherine in such a state. Naturally, some explanation was needed and, weeping all the while, Catherine told her Superior about her request and how Father Boré had turned it down. Sister Dufès was as much in the dark as ever; she knew only that Catherine was in great trouble and needed desperately to speak with Father Chinchon. Suddenly Catherine's whole manner changed, as if she had hit upon a plan, and she spoke once more in her old decisive way.

"Since I have not much longer to live," she told the astonished Superior, "I feel that the moment to speak out has come. But, as the Blessed Virgin told me to speak only to my confessor, I shall say nothing to you until I have asked Our Lady's permission in prayer. If she tells me I may speak to you, I will do so; otherwise I will remain silent."

The next morning, promptly at ten o'clock, Catherine most unusually sent for Sister Dufès to come to the parlor. Mary Immaculate had given Catherine leave to speak, to break the silence of forty-six years. The interview lasted for two hours, and so engrossed the Sisters that they remained standing the whole time without realizing the fact.

As Catherine recounted the whole story of her visions, minutely and with precision, Sister Dufès's attitude toward her underwent a substantial change. It was Catherine's moment of vindication in the eyes of her Superior, but she was too holy to relish the triumph. Poor Sister Dufès! The times when she had neglected, even worse, had reprimanded harshly this venerable confidante of Mary came crowding in to accuse her. At several points in the narrative she felt impelled to cast herself at Catherine's feet, and only her basic good sense and strong will kept her from it. What amazed the Superior most of all, perhaps, was the ease with which Catherine spoke, she who was always so shy and spoke so little.

Then Catherine came to the point: The statue must be made, the statue depicting Our Lady in her first attitude, holding the golden ball in her hands and offering it to God. Sister Dufès was completely bewildered.

"But I have never heard tell of this detail," she cried. "If you speak of such an attitude now, they will say you have grown foolish!"

"It will not be the first time they have said that of me," Catherine replied, "but until the moment I die, I shall insist that the Blessed Virgin appeared to me, holding a ball in her hands."

"What became of the ball?" Sister Dufès asked.

"Oh, I do not know; I only know that suddenly I saw rays falling upon the globe on which Our Lady stood, and especially upon a spot where *France* was written."

"How about the Medal? Is it necessary to change the design?"

"Do not touch the Medal," Catherine replied. "It is only necessary to erect an altar on the spot of the Apparition, as the Blessed Virgin asked, and to place above it her statue, with a ball in her hands."

Sister Dufès was still doubtful. "They are not going to believe you," she persisted. "Is there anyone who can confirm your story?"

"Yes," Catherine said, considering, "yes, there is someone: Sister Grand, who was secretary in the Motherhouse at the time, and who took notes of the Apparitions from Father Aladel's dictation."

Sister Dufès wrote at once to Sister Grand, and Sister Grand replied that all Catherine had said was true; she even included some rough sketches of the proposed statue which had been drawn at the time.

Whatever might be said of her, Sister Dufès was efficient. Within a few days, she had called in a sculptor named Froc Robert and work on the statue was begun. On at least one occasion she took Catherine with her to the sculptor's studio, to inspect the progress of the work. Catherine had several criticisms to make. The artist's curiosity was aroused, and he asked Sister Dufès in a low voice whether this was the Sister of the Apparitions, but he received no reply. Shortly before her death, Catherine saw the finished plaster model from which the statue would be carved. Her disappointment was keen.

"Ah," she exclaimed, making a face, "the Blessed Virgin was much more beautiful than that!"

Sister Dufès lost her temper. "You weary me, Sister Catherine," she scolded in her old accustomed way. "How can you expect anyone on earth to depict what you saw?"

Catherine's mission was fulfilled. Now she could die in peace. As the summer wore on, she began to speak openly of her death. "I will not see the New Year," she would say. Everyone scoffed, of course. How could she know the moment of death? She did know, but would not argue the point; she would merely smile and say: "You will see."

On August 15, her niece Marie brought the children to see her. As they were leaving, Catherine pressed a package into Marie's hand.

"It is a first Communion present for the little one," she explained.

"But she will not make her first Communion until May," Marie protested in astonishment.

"Put it away until then," Catherine said placidly. "I shall not be here in May."

She began to take to her bed with more and more frequency. It became necessary to bleed her from time to time, so that she could breathe more easily, and to apply leeches in the kidney area. Both these treatments were used in former days to relieve high blood pressure, as well as the breathlessness that comes with hardening of the arteries and the consequent weakening of the heart. All of Catherine's symptoms would seem to point to some cardio-vascular failure, a condition not uncommon at her age—she was past seventy—and to the complications induced by chronic asthma.

Catherine was still able to go out occasionally, usually to the Motherhouse to attend the monthly conference. On one of these visits, while the other Sisters were at dinner, Catherine led Sister Dufès into the chapel and pointed out the exact spot of the Apparitions, where the altar and statue were to go.

Once, as she climbed into the omnibus to return home—it was a feast day of Our Lady—Catherine slipped and fell. She said nothing, but a few minutes later one of the Sisters noticed that she held her hand wrapped in a handkerchief. She undertook to tease her about it.

"What treasure have you there, Sister Catherine?"

"It is a bouquet from Our Lady," Catherine said, smiling. "She sends me one like it on every one of her feasts." Upon examination, it was discovered that she had broken her wrist.

Father Chevalier had succeeded Father Chinchon as confessor at Enghien, and now he asked Catherine to write out, once more, a full account of the visions. It is amazing how well this last account agrees, even to the use of the same words and phrases, with the earlier accounts of 1841 and 1856. She had told the story many times over: Father Chinchon related that every year, as the twenty-seventh of November drew near, she felt urged to tell again the details of the vision.

Two weeks before Christmas, Catherine became so ill that she retired to her room, never to leave it again. She was not confined to bed exclusively; she found it easier to breathe if she sat in a chair from time to time. It was the beginning of the end, but her sufferings were not to be wholly physical. A certain Sister was assigned to nurse her who had neither the aptitude nor the willingness for the task. She was so slipshod, even rough, in her treatment of Catherine, that several of the Sisters were outraged and spoke their minds to the saint. Catherine refused, as always, to make the least unkind comment.

"She is not a worker," was all she would say; and there is a wry humor in the remark.

Catherine was not to leave the earth without one more encounter with the redoubtable Sister Tanguy. The Assistant entered the sickroom one afternoon while another Sister was visiting Catherine. With scarcely a word of greeting, she asked brusquely:

"Have you taken your medicine?"

Catherine replied in the affirmative, but Sister Tanguy was not satisfied. Lifting the bottle to the light, she said sharply:

"You've done nothing of the kind. There isn't a bit more missing since the last time!" And she proceeded to administer a veritable tongue-lashing to Catherine, in the presence of the visitor. Her conduct was all the more inexcusable since she knew that Catherine was the Sister of the visions. Sister Dufès had told her, with Catherine's permission. Throughout the scolding, Catherine remained silent. When, finally, Sister Tanguy finished and left the room, the saint could hold her tongue no longer. Turning to her visitor she said, again with that characteristic dryness:

"That one hasn't been to see me all day, and see the way she is when she does come!"

Every day, Catherine grew weaker. She continued to remind the Sisters that she would die before the year was out, but there were so few days left in the month that the Sisters could still not believe that she would die so soon.

One of them ventured to ask her whether she was afraid to die. Catherine answered, with genuine astonishment:

"Why should I be afraid? I am going to see Our Lord and the Blessed Virgin and St. Vincent."

Another Sister asked Catherine to beg Our Lady and St. Vincent, when she saw them, to intercede with God in behalf of certain special intentions of the Sister's. Catherine's reply revealed an unexpected naïveté and childlike humility.

"I should be glad to do what you ask, but I am not sure that I shall be able to speak the language of Heaven."

When the Sister laughingly assured the old lady that she would have no difficulty in doing so, Catherine promised to look after the matter.

On December 21, Sister Thomas stopped by to see her. The saint repeated the prediction of her death and added:

"They will not need a hearse for me." Sister Thomas was either a very guileless person, or something of a ghoul, for she gaped at the saint and asked in amazement:

"How, then, will they carry so large a body?"

"I am going to stay with you at Reuilly," Catherine replied.

"Furthermore, there will be no need of ribbons for my coffin." (She referred to the ornamental cords which, by custom, hung from the pall and were carried by the pall bearers.) There can be little doubt that Catherine had her reasons for giving Sister Thomas this particular bit of information. At Catherine's funeral, Sister Thomas was actually designated to hold one of the ornamental ribbons. She went to take hold of it, thinking to herself that this was one prophecy of Catherine's that would not come true, when one of the bearers pushed her back, saying with some roughness:

"Get back, Sister, you are in our way." She had no other choice but to obey, and so, even in death, Catherine won her point.

A few days later, an incident took place which brought trouble many years later. The nurse asked Catherine what she would like for breakfast.

"Anything will do," was the reply. Indeed, her stomach was

so upset in the mornings that she could scarcely bear to take anything but a little bouillon.

"It would be easier for me if you would mention something in particular."

"Very well, then, a soft-boiled egg."

From this very innocent conversation a rumor arose through some pious busybody, perhaps the reluctant nurse herself, that Catherine had shown a lack of mortification in asking for special food on her deathbed. The rumor persisted for nearly fifty years, and even found its way into the formal Inquiry of her sanctity, where the "Devil's Advocate" alleged it as a sign that her holiness was not always so heroic as it seemed.

The last day of the year came, December 31, 1876, and Catherine was no worse than usual. In the afternoon, in fact, she rallied sufficiently to sit on the side of the bed and chat with her niece Marie. Reaching for her old worn purse, she gave Marie the last of her original Miraculous Medals. When it was time to go Marie bent to kiss her and said that she would come to wish her a Happy New Year in the morning.

"You shall see me," Catherine answered, "but I shall not see you, for I shall not be here."

Shortly after six o'clock, she took a sudden weak spell. The Sisters were hurriedly summoned and the prayers for the dying begun. She sank so rapidly that there was no time to carry out one of her dearest wishes. She had wanted each of the little orphans of the house to recite an invocation from the Litany of Our Lady as she entered her last agony. At seven o'clock, with no struggle, with scarcely a sigh, Catherine Labouré died.

Her death brought no sadness to the house. Death is never sad in religious houses, but the death of Sister Catherine seemed to leave with her Sisters a spirit of positive joy. As they filed into the refectory for supper, Sister Dufès rose to speak to them:

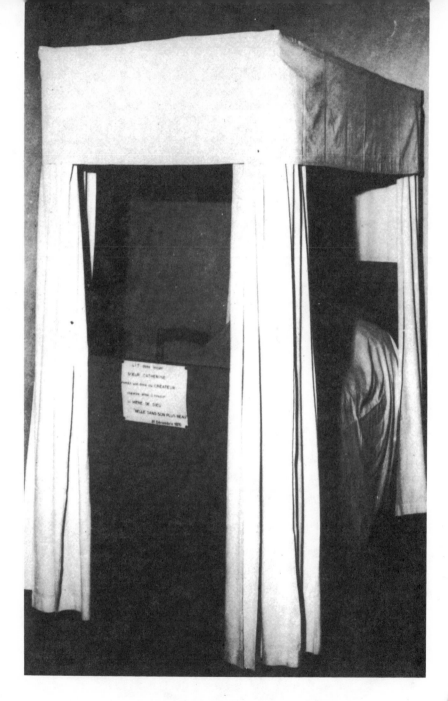

The bed in which Catherine died; the bed is preserved at Reuilly.

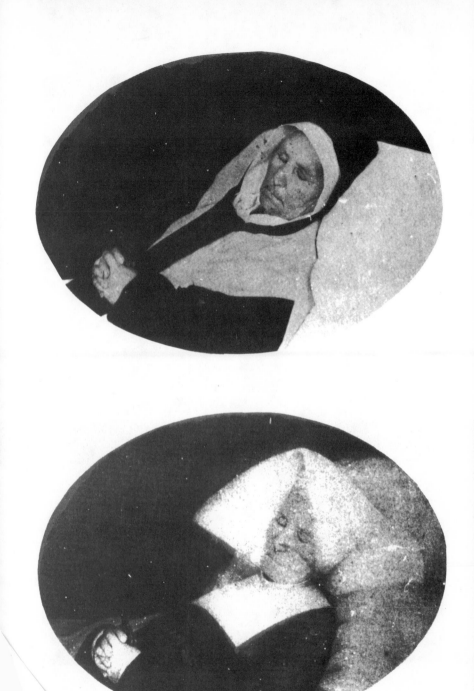

Photographs of St. Catherine after her death.

Upper left: First her body was dressed in the costume of the seminary sisters, or novices, which was the clothing Catherine wore during the Apparitions.

Lower left: Then the body was clothed in the habit of a professed Sister of Charity, and another photograph was taken.

Below: Retouched picture of St. Catherine's body after her death.

224-3

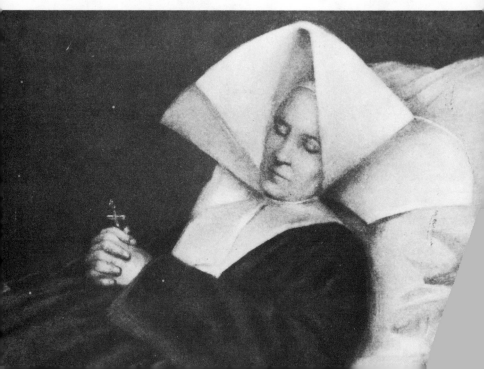

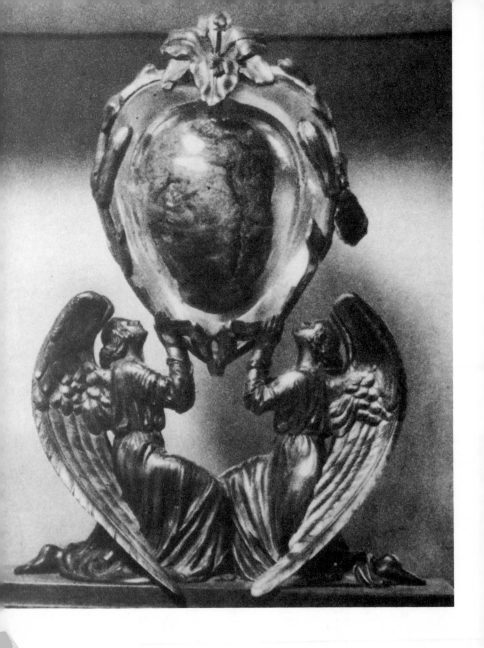

Above: The heart of St. Catherine preserved in a reliquary.
Right: The canonization of St. Catherine Labouré by Pope Pius XII on
July 27, 1947.

When Catherine's body was exhumed in 1933, 57 years after her death, a gasp of astonishment ran through the crowd; Catherine's body was as fresh and serene as on the day she was buried. Her skin had not darkened in the [...]. Her eyes were as intensely blue as ever, and her arms and legs were [...]pple as if she were merely asleep.

Left: Catherine's incorrupt body lies in the chapel of the motherhouse at 140, rue du Bac, Paris beneath the statue, "Virgin of the Globe," which Mary had requested.

Above and below: Two views of the incorrupt body of St. Catherine Labouré, showing its remarkable state of preservation.

224-7

O Mary, conceived without sin,
pray for us who have recourse to thee.

...e of the statue, "Madonna of the Medal," at the shrine of the Central
...iation of the Miraculous Medal in Germantown, Philadelphia, Penn-
...ia (475 E. Chelten Ave., Philadelphia, PA 19144). This shrine
...s many thousands of reports of favors received through the
...ulous Medal.

"Now that Sister Catherine is dead," she began, "there is no more cause for silence." And she went on to read to them Catherine's own accounts of her visions. The Sisters listened with wonder and a growing excitement, for, in spite of the guesses and suspicions of years, no one had known for sure that Sister Catherine was the Sister of the Medal. The excitement spread to the outside, as the news ran quickly through the city. Crowds began to converge on Reuilly the next morning, and clergy, religious, and laity alike, took their places in the line stretching along the sidewalk, patiently awaiting the privilege of passing by the coffin of a saint.

At the time of Catherine's death, her old friend, Sister Séjole, had been in a coma for three weeks. It was shouted into her ear that Catherine had died, and, rousing from her stupor, she cried:

"Then I must get ready!" It was as if the two had made a pact.

A saint's story does not end with death. This was the beginning for Catherine, the start of her glory. She who had lived so hidden a life belonged now to the whole world. The change had been marked the night before when, after they had washed the body, the Sisters brought in a photographer to take a picture of her as she lay in state. Someone with a rather peculiar imagination suggested that they photograph her also, dressed in the novice's habit she had worn when she saw Our Lady, and this, too, was done. There was something incongruous in the sight of the peaceful old face, lying there, framed in the costume of youth.

The funeral was set for January 3, 1877, at 10 o'clock. Sister Dufès was in a ferment. She wanted desperately to keep Catherine at Reuilly, but there was no place to bury her. On the morning of January 2, as the Superior rose for morning meditation at four o'clock, she distinctly heard a voice, which said:

"There is a vault beneath the chapel."

Sister Dufès had forgotten entirely about this vault. It was actually a storeroom, cut out of the earth, and had been boarded up for years. Hurriedly, it was opened and found to be suitable for a grave. The permission of the Superior General to bury Catherine here was easily gotten; permission of the civil authorities might be more difficult to obtain. Sister Dufès took no chances. She went directly to the top, to the wife of the President, Mme MacMahon. This great lady made the necessary arrangements promptly, and with no difficulty.

On the morning of the funeral, a large number of the clergy came to follow Catherine's body to the grave. Hardly had the funeral procession got under way when it was transformed into a march of joy and triumph. The funeral chants became songs of rejoicing. The requiem, the sad appeal for mercy, was forgotten. Impelled by the Spirit of God, the voices of the faithful trumpeted the Magnificat of Our Lady. "My soul doth magnify the Lord!" Then, "Ave Maris Stella"—"Hail, Star of the Sea!" And finally, "O Mary, conceived without sin, pray for us who have recourse to thee!" All sadness, all sorrow was gone like the mist of the morning. Amid shouts of gladness and acclaim, the humble Sister was laid to rest.

A few days later, the first cure took place. A child of ten, deprived from birth of the use of his limbs, was brought to Catherine's tomb. In a scene strongly mindful of Christ's healing of the paralytic at Capharnaum, the little boy was let down by ropes to the tomb in the chapel basement. Hardly had the child touched the stone when he stood erect and firm upon his feet. He was suddenly and wholly cured.

It was a distinct sign of God's intention to glorify His servant. And yet, the work of God is not done hastily. In His own good time, He would reveal His further plans. And so, for the time, no thought was given to the introduction of Sister Catherine's Cause of Beatification.

In 1895, it was decided to petition Rome for a feast day in

honor of Our Lady of the Miraculous Medal. To this end, the
documents recounting the Apparitions were sent to Cardinal
Masella, prefect of the Sacred Congregation of Rites. The
story impressed His Eminence deeply, especially the story of
the little novice and the humble part she played as the bearer
of Our Lady's message to mankind. Filled with admiration for
her virtue, he called upon Father Fiat, Superior General, and
Mother Lamartinie, Superioress of the Sisters of Charity, to
begin the process for Catherine's Beatification.

The Superiors hesitated. It was the spirit of their rule to
shrink from glory. Catherine herself had hidden from it all her
long life. Did God wish otherwise now? "If you do not under-
take it," the Cardinal insisted, "I shall do it myself!" There
was no longer any doubt or holding back. God had spoken in
His official. In 1895 the Cause of the Servant of God, Sister
Catherine Labouré, was introduced at Rome.

Rome does not hasten. Time counts for little with her, because her gaze is fixed upon eternity. In its bright, unending
light she ponders all her problems. Catherine was with God
just fifty years when her Cause came up for serious discussion.

Those fifty years had not been idle years. Necessary and
exhaustive research into her sheltered life had occupied them.
But now all things were ready. The members of the Sacred
Congregation of Rites were talking excitedly about "this
amazing French nun" as they filed into the study of Cardinal
Vanutelli on April 2, 1927. Enthusiastically they voted further, intensive consideration of the Cause.

Then, for some reason known only to God, things came to a
standstill. Was it perhaps to bring forward two mighty champions for Catherine? Cardinal Ehrle, former director of the
Vatican Library, and Father Ojetti, ex-secretary of the Commission of Canon Law, had both been removed from active
participation in the sessions of the Congregation of Rites
through illness. Now, hearing that the Cause of Catherine was

in difficulty, they asked to return to the Congregation, and did in truth return, to the astonishment of everyone, even of the Pope. "The Cause of Sister Catherine Labouré," they said, "is the Cause of the Immaculate Conception."

Cardinal Ehrle, more than eighty years old and unable to walk, was carried to the Vatican for the general Congregation, and read a convincing and vigorous defense of the humble Sister.

Father Ojetti, confined to his home by an advanced paralysis, wrote to the Congregation: "I can use only my right hand and my pen, and it is my will to make them serve to uphold the Cause of the Immaculate Conception!"

The action of Divine Providence appeared still more forcibly in the intervention of Father Quentin, the realtor of the Historical Section of the Congregation of Rites. He was somewhat anxious. Only three days before the second preparatory Congregation, held on March 17, 1931, his attention was suddenly drawn to the canonical inquiry made in 1836, by order of the Archbishop of Paris, Msgr. de Quélen—a document of the first importance and an inexhaustible source of information about Sister Catherine. He worked night and day, preparing the results of this great "find," overcame all opposition, and obtained by unanimous vote the triumph of the Cause of the Immaculate Conception. The day following this session, the Holy Father, rather unusually, ordered the continuation of the process. The decree on the Virtues of Sister Catherine was soon ready, and the Pope, in a moving discourse, traced a finished portrait of the Holy Sister.

The Beatification of Catherine Labouré, held in St. Peter's on May 28, 1933, ranked in magnificence with those of Jeanne d'Arc and Thérèse of Lisieux, ceremonies which left a lasting memory in Rome.

The Church now ordered the exhumation of the body of the saint. It had lain, sealed in the vault beneath the chapel at

Reuilly, for fifty-seven years. The coffin was carried to the rue du Bac, and there opened in the presence of Cardinal Verdier, Archbishop of Paris, and a number of civil officials and doctors. As the lid was lifted, a gasp of astonishment ran through the group. Catherine lay there, as fresh and serene as the day she was buried. Her skin had not darkened in the least; the eyes which had looked on Our Lady were as intensely blue as ever, and—most remarkable of all—her arms and legs were as supple as if she were merely asleep.

Fourteen years later, on July 27, 1947, Catherine Labouré was formally declared a saint and raised to the full honors of the altar. At the close of the magnificent rites, Pope Pius XII spoke words which might well be engraved as the epitaph of Catherine Labouré, for they were, in effect, the story of her life.

Favored though she was with visions and celestial delights, she did not advertise herself to seek worldly fame, but took herself merely for the handmaid of God and preferred to remain unknown and to be reputed as nothing. And thus, desiring only the glory of God and of His Mother, she went meekly about the ordinary, and even the unpleasant, tasks that were assigned to her in the bosom of her Religious family.

She was always willing and ready to give diligent attention to the sick, ministering to their bodies and their souls; to wait upon the old and the infirm without sparing herself; to act as portress, receiving all with a serene and modest countenance; to cook; to mend torn and tattered clothing; to carry out, in a word, all the duties laid upon her, even the unattractive and onerous ones. And while she worked away, never idle but always busy and cheerful, her heart never lost sight of heavenly things: indeed she saw God uninterruptedly in all things and all things in God.

Impelled by the urging of love, she hurried eagerly before the tabernacle as often as she could, or before the sacred image of her holy Mother, to pour out the desires of her heart and to make an offering of the fragrance of her prayers. Accordingly, it was evident that while she dwelt in earthly exile, in mind and heart she lived in Heaven and sought, before everything else, to mount with rapid steps to the highest perfection, and to spend all her powers in reaching it. She loved the Sacred Heart of Jesus and the Immaculate Heart of Mary with a special warmth of piety; and she was ever on the watch to influence, by word and example, as many other persons as she could to love Them.

And thus when she came to the end of her mortal life, she did not face death with fear but with gladness. Confident in God and the most holy Virgin, she took time to distribute, with a weak and tremulous hand, the last of her Miraculous Medals to those standing by, and then, content and smiling, she hastened away to heaven.

Notes to the Text

Key

PO   Ordinary Process, Cause for the Beatification and Canonization.

PA   Apostolic Process, Cause for the Beatification and Canonization.

ACMP   Archives of the Priests of the Congregation of the Mission, Paris, France.

AFC   Archives of the Daughters of Charity, Paris, France.

AVR   Archives of the Vicariate of Rome.

Notes

P. 4, L. 22	Registre d'Etat Civil de la Commune de Fain et Saint-Juste-les-Moutiers, canton de Montbard (Cote d'Or), Copy ACMP.
P. 4, L. 34	Certificat de Bapteme, extrait, April 29, 1896.
P. 6, L. 2	Crapez, p. 7.

231

P. 6, L. 7 — Mme Duhamel, witness, n. 932, Nov. 24, 1897, PO, s. 29, p. 311.

P. 7, L. 21 — Pere Meugniot, witness, Oct. 20, 1899, PO, s. 78., p. 778; Mme Duhamel, witness, n. 932, Nov. 24, 1897, PO, s. 29, p. 300.

P. 8, L. 8 — Laurentin-Roche, p. 102, footnote 9.

P. 9, L. 2 — Pere Meugniot, witness, Oct. 20, 1899, PO, s. 78, p. 779, and PA, Nov. 4, 1909, p. 1011.

P. 9, L. 25 — Pere Meugniot, witness, Nov. 4, 1909, PA, s. 72, p. 1011.

P. 11, L. 3 — S. Casaneuve, n. 917, June 1, 1897, 25, p. 275.

P. 11, L. 29 — *Ibid.*

P. 16, L. 9 — Pere Meugniot, Nov. 4, 1909, PA spec., p. 1012; *et al.*

P. 18, L. 7 — *Ibid.*

P. 21, L. 12 — *Ibid.*

P. 22, L. 27 — *Ibid.,* p. 1011.

P. 23, L. 5 — *Ibid.,* p. 1012.

P. 23, L. 33 — *Ibid.,* p. 1013.

P. 25, L. 14 — *Ibid.*

P. 25, L. 27 — Mme Duhamel, Nov. 24, 1897, PO, s. 29, p. 312.

P. 26, L. 22 — Cf. *ibid.*

P. 26, L. 31 — *Ibid;* also, Pere Meugniot, *ibid.,* p. 1016.

P. 27, L. 26 — Leonie Laboure, May 3, 1898, PO, s. 48, p. 516.

P. 28, L. 13 — P. Meugniot, *ibid.,* p. 1015.

P. 28, L. 30 — Mme Duhamel, *ibid.;* also, P. Meugniot, *ibid.*

P. 31, L. 25 — P. Meugniot, *ibid.,* p. 1015.

P. 33, L. 31 — Chevalier, p. 5; also, P. Meugniot, *ibid.,* p. 1014.

P. 37, L. 2 — Chevalier, p. 6; also witnesses PO, p. 126, 349 (Sr. Cosnard, who was told of the dream by Catherine herself) *et al.*

P. 39, L. 19 — Chevalier, June 10, 1896, PO, s. 9, p. 125; Mme Duhamel, Feb. 24, 1898, PO, s. 42, p. 437, P. Meugniot, Oct. 20, 1899, PO, s. 76, p. 780.

P. 40, L. 6 — Mme Duhamel, Nov. 24, 1897, PO, s. 29, p. 313; P. Meugniot, *ibid.,* p. 779.

P. 41, L. 23 — Leonie Laboure, *ibid; et al.*

P. 47, L. 6 — AFC, copy in Catherine's own hand.

P. 47, L. 33 — Leonie Laboure, *ibid.,* p. 517; Mme Duhamel, *ibid.*

P. 51, L. 3 — Chevalier, p. 7; cf. also Crapez, p. 38, and Misermont, p. 47.

P. 52, L. 15 — A. Donon-Laboure, June 5, 1896, PO, s. 8, p. 110.

P. 57, L. 22 — ACF, Registre des Postulants (1824-1831), p. 320.

P. 58, L. 9 — Sr. Tanguy, PA, p. 367.

P. 64, L. 23 — ACMP, *Annales,* LXVI, pp. 449-459.

P. 68, L. 10 — Autograph, St. Catherine, Feb. 7, 1856, AFC.

P. 69	P. Aladel, *Les Rayons*, 1922, pp. 223-229.
P. 72	Autograph, St. Catherine, *ibid.*
P. 74, L. 24	*Ibid.*
P. 75, L. 27	*Ibid.*
P. 86, L. 32	*Ibid.*
P. 90, L. 4	De Melun, *Life of Sr. Rosalie.*
P. 94	Autograph, St. Catherine, Aug. 15, 1841, AFC.
P. 95, L. 24	Chevalier, June 17, 1896, PO, s. 10, p. 136.
P. 97, L. 28	Cf. note for painting by Letaille, ACMP.
P. 98, L. 3	Autograph, St. Catherine, Aug. 15, 1841, AFC.
P. 100, L. 34	Aladel, Canonical Inquiry "Quentin," 1836, p. 5., pp. 10-11, ACMP.
P. 106, L. 30	Sister Dufes, PO, s. 3, p. 65.
P. 107, L. 34	AFC, Registre des Postulants (1824-1831), p. 320.
P. 109, L. 15	Sister Desmoulins, July 23, 1909, PA, s. 57, p. 822.
P. 110, L. 29	Caulfield, *Our Union with France*, p. 124-125.
P. 111, L. 7	Srs. Tanguy, Hannezo, Desmoulins, PA, p. 208, 912.
P. 112, L. 12	Autograph, Aladel, July 1834, ACMP.
P. 114, L. 11	Aladel, Canonical Inquiry "Quentin," p. 2, p. 8, ACMP.
P. 115, L. 7	*Ibid.*
P. 115, L. 14	Vachette, Canonical Inquiry "Quentin," pp. 8-10, ACMP.
P. 115, L. 16	Aladel, *ibid.*, p. 3.
P. 115, L. 31	Aladel, *Notice*, June, 1837, XVI, p. 440.
P. 116, L. 21	Misermont, *Vie* (1933), p. 119.
P. 116, L. 29	Vachette, *ibid.*, pp. 8-10.
P. 118, L. 2	Le Guillou, *Mois de Marie;* Crapez, *Vie*, p. 109.
P. 118, L. 31	Canonical Inquiry "Quentin."
P. 119, L. 12	Chevalier, p. 25.
P. 119, L. 33	*Ibid.*
P. 120, L. 6	*Brouillon du Rapport de M Quentin*, ACMP.
P. 120, L. 24	De Quelen, *Proclamation*, Dec. 15, 1836, ACMP.
P. 122, L. 32	*Ibid.*
P. 129, L. 12	Sister Desmoulins, *ibid.*, p. 828.
P. 130, L. 7	Sr. Tanguy, Nov. 2, 1897, PO, s. 27, p. 295.
P. 135, L. 2	Cf. pp. 45-47, Autograph, St. Catherine, Sept. 29, 1844, AFC. (The dates in the text are incorrect; Pierre Laboure died on Mar. 19, 1844.)
P. 138, L. 14	Autograph, St. Catherine, AFC.
P. 141, L. 31	Autograph, St. Catherine, AFC.
P. 143, L. 4	Sister Dufau, PO, p. 440.
P. 143, L. 10	Cf. PA, Sister Cosnard, p. 467, Sr. Clavel, p. 631.
P. 143, L. 31	Cf. Autograph, St. Catherine, *Livre de Comptes;* also various witnesses, PO and PA.

P. 145, L. 18	Sr. de La Haye Saint Hilaire, July 6, 1909, PA, s. 37, p. 544.
P. 145, L. 21	Chevalier, p. 28.
P. 145, L. 32	Sr. Tanguy, PA, s. 27, p. 293.
P. 146, L. 10	Sr. Thomas, PA, pp. 345-346.
P. 147, L. 20	Sr. Desmoulins, July 23, 1909, PA, s. 57, p. 828.
P. 147, L. 30	Sr. Olalde, June 18, 1909, PA, p. 336.
P. 148, L. 4	*Ibid.*
P. 148, L. 14	Sr. Tanguy, PA, p. 367.
P. 148, L. 23	*Ibid.*
P. 150, L. 6	Sr. Charvier, Mar. 17, 1899, PA, pp. 726-729.
P. 150, L. 11	Sr. Dufes, May 11, 1896, PO, p. 79.
P. 150, L. 15	Cf. Sr. Combes, July 20, 1909, PA, s. 50, p. 726.
P. 151, L. 32	Duhamel, PA, p. 417, and Meugniot, p. 765.
P. 153, L. 5	Meugniot, *ibid.*
P. 154, L. 24	Re service to her family, cf. Mme Duhamel, PA Sum., p. 319.
P. 155, L. 2	Aimee Laboure, PA, 1907.
P. 156, L. 9	Autograph, St. Catherine, Oct. 30, 1876, AFC.
P. 157, L. 3	Cf. *Manuel des Enfants de Marie*, 1868, p. 7.
P. 157, L. 33	Misermont, *Ame*, p. 266.
P. 160, L. 30	Autograph, St. Catherine, 1841, AFC.
P. 163, L. 13	Sr. Dufes, May 11, 1896, PO, 5, p. 79.
P. 164, L. 4	Sr. Cosnard, PA, p. 462.
P. 165, L. 17	Cf. Edouard, *The Green Scapular and Its Miracles*, Paris, 1923.
P. 166, L. 2	Cf. Collard, *Le Scapulaire de la Passion*, Abbeville, 1946.
P. 170, L. 19	Autograph, Theodore de Bussiere, Jan. 30, 1842, AVR; also Aladel, *The Miraculous Medal*, 1880, pp. 193-227.
P. 174, L. 31	Autograph, St. Catherine, July 30, 1848, AFC.
P. 175, L. 30	*Ibid.*
P. 176, L. 19	AFC.
P. 178, L. 12	Sr. Tanguy, p. 226.
P. 178, L. 17	P. Meugniot, p. 247.
P. 180, L. 24	Sr. Tanguy, PA, p. 398.
P. 180, L. 33	Villette, *Memoire*, 1912, ACMP.
P. 181, L. 23	Sr. Dufes, PO, p. 57.
P. 182, L. 9	Autograph, St. Catherine, AFC.
P. 183, L. 29	Sr. Henriot, PO, s. 73, p. 745-751.
P. 183, L. 32	Sr. Tanguy, PO, p. 380.
P. 184, L. 31	Sr. de La Haye Saint Hilaire, *ibid.*, pp. 823-824.
P. 185, L. 13	Sr. Henriot, PA, Sum., p. 352.
P. 186, L. 26	Sr. Pineau.
P. 187, L. 15	Sr. Tanguy, *ibid.*, p. 80.

P. 188, L. 14	Sr. Dufes, PO, p. 403.
P. 189, L. 2	Sr. Desmoulins, PA, Sum., P. 471.
P. 189, L. 13	S. Millin, PA, p. 228; also Chevalier, PA Sum., p. 305.
P. 190, L. 13	Sr. Dufes, PA, p. 195; Sr. Tanguy, *ibid.*, p. 300.
P. 190, L. 23	Sr. Dufes, PA.
P. 191, L. 21	Sr. Desmoulins, PA Sum., p. 489.
P. 192, L. 25	Sr. Cosnard, PA Sum., p. 488.
P. 193, L. 13	Srs. Desmoulins and Charvier, PA Sum., pp. 491, 505-507.
P. 193, L. 25	Gil Moreno de Maura, *ibid.*, p. 415.
P. 195, L. 6	Aladel, *Les Rayons,* 1922, pp. 223-229.
P. 200, L. 21	Sr. Dufes, *Note,* 1877, AFC.
P. 206, L. 26	Sr. Maurel, July 11, 1898, PO, s. 58, p. 606.
P. 208, L. 11	For the Sisters at Enghien and the Communards, cf. *Note* of Sr. Dufes, witness at the Ordinary and Apostolic Processes, and other contemporary material, AFC.
P. 208, L. 14	Sr. Tanguy, June 7, 1909, PA, s. 8, p. 189.
P. 208, L. 18	Autograph, St. Catherine, Oct. 30, 1876, AFC.
P. 211, L. 6	Sr. Tanguy, Nov. 2, 1897, PO, p. 292.
P. 211, L. 10	Sr. Cosnard, Jan. 18, 1898, PO, s. 37, p. 389.
P. 212, L. 22	Srs. Tanguy and Combes, PA, June 10 and July 21, 1909, pp. 198 and 736.
P. 213, L. 29	Srs. Tanguy and Henriot, Sum. PA, pp. 461-462.
P. 214, L. 14	Chevalier, PA Sum., pp. 474-475.
P. 214, L. 24	Sr. Clavel, PA Sum., p. 476-477; also *ibid.*, Srs. Clavel, Olalde, Combes, pp. 477, 478, 463, 468, 469.
P. 215, L. 25	Sr. Desmoulins, PA Sum., pp. 317-318 *et al.*
P. 219, L. 34	Sr. Tanguy, May 24, 1897, PO, s. 24, p. 267-268; Sr. Grand to Sr. Dufes, June 24, 1876, copy, AFC.
P. 220, L. 15	Sr. Desmoulins, July 25, 1909, PA, s. 56, p. 810.
P. 220, L. 29	Numerous witnesses attested to her predictions of her approaching death, PA.
P. 221, L. 6	Testimony of many witnesses, PA.
P. 221, L. 20	Sr. Tanguy, PA Sum., p. 226.
P. 221, L. 28	Autograph, St. Catherine, Oct. 30, 1876, AFC.
P. 222, L. 6	Srs. Olalde and Patrissey, PA Sum., pp. 313, 321, Jan. 12, 1897, PO, s. 16, p. 187, *et al.*
P. 222, L. 22	Misermont, *Vie,* p. 230-232.
P. 222, L. 34	Sr. Clavel, July 11, 1898, PO, s. 58, p. 606.
P. 223, L. 9	Sr. Millon, June 15, 1909, PA, s. 13, p. 238.
P. 223, L. 7	Misermont, *Graces,* p. 188.
P. 224, L. 5	Mott, June 22, 1909, PA 24, p. 382.
P. 224, L. 21	Mme Duhamel, June 30, 1909, PA, p. 464.

P. 224, L. 27   Sr. Desmoulins, July 24, 1909, PA, s. 58, p. 847, also p. 844; Sr. Millon, June 10, 1898, PO, s. 53, p. 556.

P. 224, L. 29   *Registre de la Prefectoire de Paris,* G85/23-MD; also many witnesses, PA.

P. 224, L. 34   Sr. Tanguy, Nov. 17, 1897, PO, s. 28, p. 301; and *ibid.,* June 9, 1909, PA, s. 10, p. 208.

P. 225, L. 2   Sr. Henriot, June 16, 1909, PA spec., s. 15, p. 274.

P. 225, L. 8   Several witnesses, PO.

P. 225, L. 26   Srs. Tanguy, Olalde, Combes, PA, s. 10, 20, 51, pp. 209, 341, 736.

P. 225, L. 33   Sr. Dufes, May 27, 1896, s. 7, p. 97.

P. 226, L. 9   *Ibid.;* also, *Letter,* Dufes to Meugniot, Jan. 4, 1877, ACMP.

P. 226, L. 21   Many witnesses, PO and PA.

P. 230   Pope Pius XII, Homily, Canonization, July 27, 1947.

Bibliography

Aladel, Jean Marie. *The Miraculous Medal,* ed. by Jules Charles Chevalier, tr. by P. S. [*sic*], Philadelphia, 1880.

Beevers, John. *The Sun Her Mantle,* Westminster, 1953.

Belloc, Hilaire. *Marie Antoinette,* New York, 1913.

Boyne, Mrs. P. *Life of St. Catherine Labouré,* Dublin, 1948.

Calvet, Jean. *St. Vincent de Paul,* tr. by Lancelot C. Sheppard, New York, 1948.

Carroll, Eamon R. *Queen of the Universe,* St. Meinrad, 1957.

Caulfield, Sister Marie Louise. *Our Union With France,* Emmitsburg, 1855.

Collard, M. *Le Scapulaire de la Passion,* Abbeville, 1946.

Coste, Pierre. *Life of St. Vincent de Paul,* tr. by Joseph Leonard, Westminster, 1952.

Crapez, Edmond. *Le Message du Coeur de Marie à Sainte Catherine Labouré,* Paris, 1947.

———. *Venerable Catherine Labouré,* tr. anon., Emmitsburg, 1918.

De Melun, Viscount. *Life of Sister Rosalie,* tr. by Joseph D. Fallon, Norwood, 1916.

Dirvin, Joseph I. "What Came to Light," *The Miraculous Medal,* Vol. 20, (June 1947), p. 27 ff.

———. *St. Catherine Labouré* (pamphlet), Philadelphia, 1948.

———. *Major Errors and Omissions in Jules Charles Chevalier's Biographical Notice of St. Catherine Labouré*, Dissertation for Master's Degree, St. John's University, New York, 1956.

di Sales, Gaetano. *Soeur Catherine*, Rome, 1947.

Hayes, Carleton J. H. *A Political and Social History of Modern Europe*, Vol. 2, New York, 1933.

Hazen, Charles Downer. *Europe Since 1815*, New York, 1910.

Labouré, Catherine. *Accounts of Her Visions Written by Her Own Hand, 1841, 1856*, Archives of the Sisters of Charity, Paris.

Lhotte, Céline, and Dupeyrat, Elizabeth. *White Wings and Barricades*, tr. anon., New York, 1939.

Louis-Lefebvre, Marie Thérèse. *The Silence of St. Catherine Labouré*, tr. by the Earl of Wicklow, Dublin, 1953.

Misermont, Lucien. *La Bienheureuse Catherine Labouré Fille de la Charité et la Médaille Miraculeuse*, Paris, 1933.

———. *L'Ame de la Bienheureuse Catherine Labouré Fille de la Charité et Quelques Circonstances Moins Connues des Apparitions de la Médaille Miraculeuse*, Paris, 1933.

———. *Les Graces Extraordinaire de la Bienheureuse Catherine Labouré Fille de la Charité Voyante de la Médaille Miraculeuse*, Paris, 1934.

Mott, Marie Edouard. *The Green Scapular and Its Miracles*, Paris, 1923.

Parsons, Reuben. *Studies in Church History*, New York, 1886–1900.

Sacra Rituum Congregatione. *Parisien. Beatificationis et Canonizationis Servae Dei Sor. Catharinae Labouré e Societate Puellarum Caritatis*, Rome, Positio Super Introductione Causae, 1907, Positio Super Fama in Genere, 1911, Positio Super Virtutibus, 1927.

Sharkey, Don. *The Woman Shall Conquer*, Milwaukee, 1952.

Teresa of Avila. *The Life of St. Teresa of Jesus of the Order of Our Lady of Carmel, Written by Herself*, tr. by David Lewis, ed. by Benedict Zimmerman, Westminster, 1933.

Vittenet, A. *De Saint Jean de Réome à la Bienheureuse Catherine Labouré*, Dijon, 1934.

Vincent de Paul. *The Conferences of St. Vincent de Paul to the Sisters of Charity*, tr. by Joseph Leonard, London, 1939.

———. *Regulae seu Constitutiones Communes Congregationis Missionis,* Paris, 1658, 1954.

———. *Common Rules of the Daughters of Charity,* Paris, 1658, 1954.

Wyndham-Lewis, D. B. *King Spider,* New York, 1929.

Yver, Colette. *La Vie Secrète de Catherine Labouré,* Paris, 1935.

Anon. *Annales de la Congrégation de la Mission,* Tome 36, Paris, 1871.

———. *Venerable Sister Catherine Labouré, Sister of Charity of St. Vincent de Paul,* London, 1920.

———. *Le Scapulaire Vert,* Paris, 1944.

———. *Vie, Vertus et Mort de M. Aladel,* Paris, 1873.

Index

Adelaide, Mme, 110
Affré, Msgr., 165, 173–174, 176
Aladel, Father Jean Marie, sketch of life 72–73; character and ability 73–74; reactions to Catherine's visions 74, 78, 112, 126, 176; visions as a problem to 90–91, 102–103, 107, 109, 112; relationship to Catherine as confessor 74, 100–101, 113, 129–130; his opinion of Catherine 101, 118; his slowness to act 156, 160–162, 165, 216; and the Secret 103–107, 108–109, 118–119, 181–182, 185–186; and the striking of the Medal 112–115; and the design of the Medal 95–97; as an apostle of the Medal 162; his refusal to make rue du Bac a shrine 120–121, 123; and the Children of Mary 156; and Ratisbonne 170; and the Green Scapular 165; and the "Cross of Victory" vision 174–175; last conference 68–69, 194–195; death of 194–196, 44, 71, 84, 111, 115, 118, 126–127, 132, 178, 201, 210, 219
Alphonsus Ligouri, St., 179
Ampère, André Marie, 42
Andreveux, Sr. Appolline, 165–166
Anne of Austria, 76
Apparition of July 18, 80–87, 94, 97, 99–100, 111, 119, 149, 156, 160, 176–177, 182, 186, 194, 206, 208, 210
Apparitions of the Miraculous Medal, 17, 30, 58, 70, 78–79, 87, 92–97, 99–100, 103–104, 108, 110–111, 118–119, 124–125, 135, 148, 159–161, 164, 177, 179–181, 185–186, 190, 219, 221, 227
Athanasius, St., 5
Augustine, St., 141

Baker, Father, 123
Basilica of Our Lady of Victory, 123
Baudrey, 4
Belloc, Hilaire, 75
Berchmans, St. John, 130
Bernadette Soubirous, St., 68, 87, 118, 141, 178–179
Bernard, St., 3, 8, 65
Bismarck, Prince Otto von, 198
Bisqueyburu, Sr. Justine, 74, 164–166
Blanc, Louis, 173
Blanchot, Mother, 69–70
Blessed Virgin Mary, 5, 15–17, 20, 27, 30–31, 66, 68, 70, 74, 79, 81–91, 93–104, 106–123, 126, 134, 138, 140, 148–149, 156–164, 168–170, 175–176, 178–183, 185–187, 189, 194–196, 200, 202–203, 206–208, 210, 215–223, 225–230

241

OTHER TITLES AVAILABLE

At your bookdealer or direct from the Publisher.

OTHER TITLES AVAILABLE